To Adler —

Hope you enjoy!

Dick Elbert

COP STORIES

The Few, the Proud, the Ugly—
Twenty-five Years on the Baltimore Police Department

Dick Ellwood

iUniverse, Inc.

New York   Bloomington

Cop Stories

The Few, the Proud, the Ugly—Twenty-five Years on the Baltimore Police Department

iUniverse books may be ordered through booksellers or by contacting:

iUniverse
1663 Liberty Drive
Bloomington, IN 47403
www.iuniverse.com
1-800-Authors (1-800-288-4677)

ISBN: 978-1-4502-4351-3 (pbk)
ISBN: 978-1-4502-4353-7 (cloth)
ISBN: 978-1-4502-4352-0 (ebk)

Library of Congress Control Number: 2010910394

Printed in the United States of America

iUniverse rev. date: 7/16/2010

In memory of my Mom and Dad; Dad was the best cop I ever knew

Contents

INTRODUCTION

Every cop has stories; you will hear them in the locker room, police parking lots, court house hallways, retirement parties, promotion parties, shift change parties, and especially in bars, where cops go to let off the steam. Now that I am retired and really don't have much steam to let off, I share the stories at retiree meetings, breakfast gatherings, funeral parlors and sometimes, still in the bars. Some of the stories in this book bring back memories that are not so good, but for the most part, I am proud of my career in the police department.

I started to write a book about the history of my family, the Ellwood family in the Baltimore Police Department. I soon realized that it was going in too many directions and converted to short stories. I will tell you that we Ellwoods have had quite a presence in the Baltimore Police Department going back to the early 1900s and it goes like this; David is my son and was a member of the police department until he decided he wanted some warmer weather and moved to Florida. He is currently a homicide detective with the Broward County Sheriff's Department, the apple doesn't fall far from the tree. Next would be me and you will hear a lot from me in these short stories that I have put together. I served the Baltimore Police Department for a little over twenty-five years. The next Ellwood would be my father, who is Richard senior or as we called him, "Big Dick" and as I am a junior, that would make me "Little Dick." My dad was a cop in Baltimore City for about thirty-three years and most of that time was spent as a traffic cop on a corner in downtown

Baltimore. I have a brother, John who was also a Baltimore cop and like me, was also a member of the Homicide Unit and was a detective sergeant when he retired. Then there are the cops that were on my mother's side of the family and they actually go back to the late 1800s. My mother's maiden name was Dunn and her brother, Ed Dunn, was a captain in the police department in the 1920s. His father was a cop in the city back in the early 1900s. There were a lot of other Dunns in the police department. The Dunns and the Ellwoods all originated from a great old Irish neighborhood in Baltimore known as the "10th Ward."

I joined the Baltimore City Police Department in December 1964, just after my discharge from the Marines. I went in the Marines when I was seventeen years old. I was actually too young to join on my own, so my parents had to sign for me to enlist. I was not a real bad kid, but I did quit school to join the Marines and looking back, it was probably the best move I could have made. I think I was getting in with a crowd that was not quite what you would call, model kids. They were stealing cars, drinking, hooking school, and just pretty much hanging out. I know that the Marine Corps straightened me out and gave me the direction that I needed at that time in my life. I also know that while going through boot camp at Paris Island, South Carolina, I figured out real early that the seventeen year old skinny, pimple faced, snot nose, punk kid from the 10th Ward in east Baltimore who joined the Marines was changing into a person who realized that you had to earn your way through this life.

I always knew that I wanted to be a cop, not just because I came from a family of cops. I always watched the cops in my old neighborhood and although they were a little nasty to us once in awhile, I liked the fact that they had the respect of the neighborhood. I could tell that everyone looked up to them and went to them for advice. I have to admit that carrying a gun, having a badge, and catching the bad guys were also big attractions to the job for me.

Well, it is time to get started with my short stories and as I prepare, I can't help but remember one of the old great cop shows, The Naked City which probably goes back more than fifty years. The show's signature was its narrator, who introduced each episode with the assurance that the series was not filmed in a studio, but on the streets and buildings of New York City.

After the show, the narrator would return and in a real deep and convincing voice, he would say, "There are eight million stories in the naked city; this has been one of them." Well, that's how I am going to get started, by saying that there are millions of stories that could be told by the men and woman past and present who served in the Baltimore Police Department. These stories are mine and I want to share them with you. If you have the opportunity to make it to the next Baltimore Police Homicide Unit reunion, you might hear some of them and they might be expounded on, because that's what cops do when we get together and we do it damn good.

I just want to say before we move on to the good stuff; I have absolutely laid it all out on the line with this book, The Few, The Proud, The Ugly. I am telling it like it really happened and I hope I don't offend anyone, as that is not my intentions, but if you are offended, you probably deserve it. My sole intentions with these stories are to put them in print before I am too damn old to remember them. I also want to share them with family, friends, and anyone interested in knowing how life in a police department really is.

Much of what I write about in this book has been personal for many years. Some of what I write about, I am not real proud of, but it happened and I want to put it all out there. You can decide for yourself if I am a bad person, a good person, or just a cop who tried to do the best job he could and had some bumps along the way.

I have read cop stories in recent years and for the most part, I have enjoyed them. I have also read some that are boring as hell and don't seem to project the real image of police work. I don't think that after you get done with these short stories, you will be left with the feeling that I did not tell it all. I am a person with a lot of pride in myself and in the men and women who serve and protect our streets every day. I look back on my career and can honestly say that I did my best.

I try to hold the bad language down to a minimum in these short stories, but in some parts I have to use the language to get the point across. I have eight grandchildren that might read this book one day and I want them to think well of their grandfather. I am not using the f---- word just to make the book longer, as I see in some books today. So let's get this fuckin show on the road..., sorry kids.

CENTRAL DISTRICT 1965 – THE BEGINNING

After graduating from the Baltimore Police Academy in the spring of 1965, I was assigned to uniform patrol in the Central District and like all my fellow rookie cops, I could not wait to get on the street to kick ass and take names. When I reported to the Central District in that new uniform, shiny new badge, a night stick made out of pinewood, and the best part of all, that brand new Colt revolver, hell I was Clint Eastwood and John Wayne all rolled up into one nasty looking son of a bitch. I was always proud of wearing the Marine Corps uniform, especially the dress blues, but this was different. I was about to be launched out on to the mean streets of Baltimore and solve the crime problems.

I can remember my first day on the street. I was assigned to work the area around Greenmount Avenue and Preston Street in east Baltimore and I was excited to get this assignment. I grew up in this same neighborhood and could not wait until I walked the same streets I grew up on and hear all the people say, that's Dicky Ellwood; he was in the Marines and now he's a cop. I had just recently been discharged from the Marines and I figured, hell I can handle anything after surviving four years in the Marines. I did not see combat while in the Marines, but little did I know, I was about to experience some real urban combat, ghetto style.

Well, it was about 11 AM on my first day on the mean streets of charm city and I was standing at the corner of Biddle Street and Greenmount Avenue, looking real police like, when I heard people screaming. I then saw

1

this large dog chasing some people who seemed like they were just running in circles trying to avoid the wrath of this dog or hope that he went after someone else, probably me. I could see that the dog was acting crazy and foaming from the mouth and it was a large German shepherd or mixed breed city slicker dog. When the crowd saw me, they were hollering for me to do something and my first thought was, shit, I am jumping into action and saving the day and I'm going to be a hero my first day on the job.

As I moved closer to the dog, he left the crowd and started to chase the man in blue, which would be me. I guess that might have been his favorite color. I have to admit that my first act was to run for cover behind a mailbox, but I knew that I had to do something, as this crowd was now watching the dog coming after me. The dog approached me and the foamy white ugly stuff was seething from his mouth and it was no doubt this was a mad dog situation and a pretty big mad dog. As he was about to attack me from about five feet away and in what appeared to be a leaping position, I drew my gun and shot him. I hit him in the side and I was surprised that it only seemed to piss him off and I don't know why I was surprised, because this was the first dog I had shot. We didn't do dog shooting in the Marines.

About this time, people were running and screaming when they heard the shot, not that the sound of gunshots was a rare thing in this neighborhood. It was probably because it was daylight and a crazy cop was shooting at a crazy dog. As the dog approached me again, I shot him again and this time it took its toll and he fell to the ground, but was still kicking. I stood over him and was going to take him out of his misery with a head shot, but that's when my sergeant pulled up with about three other patrol cars that had gotten a call for a shooting. The sergeant was furious and this was actually my first encounter with him and I knew it would not be good, as he screamed, "What the fuck are you doing shooting this dog? You think you are still in the Marines?" Being brand new and a little intimated by the sergeant, I said, "Sarge, they told us in the Police Academy that one of the times we could use our gun was to shoot a vicious wild dog." Well, the sergeant, who came off as the grumpiest and nastiest looking son of a bitch you ever wanted to see, became more upset. By this time, I noticed that the dog was just lying there and it was no doubt, he was dead. Well, the same old crowd that was earlier screaming for my help turned on me and started screaming obscenities at me, like you dog killing son of bitch or things similar to that, except they were much nastier.

This incident would turn out to be my first introduction to police work that would show that no matter what you did, someone would usually be pissed off at you. The bottom line of this story is that the sergeant busted my ass in front of the other police officers and the crowd and told me that I did not use good judgment. He said that with all those people around and me firing my gun that was not quite the approach cops take. He, however, did not go into what the correct approach would be and I can bet his fat ass would have shot the dog also. He later told me that because it was daytime and with a large crowd around, the bullet could have ricocheted and someone could have been killed.

When I came back to work the next day, all I could hear when I walked the post was some quiet talk from the residents like, there's that cop who shot the dog. I later found out from a veteran cop that if you shoot a dog, you probably should shoot him in the head and preferably between the eyes for a fast kill or if the sergeant had his way, I guess just beat him off with the night stick until help arrives.

If I had it to do over, I would probably do the same thing, because the thought of that dog biting the hell out of me, just does not sit well. I can handle an irate sergeant, but I can't handle lots of dog bites and eventual rabbi shots, that's not what I signed up for. I think this was the first time that the great advice that my dad gave me kicked in. He said, "You can always get another job, but you cannot get another life" and this advice would come into play many more times from that day forward.

First Assignment – My Old Neighborhood

After surviving little things like the dog shooting incident, I settled down and felt more comfortable walking the same streets that I grew up on. I don't think many cops get that privilege. I knew every alley, every street, every hideout, and most of the bad guys. It was weird walking in the same neighborhood where you did a lot of crazy things while you were growing up and for the grace of God, did not get caught. My first few days, I saw some people that I had not seen for years and I also saw some of the guys that I had grown up with, hung out with, and took some friendly kidding from them.

I walked a beat in that neighborhood in the days when we did not have any police radios or any communication with other cops, other than the call box and the call light. The call light was just a pole with a yellow light on it that blinked when the police dispatcher wanted you to handle something on your post or another police officer wanted to get in touch with you. I look back on that system and wonder how it ever worked, but it did. The light would blink and you would walk to the nearest call box and call in to the police dispatcher. The dispatcher would give you a call to an address on your post for anything from a domestic disturbance, disorderly person or a serious call, like a stabbing or a shooting. It sounds silly, but you would than walk some distance to the location and handle the call. I guess in a good way, sometimes when you got a call for a disturbance, by the time you got there, it was usually over. I know today when a cop gets a call and it is serious, they get several cars to respond to the location, but back than when we got a call, we were on our own. When we got there, we handled the call and than just went back to walking the post and walk we did. I can't begin to tell you how many miles we may have walked during a shift. I liked the walking part because I had just got out of the Marines and was in great shape, but for some of the old timers, it was not easy.

The tradition in the police department was that when you first came on the job, you walked for several years, until an opening came up in what was called back then, the radio patrol. The radio patrol was comprised of five radio cars that patrolled the entire district and would get the calls that would need a quicker response. The guys that worked those cars were senior guys and they all looked old to me and most were fat from sitting in a car for years. On occasion, you would be loaned out to work a radio car if the regular guy was on leave and that was an experience in itself, as most of them were chain smokers and I did not smoke.

I can remember my first experience in a radio car and the regular guy smelled of smoke before we even got in the car. He pulled what I later found out to be a trick they did with rookies that were in the car for the first time. On this occasion, the driver was Bob Rose and his nickname was "Pigpen", so that should give you some idea of where I am going with this story. He pulled up to a coffee shop and just pointed to the shop and said in his probably cancer ridden throat, "Black, no sissy shit in mine." Being a quick learner, I knew that meant no cream or sugar. I went in the shop and ordered two coffees, one black and one with the sissy shit in it. The lady behind the counter looked like something out of a real old horror movie that I had seen. She had a cigarette in her mouth with an ash that looked about three inches long and I watch and just waited for that ash to fall, but it never did. She asked me if I was new and also asked if "Pigpen" was working. I told her that he was working and she pushed the coffees towards me. I started to reach for my money and she said, "Put your money away sweetie, cops don't pay for anything in this place." I thanked her and went out to the car, where "Pigpen" had already lit up a real nasty smelling cigar. I handed him his coffee and I took the lid off of mine and that was a big mistake, because "Pigpen" was about to welcome me to the police department in his own sick way. He floored the gas pedal and the coffee went all over me and I mean it got me everywhere a coffee could go. Well, good old "Pigpen" laughed so hard he had to eventually pull the car over. After his belly laugh that rocked the whole car, he said, "Son you have just learned your first lesson of working a patrol car, don't take the fuckin lid off your coffee." He went on to preach to me the science of drinking a coffee in a police car. He showed me that you only break the small piece on the lid and drink through that opening, so that when you get a call and have to move out quickly, the coffee will not spill on you. As I sat there with my sissy shit coffee all over my very neat and clean uniform, I could not help but to think, I hope this bastard dies a slow death from cancer of the throat and when he does, I am going to the graveyard and pour my coffee with sissy shit in it, all over his sorry ass.

I did not look forward to getting loaned out to the patrol cars; I was very content to walk a foot post. Hell, I could go in a coffee shop, sit down and drink a coffee like a human being and put all the sissy shit I wanted in my coffee. When I walked, I knew I did not have to listen to "Pigpen" and smell the nickel cigars that he smoked.

Back in those days when nearly the entire shift walked a post, you had to be a smooth talker to get yourself out of some serious situations, like domestic disturbances, where it got pretty hot and heated. The husband was usually drunk and the wife would be screaming what a bum he is and wants him out of the house. If the occasion presented itself where you had to make an arrest, you had quite a situation on your hands. You had to walk the arrestee to the closest call box and call for a paddy wagon to take the arrestee to the station to be booked.

I can remember taking people to the call box and they would fall down several times on the way and you had to pick them up and keep on going and some of them decided that on the way, they wanted to fight. I have to say that in that neighborhood I did get plenty of help when I needed it, from my old buddies and neighbors that I grew up with and just some good decent people. There were plenty of decent people in that neighborhood in spite of the neighborhood being a very high crime area. Seeing all the white families moving to the suburbs bothered me, because when I left to go in the Marines, the neighborhood was still one of the best in the city. It was a place you would love to raise your family.

The neighborhood had everything a family would need; parks, schools, churches, stores, funeral parlors, bars, and bakeries...oh did we have some good bakeries. There was one bakery on the corner of Greenmount and Preston Streets, called Lindingers and it was the greatest. I can remember standing on that corner when I worked the midnight shift and the bakers would come to work about 4 AM and start to make the cakes and doughnuts for the day. I was twenty-one and weighed about a hundred and forty pounds and I knew early in my career that if I picked up one bad habit that cops do, it would be eating doughnuts. I would work my way to the front window and wave to the bakers, knowing they would invite me in, especially when it was cold.

As soon as you stepped in the place, the smell took over like a drug and there was a place in the back where I could sit and get warm on cold nights. I would eat a few doughnuts right off the assembly line and they were hot and some of them you did not even have to chew, they just slid down your throat. I am still a doughnut eater and if I sit back and think of Lindinger's Bakery, I can still smell those honey dips and those chocolate doughnuts with the icing still warm...this is torture just writing about this and I need to move on.

I can remember one of the most bizarre and uncomfortable situations that I had while waking that post, was when I walked into Swartz's Tavern, which was owned by the father of a guy that I grew up with in that same neighborhood. It was about 7 PM on a summer evening and I walked in the bar and old man Swartz was behind the bar. He greeted me kindly, by saying how pleased he was that I was on the police force and back working the post where his bar was and how safe he felt. He asked if I wanted anything and I took a soda and stood down the end of the bar talking to some old friends. While I was drinking my coke, I noticed that Mr. Swartz's son, Harry, was sitting at the bar and was drinking beer. Well I knew for a fact that he was not twenty-one, which meant he was not old enough to be drinking. I found this unusual that his father was serving him beer, especially while I was standing in the place. When Mr. Swartz came down where I was standing, I told him that I didn't think Harry was old enough to drink and Mr. Swartz laughed and said, "Hey, don't take this police job so serious." Well, when he said that, apparently he did not know how serious I did take the job and was about to find out. I walked down to Harry and told him that he would have to leave because he was not old enough to drink. Well, he sort of laughed a little and said, "I can't believe this is the same guy who grew up with my brothers and drank beer when he was a teenager." I told him that I was leaving the bar and walking around the block and when I come back and he was still there drinking, I was locking him up for drinking under age. It also meant that I would have to lock up his father for serving minors.

I left the bar and walked around the block. When I came back to the bar and walked in, Harry took a beer and put it up to his lips. He looked directly at me and gave me a little shit-eaten smile that he had. I walked over to him and told him that he was under arrest and had to come with me and he laughed a bit. I grabbed him by the rear of his pants and started out the door. His father came over and asked me if I was kidding and I said that I did not take this job to kid with people. I took the job to enforce the laws and especially when it is a blatant violation like what his son had done. I further told him that he should close the bar, because as soon as I got Harry to the station, I was coming back for him. Well, he went ballistic and told everybody in the bar to get the hell out.

I sent Harry to the station after taking him a short distance to the call box and then I went back to lock up Mr. Swartz. Needless to say when I went back and locked up Mr. Swartz, he had some choice words for me on the way to the station. I took it in stride, because I actually liked Mr. Swartz and had some fond memories of him and his family when I was growing up in the neighborhood. I charged him with serving minors and I charged Harry with consuming alcohol while being a minor and both of them made bail.

Well, the next day when I went to work, the word was all over the neighborhood about me locking up old man Swartz and his son. I made it a point to walk around for awhile to see what the mood was and then I could not wait to go in Swartz's Tavern to see what they had to say. I was kind of surprised when I walked into his bar, no one looked up and no one said anything to me, except for some old man who was quite in the bag already. All he said was, "Watch out here comes the sheriff and he locks up his old buddies." I ignored this guy, except for telling the bartender not to serve him anymore, because he had enough and I am sure that pissed him off real good. The bartender told me that the guy only lived about one block down the street and he could walk home. I told him that it did not matter where he lived, he was not to be served and in the future if someone is sitting at your bar and is drunk, you need to stop serving them.

It was about one week later when I went to court on the charges against Mr. Swartz and his son, Harry. The case was called and the sitting judge was Sewell Lamden, who was strict and moved quickly in his courtroom and did not want to hear any nonsense from the accused. I testified about what happened leading up to the arrest and then the judge asked Mr. Swartz if he had anything to say. He told the judge that he thought I was kidding when I told him that I was walking around the block and coming back to see if Harry was still in the bar drinking. He told the judge that his kids grew up with Officer Ellwood and I had been in his bar drinking when I was not twenty-one, which is true. After he was done talking, the judge told Mr. Swartz that he did not want to hear about what Officer Ellwood did prior to becoming a police officer, that it had nothing to do with the current charges against him and his son. The judge told Mr. Swartz that I did not have to walk around the block; I could have locked Harry up on the first visit to the bar. The judge found both of them guilty and fined Harry fifty dollars and court cost and fined the father, one hundred dollars and court cost and told Mr. Swartz that the liquor board would be notified about the liquor violations.

I did not make any new friends in that neighborhood because of that incident, but looking back on it, it was probably the best thing that I could have done. I think that going back to police a neighborhood that you grew up in can be tough and this incident showed others in the neighborhood that I was there to enforce the law, do my job, and not just be one of the guys from the old neighborhood.

I enjoyed working in my old neighborhood, because it gave me a sense that I was doing some good for the people that I knew and maybe if I worked real hard, I could keep the neighborhood safe and make a real difference. I made a lot of new friends while working that neighborhood and every street and alley that I walked in brought back memories of my childhood. I felt really accepted and needed when the older people who knew me as a kid, would ask me to come in for a coffee or something to eat and being a skinny cop, I took most of them up on the offer. I also had the pleasure of having an uncle and aunt who still lived in the neighborhood and this was great, because I would go there sometimes and have breakfast or lunch or just sit and take a break. I guess I can tell it now, but they gave me the key to their house and when I worked the midnight shift and after about three in the morning, I would go in and sit on their couch and could look out the front window to watch people. I can also tell you that some early mornings when the weather was real cold, I would go inside and sit on the couch and doze off for a few minutes. I could not sleep for any length of time and I guess that was from my Marine training, where if you slept on your post and got caught, you would get a court martial. In 1965 when I walked the post, most of the other cops who worked alongside me, would go somewhere when working the midnight shift and get some sleep. I knew cops that slept in the back of a cab company, in the basement of a liquor store, and there was one who had the keys to a church and actually slept in the church on a pew. I really don't think it was anything wrong with those guys sleeping, but a few abused it and you would not see them on the midnight shift from about three in the morning, until they were getting relieved at about eight o'clock. I can honestly say that most of the cops in the squad stayed on the street in some pretty cold weather, because the bad guys were not dumb and they knew when the cops were not around and that was the time to take advantage and break into the businesses on the post.

In the summer time it was different, because most of the houses in the neighborhood still did not have air conditioning and people were out all night sitting on their marble steps or "stoops" as they called them, trying to stay cool. When you have the combination of hot weather and a certain bunch of people who drink most of the night, you have the formula for some big trouble. I knew people in that neighborhood that were the nicest people in the world, but when they had a few drinks, they turned and caused a lot of trouble that they would admit later was the result of their drinking. I was always careful with the people you encountered that were drinking, because they did not really fear the cops at that time, maybe later when they sobered up, but not when they had the booze in them. I am not bragging, but I think I handled drunks pretty well and when they needed to be arrested, I would always try to get them on the ground where you had some control as you placed the handcuffs on them. I knew that the longer you debated with a drunk, the worse it would get and for the most part it got out of hand real quick.

I learned some things in a hurry in that neighborhood; don't reach into someone's pants pockets too quick. I was locking up a drunk one night and he was on the ground, not so much struggling, but just sort of thrashing around and I reached in his pants pocket to see what he had. I found out real quick what he had and it was an open pocket knife and it went into the right side of my hand. I didn't feel the pain at first, because it was real sharp and it got the fatty part of my right hand. I started to pick this guy up and that's when the blood started to pour from the wound and I mean it poured. I wrapped a hanky around my hand and a passing car stopped to help me, because this guy I was locking up was dead weight and with the bad hand, I could not lift him. Someone called in and the wagon responded and took this guy to the station house and he was charged with being drunk in public. I did not charge him with the stabbing, because it was actually my fault for not being a little more careful. I went to Mercy Hospital and got my hand stitched up and was ready to go back on my post when the grumpy old sergeant showed up at the hospital and told me to take the rest of the night off and go home. I told him I was fine and wanted to stay at work and he gave me that nasty look and said, "Son, take advantage of a bad situation and make it a good situation and go home." I kind of looked at him wondering what the hell he just said, but I knew better than to ask and I went home. I actually saw this drunken guy a few nights later and confronted him and he absolutely did not remember the incident and I believe him and he apologized for the hand injury.

I made a lot of lockups in that neighborhood and I think I had the respect of the older people and probably most of the kids, but there will always be the few who always want to try you and push the button as far as they think they can. When I worked the day shift in the warm weather, I really enjoyed watching the kids play baseball on the makeshift ball field that they used behind the Kennedy Playground on Chase Street. The ball field was the same ball field that I played on as a kid only about seven years earlier. I instantly made friends with most of the kids playing baseball. When I told them that they were playing on the same ball field that I played on when I was a kid, they thought that was real cool.

I can remember watching the boys one summer day and they asked me to play. It must have been about ninety-five degrees, just a scorching day. I guess they were real short of players and desperate. I at first said no and then after seeing how much fun they were having, I said what the hell, give it a shot. I piled my gun, hat, and other police equipment along the fence and I actually felt safe that no one would mess with it while I was playing. I also kept one eye on the ball and the other on my stuff. I told them I would be the pitcher, figuring that it would not require much running and thus I would not sweat as much. Wow, was I ever wrong!

I played about one hour and I was dripping wet with sweat and finally had to tell the boys that I had enough. The boys kept playing and if they were like me and my buddies when we were young, they probably played until it got dark. I was heading for the first place I could find with an air conditioner. I was walking toward Greenmount Avenue when my sergeant pulled up in a car and rolled the window down about one inch, so the cool air would not escape from his car. He said in that great grumpy voice, "What the hell happened to you?" I mean I was wet from my head to my ass, but at that point I could not think of anything but the truth. I told him that things were quiet and I played some baseball with the neighborhood kids over at the Kennedy Playground. He didn't say much, he just sat in the car, shook his head and then he said something that just didn't sit well with me. I guess it was the era of the 60s, but I never liked it then and still don't like it today, he said, "You know son, you ain't gonna change those little black bastards, they all hate cops and playing ball with them ain't gonna prove shit." I am not sure of my exact response, but I started to just walk away. I was upset and I was sort of mumbling to myself that maybe he should get out of that car sometimes and give it a try. I don't think he heard me, but he did say, "What did you say son?" When he called me son, I was thinking, I am not your fuckin son and I pity the poor bastard that is. I walked back to the car and for a moment I thought I was going to really go off on this fat piece of shit, but I didn't. I just told him that he was wrong and those kids probably never had a cop take time to talk to them, much less take off his gear, and play ball with them. He just made a grumpy sound and rolled the window up so that the cool air did not escape and cause something drastic to occur, like a sweat bead on his bald head.

I loved that neighborhood, which was actually known as the "10th Ward." Back in those days, the city was broken up into "Wards" and the most famous was the "10th Ward." I have lived in Baltimore all my life and I have never heard anyone mention the ward they lived in, other than the people that lived in the "10th Ward." If you lived in the "10th Ward", you were proud of it and made sure everyone knew it. I loved it when I was growing up in it and had the same feelings when I walked the post as a police officer. I learned so much about people and as the neighborhood changed and started to deteriorate, it hurt me to watch it happen. I worked the area long enough to see the changes that took place and for the most part, they were not good changes. I saw the decent law abiding people, both black and white move away to the suburbs or other areas of the city. I know that they did not want to raise their children in what was quickly becoming a drug infested and totally crime ridden neighborhood.

When I walked that post, I would make it a point to walk by Saint John's Catholic School on the corner of Eager and Valley Streets, which was now vacant. I could stand on that corner and it would bring back memories of my first eight years of Catholic education. We lived about one block from the school and we walked to school every day. There were six kids in our family and we went home every day for lunch, I don't know how my mother did it. I can remember being in the first grade at Saint John's and as I was a left hander, the nuns would smack me on the hand when I was writing, trying to get me to be "normal" and switch to the right hand like the rest of the class. I am still a lefty, but play all sports right handed. I guess they sort of succeeded, but I have never understood why they wanted to make left handers switch to the right hand; I don't think they knew either.

I would walk by the church that was across the street from the school and it was now empty and not being used as a Catholic church any longer. The church had been in operation for over a hundred years. I remember the days when I was an altar boy and walked from my house to the church almost every day to assist with Mass. I loved being an altar boy and at one point in my early life, I thought for sure that I would be a priest. I still to this day, when I am in church, watch the altar servers and make sure they are doing their job right. I have a great deal of respect for priest and I think I would have been a good one. I don't think I could have kept up on all the schooling that goes into being a priest. My attention span in school was not the greatest. I guess if I were in school today, they would load me up with drugs and everything would be fine. I am proud that I did get my high school completed in the Marines and also later in life got an Associate's Degree from a community college, even if it did take seventeen years.

Sometimes on the midnight shift while I was walking my beat and things were quiet, it would be the best time for me to reflect on growing up in the old neighborhood. The neighborhood was safe, clean and everybody knew each other. I don't think we ever locked the doors at night. The only bad thing about living in a great neighborhood like ours was that because everybody knew each other, you couldn't get away with anything. I can remember getting in a little trouble, like maybe playing football in the street and running from the cops when they came around, knowing that they would take your football. Hell, I don't know why I was running, because all the beat cops knew my father, who was a cop. If they wanted to, all they had to do was come to my house and tell him and the punishment was worse than what they would have done to me. When I was about sixteen, the big thing on the weekends was getting some local bum to get us beer. If the cops caught you drinking the beer, they took it and smacked you on the butt with the strap of the nightstick.

I learned how to shoot "craps" from the older guys in the neighborhood. When they were shooting dice in the alley they would give me fifty cents to be the lookout for the cops. The cops would get smarter each time and find ways to come through the alley where the game was and they really didn't care about anyone gambling. The cops would start hollering as they got close to the game and everyone including me would run. They would just pick up the money on the sidewalk and walked away a little richer. I used some of those old police tactics when I walked in that neighborhood. You gotta go with what works.

I knew when I started that when you police in any neighborhood, you have to pick and choose what you consider as acceptable behavior. It's not that you are the judge and jury of those people, but some activity, though unlawful, has to be acceptable or you will not be effective. If I walked down the street on a hot summer night and a large group of guys were outside a bar, I really did not have a problem with that, although there was a city ordinance that stated that no one was to congregate within fifty feet of a bar. I figured if they were in front of the bar, at least I knew where they were and if they were not loud or bothering anyone, what was the problem. Hell, it was their neighborhood and as long as they were peaceful, why not stand anywhere they wanted to.

The only problem with the way I policed the neighborhood was that the cops working on the opposite shifts from me may have different thoughts on how they were policing the same neighborhood. After a period of time, the residents knew each one of the cops on the beat and they knew what was expected and what was acceptable when any particular cop was working.

A good example would be that although I allowed guys to stand on the corner near a bar, I had a cop that worked the shift after me and he would lock guys up for the standing on the corner. He even went as far as to paint a line in each direction from the entrance to the bar marking the fifty feet that they could not congregate. Sometimes when I saw a group of guys standing on the corner, I would cross the street to talk to them and before I got there, some of them that did not know my policies and would run.

I guess you would think that when you walk a beat in a neighborhood you would just enforce all the laws and ordinances without any questions. I did not think that way and maybe I was different, but it worked out for me and I was the one that was walking the beat. The area you walked was like your little piece of the city and you were the sheriff of that little piece of the city. I think your survival depended on how you treated people and could you rely on some of them if you were in trouble. I was not a pushover by any means, but things like someone just drunk on the street trying to make it back to their home, that did not bother me. Hell, I can remember on occasions helping some drunks to get to their house. I also did not have a problem with things like gambling on pinball machines, playing cards inside a bar, or even shooting dice in the alley. I did try that old cop trick once, when I saw guys shooting dice in the alley and you know what, it works. I know I must have picked up at least ten quarters when I chased them out of the alley.

I could go on with lots of stories about walking the beat in that neighborhood, but we would be here for quite awhile. I know that I made a difference in my years working in that area. I tried to be sensitive to the ever changing makeup of the neighborhood. I loved to tell new families moving in, that not only am I the cop that walks the beat, but I also grew up at 835 East Chase Street, right in the heart of my post. I really can't explain the feeling of being in that neighborhood years later, sitting on the marble steps of 835 East Chase Street on a hot summer night, talking to the new residents of that house and asking questions about the rooms in the house. The kids probably thought I was kidding, until I told them the complete layout of the house, including the areas where there were ghosts. I only add the ghost thing, because when we were growing up and living in that house, we swore that there were ghosts in some of the rooms and especially in the dirt cellar.

I still at times ride down to the old neighborhood and ride around and think about growing up there and the days that I walked those streets as a very young police officer. The neighborhood is bad now and when you ride through, you better not make a whole lot of stops. I see people looking at me and probably thinking to themselves, who the hell is that white man, he is either crazy or he is a cop.

I always tell my brothers and sisters that if I could turn back the hands of time, I would move back to that neighborhood in a heartbeat. There is nothing like growing up in the inner city. In today's world, nobody knows their neighbors and kids need their parents to ride them to all their activities. I now live in a community of townhouses and other than the people on my left and right, I could not name another neighbor. I go to some social functions these days and I hear people say they grew up in the "10th Ward." I know they didn't, but hell; it was such a great neighborhood that I don't mind that they want people to think they did. I could catch them lying if I asked about some of the guys that grew up there, like; "Spike", "Shorty", "Mace", "Bro", "Boneyard" and "Little Hawk", just to name a few and of course me and I am not telling what my nickname was back then.

I Locked Up My Childhood Hero

I have told this story many times over the years, but it was not until about three years ago that it became a big deal. It was a very hot night in June 1966 and I guess the temperature was in the high 80s and very humid, a typical Baltimore summer night. On this particular night, I was assigned to the area of Charles Street and North Avenue, because they were short in that squad and this was an area that I had not worked in before. The area consisted back than of some very nice restaurants and fancy night clubs. Some of the restaurants were the Harvey House, Eager House, China Clipper, One West, Blue Mirror, Marty's Park Plaza, and the Chesapeake Restaurant.

On this particular night, I was standing at the "call box", which as we now already know was the only means of communication for police officers and police dispatchers. I was standing there and it was a little before 11 PM when I heard a group of men coming down Eager Street toward Charles Street. I could tell they were coming from the Eager House Restaurant which was a pretty high class restaurant. The owner of the restaurant, Bill Tutton, loved to smooze with celebrities and sports figures. The rowdy group was walking directly toward me and it was obvious they had been drinking. As they got closer, I could not believe my eyes. It was my childhood baseball hero, the great Yankee, Mickey Mantle and he was the loudest of the bunch. The others in the group were sort of assisting Mantle and actually holding him up, one under each arm. When they got within a few feet of me, my hero fell on the sidewalk literally at my feet. I guess in a different situation and a different

17

time, I would consider this a miracle, except for the fact that everyone in the group was laughing and they tried to help Mickey Mantle to his feet. I asked one guy who appeared to be sober what was going on and he said they were going back to the Sheraton Belvedere Hotel which was just one block away at the corner of Charles and Chase Streets. He said, they were all New York Yankee ball players, but I knew that long before he said anything. I was aware that baseball teams coming in town to play the Baltimore Orioles stayed at the Sheraton Belvedere Hotel and they did have a curfew time to be back at the hotel. Having never worked this post before, I had very little chance to see any celebrities, much less half the Yankee ball club. I was a little excited, but knew I had to keep my police hat on and not my baseball cap.

At this point, I was not sure how I would handle this and different scenario's came to mind. Would I lock up the great Mickey Mantle or just ask for his autograph and just chalk it up as one of the greatest moments of my life. The other Yankees with him were trying to assist him to his feet, but Mantle was bigger than I imagined and they were having trouble getting him upright. The others in the group were to the best of my memory, Whitey Ford, Clete Boyer, Ralph Houk, Bobby Richardson, Joe Pepitone, and a few others, but I didn't recognize their faces. I knew all of these Yankee ballplayers because I either had their baseball cards when I was younger or saw them on TV or in person at Memorial Stadium playing against the Orioles. Mantle was becoming very loud, just slurring his speech and no one could actually determine what he was trying to say. I knew that I had to do something, because others walking in the area, also recognized that these guys were Yankee ballplayers. The scene started to draw a crowd from the many people in the area leaving the restaurants and they seemed amused, but like me, also excited to see Mickey Mantle. I don't think they so much enjoyed seeing him on the sidewalk, but this was Mickey Mantle, the greatest ball player of that time. I asked the group of guys if they could either physically carry him back to the hotel or get a taxi or something to get him off the street. Mantle spoke up at this point and said, "I don't need any fuckin help, I can walk." Well, to be honest, he could not walk real well and when he tried, the others just laughed and it was getting a little out of control. I told the group that if they could not get him to cooperate, I would have to lock him up for being drunk in public. Well, this brought much more laughter from the group and especially from Mantle who was falling all over the place. As the crowd in the area was getting larger and also laughing, I repeated my prior statement to the group and no one responded, so I used the phone in the call box and called for a "wagon."

I don't know, now looking back on the incident, if the group just thought this young rookie police officer was out of his element or star struck by being around the New York Yankees. I needed to end it right away. When the police wagon arrived, it was manned that night by two veteran cops who at that time seemed like they were in their sixties, but when you are twenty-two, everyone looks like they are old farts to you. I told the wagon men I was making an arrest and asked that they transport this guy to the Central District station. One of the more senior cops working the wagon, looked at Mantle and said, "Do you know who this is?" and I replied, "We have already been through this and yes, I do know it is Mickey Mantle." Mantle was then placed in the wagon for the trip to the Central District station and to be honest, he kept on laughing and probably didn't even know where he was going.

I talked to the others in the group who were now taking what I had to say much more serious than they had been. They were a little stunned at what had just happened and one of them said, "Son, I don't know how long you have been a cop, but I think it is over for you." I tried to not have any additional conversation with the group and suggested they just leave the area. The others in the group said they were really trying to get him back to the hotel because they had an 11 PM curfew, but I really don't think they made much of an effort to get him back at all. They said they had played a ballgame earlier that day against the Orioles and were scheduled to play the next day at Memorial Stadium. I explained to the group where Mr. Mantle would be and told them I really had no choice but to arrest him. They said they would go back to the hotel and then someone from the Yankee organization would come to the police station to check on Mantle.

To get to the police station in those days, you drove your own personal car. I was due to get off work at midnight anyway but now I knew I would be working late. On the way to the station, it kind of hit me that I had locked up the baseball player that I had worshipped as a kid, Mickey Mantle. I was locking up probably the greatest baseball player of that era or at least in the past twelve or so years. I was locking up number "7", who had played for the New York Yankees since probably 1954 and appeared in twelve World Series. Mickey Mantle, who was a hero to all young boys and loved by every kid on the playground when I was growing up. I know all my old buddies would kill for the opportunity just to see him, much less be as close as I was on that night. We all tried to play baseball like Mickey; we would try to run like Mickey, hit like Mickey, bunt like Mickey, and play the outfield like Mickey.

As you can imagine, my ride to the station house was turning out to be a very troublesome ride. I was thinking while I was driving, what would the guys I grew up with think about me locking up Mickey, would they ever talk to me again and what about my Dad, who absolutely worshipped Mantle. I have checked Mickey Mantle's stats from back in those days and this guy was one incredible ballplayer. He had a lifetime batting average of two hundred and ninety-eight. He also had twelve appearances in the World Series and was probably the greatest switch hitter ever. He had five hundred and thirty-six lifetime home runs, eighteen homeruns in World Series appearances, and all star appearances from 1952 to 1968. He was the Triple Crown winner in 1956 and had numerous Gold Glove awards. He was inducted into the Baseball Hall of Fame in 1974.

I also know these many years later that Mickey had some real alcohol problems, business failures, and divorce. But before he died on August 13, 1995 at the age of sixty-three, he did some remarkable things with educating people about alcohol abuse. I would often over the years after the arrest, see him on television and that would bring back the whole unfortunate incident.

Well, I arrived at the Central District and entered the booking area to find a crowd asking for Mantle's autograph. I was actually amazed to see that he was standing and looked sober. As I walked to the booking desk, I will never forget all the stares from other police officers who were preparing to go out on the street for the midnight shift. If looks could kill, I would have been a dead man. I never really got to talk to Mickey Mantle that night and as I looked at him in the booking area, he appeared to have pulled himself together. He had that slight smile on his face, the same smile that was on my baseball card. As I was about to do the paper work for the charges, I heard Lieutenant Bo Fink, an old crusty sort of guy who had been on the job for many years, holler to me, "Get over here son!" The lieutenant was an old time cop, who liked to take a little snip of the booze, even when he was working. He didn't care who knew it and that was always obvious from his breath. He was probably at that time about sixty years old, although he looked much older, and I think he was getting ready to retire from the job. He was a good shift lieutenant and was always fair with any discipline he had to give out; although, I don't think that happened that often. Well, when I went over to him, he said, "Sit down son, we need to talk." I sat down and before he could even pull up a chair, he said, "Do you know what the fuck you have done?" I was a little surprised by this, but I don't know why, because it was about 11PM and he had probably been drinking most of the shift and the closer he got to me that was obvious. He was fumbling to say something else, when I said, "Yes sir, I made an arrest of Mickey Mantle for being drunk in public." He was still standing, or at least trying to and leaning over the desk and said, "Son, you have made an arrest of the greatest baseball player of our times." Being just twenty- two years old, I felt like I was being scolded by my dad or even worse, by a Marine drill instructor. I knew this was bad, but I also knew that I did not do anything that would have gotten me into trouble. I only made an arrest, even if it was Mickey Mantle; it was still just an arrest. Lieutenant Fink never did sit down and just walked around the table, holding on to the edge at all times and scratching his head. A few times he pounded on the table, just to keep my attention or maybe to let some others who were outside the door think he was really laying into my ass. He finally sat down and leaned over and said, "Son we have got to fix this situation, don't we." I might have only been twenty-two years old, but I knew by the way everyone was acting, especially the lieutenant that we really did need to fix it. He waited for a response and he probably could tell I was getting very upset. He assured me that everything would be okay and then he said, "We are just going to take Mr. Mantle back to his hotel and forget this whole thing happened." He did ask me if it was okay with me and of course I said, "Yes sir." Back in those days you could do things like that, but I know in today's world it would have been different, you would have had cameras and reporters all over the place and it would have been headlines in the morning paper and all over the sports networks.

Well, Mickey was driven back up to the Sheraton Hotel in a police car and I went home and everyone was happy. I was single at the time and living in an apartment. I remember getting home and taking off the uniform and flipping on the TV, hoping that I would not hear anything about Mickey Mantle being arrested. I got home about 1 AM and after several beers, I was still awake at 4 AM and I was starting to calm down. I was wondering if I still had that baseball card of Mickey Mantle. I eventually fell asleep with a little help from the beer. The next day which was Sunday, I was working and had to be in the station house for 3:30 PM roll call. I left the apartment about 2:30 PM and on the way to the station, I turned on the radio to station WBAL who carried the Oriole games locally. I am not making this up, but as I adjusted the volume, I heard the announcer say, "Now batting for the Yankees, number seven, Mickey Mantle." At this point if I said he hit a homerun, I would be lying. I really don't remember what happened, but the mere fact that he was playing major league baseball after a night of drinking was astounding to me, but I am sure it wasn't the first time it happened in his long career.

I have kept this story pretty much to myself for many years, mainly because as years go by and they go by quick in police work, you just forget some stories. I guess I figured it was something that happened and it was no big deal, at least until a few years ago when I told the story to bunch of guys at a police reunion. The guys just looked at me and said, "Tell me you are kidding." Well I was not kidding because it did happen and I have been asked if I kept any of the paper work or did I get his photo or did I get his autograph and the answer is no to all. Mickey was never photographed, never fingerprinted, and no paperwork was ever done. I did make some notes in a little black book we called a lookout book, but that has been discarded over the years.

I only wish that I would have had the chance to talk to him or maybe ride him back to the Sheraton Hotel that night. Maybe he would have given me an autograph, a signed baseball, an old Yankee shirt, or maybe we could have gone in the bar in the Sheraton and had a few drinks. I guess I could have gone to the game on Sunday and when he came to bat, I could have hollered,

"Hey Mick, it's me, the guy who locked you up last night." I don't think that would have been a good idea, the whole stadium would have turned on me. Mickey might have been playing in Baltimore, but he was always cheered when he came to bat, no matter where he played.

I still have the greatest respect for Mickey Mantle and he remains my favorite baseball player of all time with Brooks Robinson running a very close second. I often wonder if Mickey Mantle were playing today, what records would he break and what kind of salary he would demand. There have been a lot of great ones that have come along since my baseball hero played in the 50s and 60s, but there will never be anyone like number seven, Mickey Mantle. I thank the wise old lieutenant for making the right decision back then. By the way, the Yankees finished 10th in 1966 with 70 wins and 89 losses. The Baltimore Orioles finished on top with 97 wins and a 63 loss record and went to the World Series. They beat the Dodgers four straight in the World Series, so 1966 turned out to be a pretty memorable year for the Orioles and certainly a year that I will never forget.

SHOOTOUT AT BERNIE LEE'S PUB

In April 1969, my partner, Joe Bolesta and I were on a stakeout inside of Bernie Lee's Pub on Chase Street, just off of Howard Street in the center of downtown Baltimore. The reason for the detail was that someone had broken into the pub for six weekends in a row and they all occurred in the early hours of Sunday morning. We went inside the pub about 10 PM on a Saturday night, because the pub had a license that they had to close at 11 PM. We were dropped off at the bar by another cop, so that no cars would be in the area when all the patrons left at 11 PM. After the patrons and the owner left the bar and locked the front door, we commenced to drink a few Rolling Rock beers and made some sandwiches. The owner told us to eat and drink whatever we wanted, so we did.

At about 2 AM in the morning, my partner laid down on some chairs he had put together and he had a shotgun lying across his chest. Joe was six feet, four inches tall, so he needed a few chairs and it was a sight to see. I just sat in a chair and neither of us thought anything would happen and were we ever wrong.

About 3:30 AM, being the only one that was totally awake, I heard the glass break on the second floor of the bar. I will never forget that sound and I am very glad that I was awake. Actually I think Joe was awake also. We usually rest our eyes, but it is not real sleep, cops learn this early in their careers. We both took the assignment very serious, like we always did. We didn't just drink beer, eat sandwiches, and figure nothing was going to happen, it happened for the previous six Sunday mornings, why not this one.

I knew right away that someone had just broken into the bar and I could now hear footsteps on the second floor and although we saw some mice in the place earlier, they don't come that big. My partner appeared to be totally relaxed and although he was not sleeping, it did not appear that he heard the glass break. I did not want to startle him, so I covered his mouth and whispered that someone just broke in and was walking around on the second floor. At this point, we could hear the person coming down the steps and whoever it was; they would descend directly where we were positioned in the middle of the bar.

It should be noted that this was a very old bar and also very small, probably about twelve feet wide and sixty feet long. The bar was a typical old Irish bar and most of the construction was wood. With each movement from this person coming down the steps, which seemed like a lifetime, training goes out the window and survival tactics kick in. This person was proceeding down the creaking wooden steps and would eventually be in the same room where we were. Every step produced a distinct sound from the steps and as he got closer to the bottom, the cracking sound got louder and my heartbeat felt like it was coming through my chest. It's one of those moments in police work that you think; maybe I should have taken that job at the pickle factory. I quietly told my partner that we were too close to use the shotgun and the best approach was to use our revolvers. We did not have any lights on in the place and when the steps stopped creaking and cracking, a large dark figure hit the last step and he turned directly facing us. We could see a shiny object in his hand and it was so dark in the place, I don't know if he even saw us. On complete instinct and without hesitation, we opened fire on the large dark figure and from the prior stillness of the night, it turned into what sounded like a firing range and the only light now was from the sparks as the bullets left our revolvers.

It seemed like the gun shots went on for a long time and because it was so dark, we did not know if we hit our target or not. At first it appeared that we did not, which would have been impossible. The intruder ran toward the front door and jumped right through the window and I was thinking, damn, this son of a bitch is going to get away and how in the hell would we explain that. We were stunned at first and thought all our shots may have missed him, but Joe was an expert shot and I was just average. The room was twelve feet wide, hell we could have hit this bastard with basketballs. We had a hard time opening the front door and when we did, we were somewhat relieved. We found a black man about fifty feet down the street and he had been shot several times. I can still remember how quiet it was on the street that early morning and apparently no one had even heard all the shots from within the bar. As I approached the man with my gun still in hand, I knew then that we hit our target many times. I had mixed feelings, I knew that we had accomplished our mission, but I could not help to feel sadness for this guy as he literally took his last breath as I knelt over him. Here I was in the still dark hours of the morning kneeling next to someone I had never met and because of his stupid actions, we took his life. No police officer wants to have these moments, but Baltimore was a nasty city back then and still is today. We called for an ambulance, but this was just a formality. This guy was dead on the sidewalk and now the scene became eerie, but that's life in Baltimore. You take your chance as a bad guy and sometimes the good guys are there to stop you and life goes on in charm city.

In today's world, when a cop shoots and kills someone, they are placed on leave and they receive treatment for Post Traumatic Stress Syndrome. Hell, back then when you killed someone, you wrote the report, had a few drinks with your buddies, went home to your family, read about it in the paper, watched it on TV, and a few hours later you were getting ready to come back to work. I guess the therapy back then was all your cop buddies congratulating you for getting some scum bag off the streets of Baltimore.

When I went in the next day for work, it was as if I was a celebrity. The guys were all patting me on the back and I guess that was our way of handling things like that. I find it funny when you talk to people that are not cops and they say things like, "Man, if I was a cop in the city, I would shoot every son of a bitch that messed with me." I don't even respond to a statement like that, because first it makes no sense and second, the people who make statements like that, would not have the balls to walk the streets of Baltimore or any crime ridden city.

Back in those days when a cop shot and killed someone, they had to go to homicide court to see if the judge would rule the shooting justifiable. We went to court on that Monday and the judge was Mary Arabian and it was a known fact throughout the police department that this judge really did not like police officers and the feeling was mutual. As the senior police officer on the case, I testified in court to the facts surrounding the shooting and what led up to us being in the bar. I testified to the judge in detail, just the way it had happened and the Assistant State's Attorney, Dick Welsh told the judge that in his opinion, it was definitely a justifiable homicide. Well, the judge was scrolling through some papers and had that look on her face that she was not listening. She looked up and said, "I have a question." She said the reports that she was reading stated that the deceased person was shot eleven times and that fact is verified by the autopsy report. She than looked directly at me and said, "Why?" I was not sure what the question was and I said, "Why what?" and that sort of upset her. She said, "Why was he shot eleven times?" Without thinking about how the answer would sound, I said, "Your honor that was because my partner had a six shot revolver and I had a five shot revolver." She gave me that look of disgust that she had perfected and said, "I guess you are telling me that if you had a six shot revolver, the deceased would have been shot twelve times" and I said, "Yes, your honor." Well, she went off on a tirade saying that she thought this was "overkill" and it could have been handled differently. The states attorney who later in his career became a judge, Dick Welsh, told Judge Arabian that what these two police officers did was proper within the law and they did not know what the deceased intruder had in his hand when he came down the steps. He also said that the break in at the bar was a felony and the officers acted properly in preventing the escape of a felon and fingerprints have verified that this person had broken into the bar on several other occasions. I seriously, at this point thought that the judge was going to have the case sent to the Baltimore Grand Jury. She made us sweat it out a little and then reluctantly, she said, "I have no choice under the law, but to make this a justifiable homicide, but I would advise you two officers to try to use some better judgment in the future."

I stood there biting my lip and wanted to tell her that maybe in the future she should accompany us on these situations and let us know when the proper time would be to protect our lives, instead of sitting on the high and mighty throne second guessing what police officers do every day on the streets of charm city.

It was written up in the newspaper the next day and nothing happened to us, but it was scary for awhile in the courtroom because the judge had the power to hold the case over for the Baltimore Grand Jury. It would have also meant a suspension from the job for a period of time and all the unnecessary attention that goes along with it. Needless to say you never know what a grand jury made up of people living in the inner city of Baltimore would have decided. Maybe they would agree that is was overkill, whatever the hell overkill is, if you're killed, your dead, whether it was overkill or not. How many bullets does it take to stop a man...not sure, but in this case the answer is eleven. Oh yeah, the shiny object in this burglar's hand turned out to be a coke bottle, which should be a lesson to the bad guys, DON'T COME TO A GUN FIGHT WITH A COKE BOTTLE...

NEXT SHOOTING...

Well, as fun and games went on in the city it was about two months after the shooting at Bernie Lee's Pub, that I got involved in another shooting. I was working in uniform and patrolling a foot post in the area of Mount Vernon Square, which was a park that surrounded the Washington Monument and a hangout for "Hippies."

It was about 9 PM and I was walking on Saint Paul Street, near the park when I saw this guy breaking into a car. I could clearly see that he had a screwdriver and was prying open the window to the car. I watched for awhile and wanted to make my approach and actually get him inside the car which would be an advantage for me and I would not have to chase him. He was having trouble getting into the car. He broke the side window and reached in and grabbed something from the seat. I figured this was the time to approach him and make the arrest. You always try to think of the best way to do this and minimize chances of getting hurt. I walked toward him and he took off running, with the screwdriver in his hand and me in pursuit. I saw him run into an indoor parking lot just off of Saint Paul and Mulberry Street. It was nighttime and it was really dark inside the garage. I did not call for assistance at that time, as I actually thought he got away, but I wanted to make sure. I walked into the garage and was about to give up on him, when all of sudden he jumped from behind a cement post and punched me in the side of the head with his fist.

I am not sure why he did not use the screwdriver on me, because he certainly had the opportunity to do so. He stunned me for a minute and actually scared the shit out of me. I could see where he was running and he still had the screwdriver. I remember him hollering to me, "Leave me the fuck alone" and I was thinking, why should I leave him alone, he just smacked me in the face and his ass was going to pay. I am not sure why he did not use the screwdriver on me in the garage, but I am glad he did not. If he had used it, I might not be here writing this story or I might be writing it in Braille. I know he punched me with the same hand that had the screwdriver in it and just missed my eye. I chased him down Mulberry Street toward the front of the Baltimore Sun building, which is our local newspaper. I was surprised that I was keeping up with him and I am sure he was also. I hollered for him to stop and when he did not, I fired one shot and struck him in the back. I was actually surprised, because I was not that good of a shot. When he fell to the ground, I was thinking at first that he might have fallen, but with him not moving, I knew that I had hit him with the one shot. I approached him and at the same time, I called for assistance. When I got to him, I leaned down to see if he was breathing and as I was leaning over him, a newspaper reporter came out of the Sun Building and snapped my photo. Before I could stop the photographer, he ran back into the Sun Building with his camera and my photo.

Needless to say, the next morning on the front page of the newspaper was that photograph, with the caption stating, "Police Officer Shoots Another Suspect." The photo showed me leaning next to the dead guy and as some photos do not depict what is actually happening, the photo shows me holding my gun close to the dead guys head, as if I were going to shoot him again. The article went on to say that I had shot and killed two people in a period of two months and it talked about the shooting at Bernie Lee's Pub.

I remember that night while waiting for the morgue wagon to arrive, my shift lieutenant, John Lauer arrived on the scene. I remember he was an old bald-headed man, who's only real claim to fame as a police officer was being very neat and that is why we called him "Mr. Clean." Without even asking why I shot the guy, the lieutenant said "Son, you have got to stop shooting everyone who gives you a problem." I was stunned that he said that and could not believe that would be a comment from a supervisor and neither could the other officers who were standing around the shooting scene. As you can imagine when you have to shoot someone, it is a very traumatic experience and the last thing you want is some bald-headed bastard telling you not to shoot your gun, especially when they don't even have all the facts. I guess it would have been better if the bad guy had stabbed me in the face or taken out one of my eyes. I guess for that piece of shit lieutenant that would have been a better reason for me to waste the son of a bitch. I disregarded what the lieutenant said and wrote the report just the way it happened and thank God I had support from my sergeant and the rest of the shift.

I had another trip to homicide court, but it was a different judge and it went fine, although I was kind of nervous because there were a lot of newspaper reporters in the courtroom. I think they were just waiting for me to slip up and say the wrong thing. No one could say this was overkill, because there was only one shot fired and I still had the marks on my face from the punch when I went to court.

I have often thought about that shooting because I was not a very good shot with the police revolver and I was actually running when I fired the shot. When I would go to the police pistol range to qualify, which we had to do every year, I would usually shoot low scores and just about qualify. The shot that I fired at this guy was what you would call a center mass shot at the pistol range, which meant dead on in the center of the back. I actually thought I would just scare him and he would stop, I didn't mean to scare him that bad. I had police officers and some pistol instructors later congratulate me on being such a great shot and that could not be any further from the truth. I think it proves that no matter what you shoot on the pistol range under perfect conditions, it will never be like real life conditions on the street.

I remember being called into the Internal Investigation Unit a few weeks after this happened and they were questioning me on why I did not fire a warning shot at the fleeing suspect. I was prepared for this question, because it had come up in homicide court and the reason I gave, which was backed up by the state's attorney's office, was that the fleeing person had committed the crime of larceny from a vehicle. Also, when he struck me in the face, that was a felony and I was preventing a felon from fleeing and the need for the warning shot was not necessary.

It was about one year after this shooting that the police department changed their policy on firing your weapon. The change was that there would be no more warning shots fired under any circumstances. If in the line of duty, you had to use your weapon and you had good cause, you were to shoot to stop the fleeing person or to protect your life. I assume all these years later, the guys on the job now, don't even know my name, much less the fact that I changed the rules of engagement.

There are many euphemisms used by cops when they have to use deadly force, like; "Light him up", "Smoke him", "Waste him" and all cops know that they are expected to be prepared to kill. They also know that they will be judged by the public, the press, their department, the courts, even their family, and most importantly, themselves. The act of taking a life, usually only takes a moment, but is reviewed for infinity. The reality of killing a person is never what we expect, despite all the training received. No police officer wants to take a life, but it sometimes comes with the territory. Most thugs that are armed with weapons know that when they present that weapon when confronted by a police officer, they usually come out on the short end of the stick. On the occasions that I had to use deadly force, I did not hesitate. Bad guys know that cops have guns and real bullets, so why in the hell would they want to fuck with us, go figure.

POLICE OFFICER OF THE YEAR - 1967

My first two years on the Baltimore Police Department, I walked a post in a really bad neighborhood around Greenmount Avenue and Preston Street and we have talked a little bit about that already. In 1967, I was moved over to a pretty decent foot post around Charles and Eager Streets. The new post was in the same area that I had made the lock up on Mickey Mantle. When I first started there, I did not think I would see much action since the post was mostly commercial with some homes and apartments scattered around.

I got assigned to the new post because of a sergeant by the name of Francis X. Donahue, who lived in the same 10th Ward Irish neighborhood that I grew up in. My dad who was a cop for thirty-two years helped him get on the police department back in the late 50s, as he did with a few others from my neighborhood. I can remember when I was very young, some men in the neighborhood got on the police department because my dad knew the police doctor and could work some magic to get them on. I remember that Francis Donahue was a very short guy and he was probably about five feet, six inches tall on a good day. Back then, to get on the police department you had to be at least five feet, nine inches tall to even be considered for acceptance on the job. I recall my dad telling Francis Donahue to stand on his tippy toes when he went back for the final physical. Donahue got accepted on the department and apparently the tippy toes worked and that's because dad had already talked to the police doctor. My dad did things like this for guys trying to get on the job, because he was well respected in the police department and could make things like this happen.

When I went to the Central District in 1965, Sergeant Donahue made it a point to welcome me to the district and took me aside and told me that he owed me a big favor for my dad getting him on the job. My new assignment to Charles Street was his way of paying my dad back and he made me promise that I would tell dad that he made it happen. It's really funny how things work out like that. I know there are some retired cops that are very thankful for my dad helping them fulfill their dreams of being a cop.

Well, I received Policeman of the Year award in 1967 and how I got it was really interesting. On an extremely cold Baltimore night, I was standing at the call box at Maryland Avenue and Biddle Street, waiting to make my hourly call to the police station. On a very calm, cold, quiet Sunday night about 10 PM, I was looking north on Maryland Avenue. I could not believe what I was seeing. From where I was standing, I could see someone, just a figure crawling out of a 2nd floor window of a row house on Preston Street, which was about a city block away.

As I walked closer, I took off my police hat with that big shiny badge and took up an observation spot in the alley. From my vantage point, I could see that several people were loading a van with things from the rear of the house. I waited until they loaded the van and then approached them. I am not sure why I did not call for assistance; I guess I would have had to return to the call box for that, because we did not have walkie-talkies back then.

As I approached the van, it started to drive away and for some reason, two people jumped out and took off on foot, north on Maryland Avenue. I could not chase the van on foot, so I took off after the two runners and the chase was on. As they were running, they did a very smart thing and split up and I stayed with one. In the 1700 block of Maryland Avenue, I realized I was losing ground. I fired two shots over the runner's head and to my surprise, the runner stopped. I approached the person and as I was placing the cuffs on, I realized it was a female that looked like a man, but nevertheless it was a female and I was shocked. My shots had apparently drawn some attention and a nearby police car cruising in the area came to my aid. We returned back to the original scene and found that the house on Preston Street had been

34

broken into by breaking and entering through a window on the second floor. I had obtained the license number of the van, as I had a good memory back then. I also had a good description of the van and it was stopped about thirty minutes later in northeast Baltimore and the occupants arrested.

To make this short story truly short, four people were arrested. Two were in the van, the one I caught and one was picked up later and they were all females and admitted lesbians. This conclusion was no doubt and very obvious from their dress and overall appearance. It was later determined that people in the area that had their homes broken into, said they had seen several men in the area prior to the thefts. Obviously the females were mistaken for men because of the way they were dressed and without seeing them up close, you would certainly mistake these ladies as being men.

After some in-depth questioning, two of the females started to talk and after a very lengthy statement, they eventually admitted to many burglaries in Baltimore and surrounding counties. In the days following and after additional investigation, with the help of the detective unit, it was determined that the group had committed roughly one hundred and twenty burglaries in the city and several counties.

I have to say that I had a lot of help on this case from several veteran detectives, due to the fact that the burglaries were widespread. After a trial and conviction of all the female burglars, my captain submitted my name for the American Legion Police Officer of the Year Award. I won the award and had a nice ceremony and received movie tickets for a year, Coca Cola for a year, and a plaque. The ceremony was held at the American Legion Post #20, in the Hamilton section of the city. The gifts don't sound like a whole lot, but back in those days when I was probably making six thousand dollars a year, every little bit helped. I am very proud of that award and although over the years, I did receive other awards, this was the first and you always remember the first of anything.

It was really rewarding to be recognized early in my police career. I guess in any job, it is always nice to be recognized for good work. I can remember early in my career, I would be at roll calls and the shift lieutenant would read out about certain cops that always made good arrests. It seemed like it was the same names always being read out for catching a burglar, stopping a stolen car, or just being recognized for some type of outstanding police work. I knew that I wanted to be included with the elite in the district and having the gung ho mentality of a Marine, that I wanted to be a cop that everybody looked up to and said good things about. I came to realize that some cops stood out and really wanted to do the job and others just showed up for work and were just drawing a pay check.

I was fortunate that during my days walking a foot post in bad neighborhoods, there were many dedicated and gung ho cops that loved the police department and were always there for me and their fellow police officers. When you police in rough areas, which Baltimore had many, you have to have the confidence that if you get into a situation that could cause you some harm, your buddies are there for you. I knew that when I would hear a police officer call for help, I would do whatever it took to get there as fast as possible and I would expect nothing but the same from my fellow cops.

I still have that American Legion plaque on the wall in my basement and after all these years, it always reminds me of the early days on the job. I have been fortunate to get other awards along the way in my career on the department, but that one will always be special.

THE BALTIMORE RIOTS - 1968

As much as we all would like to forget the riots of 1968, it is a time that is etched in my memory forever. It was a very turbulent time of much unrest, not just for Baltimore City, but about one hundred and twenty-five cities around the country. Race relationships were still not very good in Baltimore City prior to the riots and when Martin Luther King was assassinated in Memphis on April 4, 1968, that was the tipping point for blacks in Baltimore and around the country.

On April 6, 1968, all hell broke loose in the city and continued until about April 14th. In the anticipation of the rioting, the Governor of Maryland, Spiro Agnew had called in the National Guard and five hundred Maryland State Police to be on standby on April 5th. I was working the 4 PM to midnight shift on April 6th when the riots started almost simultaneously on both the east and west sides of the city. It was a fairly quiet shift and we had heard rumors most of the early evening hours that there may be some trouble in the black sections of the city because of the assignation of Martin Luther King. Well, about 7 PM, we started to hear calls over the police radio for windows being broken on the west side and stores being looted and then the same for the east side.

I was in the Operation Squad in the Central District at the time and all our patrol cars were sent to Gay Street in east Baltimore where a staging area had been formed. Police were being dispatched from that site to areas of looting and burning all over east and west Baltimore. The looting eventually spread to other parts of the city. It was like it just mushroomed and soon the calls were so overwhelming that we would take four or five calls at a time. While we were responding to those locations, you would get additional assignments over the radio and it was literally impossible to keep up. Soon it was obvious that this type of response was not working, as the police department could not handle the volume of calls coming into the central dispatch. We were later called back to the headquarters building and just put in police cars in groups of four and roamed the city trying to stop as much of the burning and looting that we could, but it seemed fruitless. It lasted all night and the entire police department was held over and I did not go home until about noon time the next day.

I was called back to work about 6 PM and never went home after that for three straight days. Finally a curfew was put in place in the city from 8 PM until 8 AM the following day. The curfew seemed to work a little; at least it gave us an opportunity to get some rest. You could set your watch in the morning when the rioting resumed. It was as if they were standing in their homes and when the clock struck 8 AM, they were out the door.

I was in a patrol car with three really good cops and very close friends of mine; it was Steve Danko, Doug Cash, and my regular partner, Joe Bolesta. I can tell you that if you are going to be in anything that resembles combat, you could not have picked a better bunch of cops. All of these guys were not only fairly big, but they could handle themselves pretty well and were not afraid to jump in the middle if you needed help. We were all very good friends both on the job and off the job. I think this worked out well, because we knew each other's family and one thing was certain, we wanted to make sure each guy went home safe after our shift or in this case, after the riot.

During the days that followed, I saw some things that were incredible and having been in the Marines for four years, this was now the combat that I never saw. Most of the liquor stores and grocery stores were looted first and then any store in their path became a target. It was so bad that most businesses were just a shell after a couple days of looting and burning. The routine got to be, that we just pulled up on some stores and watched the looters run from the store with their loot. I saw a mother lifting her young child up to reach a shelf in a burned out grocery store that had something she obviously wanted and could not reach. I remember that she just looked at us, gathered her child and the loot, and just walked away. There were so many arrests that we were told to stop making lockups for minor offenses. Most of the arrested were taken to the Civic Center in downtown Baltimore and just held there on the main floor with police guards all over the place.

It was later estimated that fifty-five hundred arrests were made during the riots. The break down was thirty-three hundred for curfew arrests, nine hundred and fifty for burglary, six hundred and fifty for looting, three hundred and ninety for assault, five for arson and it was estimated that twelve hundred fires were set. There were also some deaths from the riot. There were seven deaths of which six were in a fire and one was from a gunshot. The city later reported that the estimated damage done by the 1968 riots was over twelve million dollars and that was in 1968 money. Baltimore was not alone with the riots, as most large cities around the East Coast had their riots also and the damage was just as severe as it was in Baltimore.

The riots scarred the city for many years after and the rebuilding was very slow, both in structures and police relations. If you go to some areas of the city today, you will still see the remnants of the 1968 riots. Even today when I am riding through the city, I can recall those terrible days and wonder how far have we have really recovered.

Race relations after the riots were at their worst, the city was still very tense and incidents of assault on police officers were at their highest. The cops, for some reason were seen as the enemy and actually we were not the enemy, we were the peacemakers. I also know firsthand that in a riot, no one wants to stop the violence long enough to talk. It seems much easier to just join the crowd and get whatever you can. I knew of small grocery stores, liquor stores, barbershops, churches, retail stores, and many other businesses that never recovered and either reopened in the suburbs or just completely went out of business. Lots of livelihoods were destroyed and the most interesting part of the destruction was that most of it occurred in the black community, which was already suffering from crime, poverty, dysfunctional families, and the lack of the types of stores that were burned. After the riots ended, you could ride through the areas of Baltimore that were hit the most by the riots and it looked like a war zone and for the most part, that is exactly what it was.

The only problem I saw during the riots with the National Guard and the Maryland State Police patrolling the streets, was that they were not very much help to the police department. Although you would not know that from newspaper accounts which made them out to be the saviors of the city. For openers, the National Guard did not have any live ammunition for their rifles and they did not know how to get around in the city. You need to remember, this was 1968 and there was no GPS. I know they had maps of the city, but by the time they figured out how to get somewhere, it was looted or burned to the ground. The rioters did not seem to give a damn that the mighty army was patrolling the streets, because they knew the streets better than the army and could out smart them.

One night just before curfew, we were patrolling in the 900 block of Whitelock Street in west Baltimore when we saw an army platoon lined up in the middle of the street. At first glance, they looked real impressive. They had rifles at the ready position, formed in a nice wedge in the middle of the street and their uniforms looked spiffy. They were trying to disperse a very large and disorderly crowd. The crowd's main objective that night was to finish looting the few remaining stores in that block. We got out of our patrol car and walked in the rear of the army ranks and we were just going to observe how they handled themselves. The crowd of bad guys was getting larger and they started to throw rocks and bottles at these neat looking army dudes. We knew things were going south in a hurry, but we did not want to step in and steal any thunder from the army. The situation was changing rapidly. The lieutenant in charge of the platoon screamed out an order, "Fix bayonets" and being a former military man myself, I was thinking they are going to stab the shit out of this crowd and I needed to stop that right away. My partner had a shot gun and I took it from him and fired two shots over the heads of the army guys in the direction of the rioters. Well, I am not sure who the hell we scared more, the rowdy crowd or the army guys, because the army did not know we were behind them and the crowd thought that the army now had some live ammunition. At this point, everybody was running: the army one way and the rioters another way. I don't know if you have ever been around when a Remington twelve gauge shotgun has been fired, but it will certainly get your attention quick. After the rowdy crowd dispersed, the young lieutenant in charge of the army unit came over to us and told us that his men did not have any live ammunition and he was about ready to charge the crowd with the fixed bayonets. I was not sure where this lieutenant was from, but I gave him a quick ghetto education, especially the part where people in that neighborhood were not afraid of knives and would have probably taken your bayonets away and kicked your butts. He said that he knew things were getting out of hand and thanked us for showing up in time and asked why we didn't let him know we were behind his unit. I told him that I wanted to fire the shotgun to give the effect that it came from your guys and maybe they would not screw with you the rest of the night. In all my years in the police department, I found that the greatest equalizer to a rowdy crowd was the shotgun. You did not even have to fire the shotgun, all you had to do was rack the round into the chamber and that sound was enough to make any person with any sense take off.

The riots of 1968 did not really prove anything or accomplish anything for the black community. In my opinion it only made the divide between whites and blacks more evident. It took many years for neighborhoods to rebound and rebuild, but many did not and have not, still to this day. I always wondered why people would destroy the very things that get them by in their everyday life, especially in neighborhoods that depend on small businesses. I know that during the riots many people gained material things at the expense of the death of a person that preached nonviolence. Did the fifty-five hundred people that were arrested in the 1968 riot in Baltimore really care about Martin Luther King Jr., or was it just an opportunity to act crazy, loot, and burn their city? I think that all the police officers that worked during the riot can answer that question.

After the rioting stopped in the city, all the so called, men of the cloth appeared and all the bullshit started. Where in the hell were they when we needed them to stop the looting and burning? After the riot, the city politicians and do-gooders came out of the woodwork and filled the TV all day and night with reasons for the riot: the black children don't have any playgrounds, no basketball courts with lights so they can play late into the night, no athletic centers for sport activities, no books in their schools, no free breakfast and lunch at school, no trash pickup, not enough police in their neighborhoods, no jobs, no free ice cream...I ran out of no's, so I threw in the ice cream thing. I did not hear any of the preachers or politicians talk about having a liquor store on almost every corner in east and west Baltimore: a drug dealer on the corners that did not have a liquor store, no fathers in the homes, nobody staying in school long enough to get a good education, and fourteen year old girls missing school because they have to babysit children... their own.

It was certainly a sad day in this country when Martin Luther King Jr. was murdered, but he would not have wanted his people to commit acts of violence. He would have rather they continue the mainstay of his preaching, which was that within the center of nonviolence stands the principle of love. I think we have come a long way in our efforts to make race relations something that Doctor King would have been proud of and his famous quote, "I have a dream that my four children will one day live in a nation where they will not be judged by the color of their skin, but by the content of their character," is getting real close to reality and just think how proud he would be that a black man is president of this great country.

CENTRAL DISTRICT VICE SQUAD - 1970

In 1970, I was asked to work in the Central District Vice Unit which investigates various vice activity, such as prostitution, liquor violations, and gambling. In those days, the sergeant in charge of the unit asked for the men he wanted in the unit and the assignment usually lasted about three years. The sergeant in charge of the unit in the Central District was Pete Bailey, who was a top notch guy and anybody that would be asked to work in the unit with him, would certainly jump at the chance. The unit actually had two sergeants and each sergeant had two men. One unit would work the day shift, which was 8 AM to 4 PM and other would work the night shift, which was 8 PM to 4 AM and would switch shifts every two weeks. When I was asked to go in the unit, I was thrilled to find out that my partner would be Joe Bolesta. I had worked for awhile with Joe in patrol and you could not ask for a better partner. He was an excellent cop and later in his career would move rapidly through the ranks to the position of Deputy Commissioner, which is one step under the Police Commissioner.

Looking back on it, the three of us were very effective in the Vice Unit and we made some excellent cases over the few years in that unit. The units were compared with other units throughout the city, as far as monthly stats went. In each police district in the city there was a Vice Unit and the captain of the district always wanted to be at the top at the end of the month with arrest statistics. We were always at the top each month and some of that could be attributed to the fact that most of the prostitution in the city was occurring in the Central District.

Also, with the "block", a nighttime adult entertainment area in the Central District, we had no problems making arrests for prostitution and liquor violations in and outside the strip joints on Baltimore Street. Back in those days, there was no legal Maryland Lottery and all gambling was illegal and we made plenty of gambling arrests each month. Looking back on it, it now seems silly that we arrested people for taking bets on the illegal numbers racket, because most of the arrests were the small people and not the guys that were at the top of the organization and making all the money.

I have too many great stories about the days I worked in the Vice Unit to try to include them all in this book, so I will pick some of my favorites. I hope you enjoy them and they are all true, hell, who could make up stuff like this.

One night we were on the "block", which was an area that extended about four city blocks on Baltimore Street in downtown Baltimore from Fallsway west to about Guilford Avenue with strip clubs on both sides of the street. On this particular night we were in a strip club called the Gay White Way, trying to make an arrest for soliciting for prostitution. Lockups for prostitution could be made in any club on the "block", but this night we singled out the Gay White Way, because we had received some complaints about blatant prostitution in that joint.

When you enter the strip clubs on the "block", the lighting is very dim and this is so some sex acts can take place either right at the bar or in the back of the club. Another reason for the low lights was obvious once you entered the bar and saw some of the ladies of the evening, hell, if you saw them up close, you would want to shoot the lights out.

I was with my partner, Joe Bolesta, and when we entered the club we went to different ends of the bar looking to make a couple arrests for prostitution. We did enter together, but by sitting at different spots at the bar, we had a better chance of appearing that we were not together. We were close enough so that we could watch each other across the bar. Pete Bailey was our sergeant and he was outside the club and said he would give us about fifteen minutes and then he would come in to see how we were doing.

I sat at the bar and was immediately approached by a very scantily clad, seemingly attractive young lady; remember what I said about the lights. She asked me to buy her a drink, as she maneuvered a set of very large breasts onto my shoulder. We ordered drinks and now having known this broad for about thirty seconds, she has her very small hands on my very small private parts. I made a move for my wallet; she made a move with her hands and all the sudden my small parts are getting bigger. I need to point out that I was about twenty-seven years old at that time and my partner was about thirty and if I have to say so, we were fairly good looking guys.

Well, not too long after this young lady sat down and got her drink, she asked me if I was looking for some fun. Hell, I was thinking, I am having fun already, how much better could it get. I asked her, how much the fun would cost and she said, "Fifty dollars for anything you want me to do." The proposition seemed reasonable to me, knowing that I was going to lock her up anyway. I said, "That's fine" and I was finishing my drink and trying to get my partner's attention.

My partner and I always had a prearranged signal for when we were going to make an arrest in a bar. The signal was that whoever was making the arrest would pull on his right ear to let the other guy across the bar know you were solicited and about to make the arrest. No matter what happened, it was important that neither one of us would lose eye contact with the other for safety reasons. I am sure you understand that it could be a problem giving the signal with a very attractive female kind of pulling on certain parts of your body.

With all the distraction going on with this young lady, I pulled myself together and remembered that I was a cop. I knew what my mission was and I pulled on my ear and my partner nodded and started to walk around the bar to assist me with the arrest. When he got close, I pulled out my badge and announced to the young lady that we were cops and she was under arrest for soliciting for prostitution. I probably should have made sure she had released her hand from my crotch before I announced that I was a cop, because she sort of yanked on it, before releasing it. She started screaming and the nightclub bouncer, a pretty big dude, came over and with the bad lighting, apparently did not see my badge and may not have thought we were really cops. He pushed me and I pushed him and a fight broke out. I don't think anyone at the bar knew we were cops and before you knew it, the whole place was fighting. It was actually pretty neat, like something you see in an old western cowboy movie. The whole joint was fighting. I saw the sergeant come in the club and he jumped right into the battle and he told me to just grab the girl I was arresting and get her outside the club. I had to wrestle her to the ground and then I grabbed her by the right leg and pulled her to the door and onto the street...or so I thought.

When I got through the door and out onto Baltimore Street, I was shocked to see that all I had was a leg and yes, I was really scared. I was thinking, did I pull this bitch's leg off, am I that strong or just what the hell was going on. What actually happened was, this lady was an amputee and had a wooden leg. In the excitement during the fight, when I thought I was pulling her outside, I in fact only had her wooden leg. Well, you can imagine how I felt standing on the street with a leg in my hand, but the fight was still going on and I went back in the bar to help out. I knew she was not going to run too far on one leg, or hell, maybe she carried a spare for just these kinds of occasions. By this time uniform patrol cops had come to our aid and several arrests were made.

When things settled down in the bar, it was not hard for me to find the lady I was trying to arrest, since she was the one sitting down on the sidewalk holding a leg, which she had gone and retrieved. I helped her up and she strapped her leg on in front of me. We took her to the Central District and booked her for soliciting for prostitution. Several others were charged with disorderly conduct and the bartender was charged with assaulting me. The rest of the night was hilarious, as we laughed quite a lot, over a few drinks about the strip club fight and especially the part about the leg coming off the prostitute.

I will end this story with telling you about the court proceedings the next day. The judge was Robert Gerstung, who was very familiar with me and our unit. We were in his court almost every day with prostitution or gambling arrests. I approached the bench to testify and the lady was brought from the rear cellblock where she had spent the night. Now in the light of the courtroom, she did not quite look as good as she did in the very low lighting of the strip club the night before. I testified about being solicited for prostitution. I did not mention the part about the leg, because I did not think it was relevant to the arrest. When I was done testifying, the judge asked her if she had anything to say and boy did she have something to say. She said, "Your honor I did solicit this bastard for prostitution," pointing to me, "But he didn't tell you he pulled my fuckin leg off." With that she pulled up her dress and showed the judge her wooden leg and this was a sight to behold. I don't mean to talk bad about people's appearance, especially an amputee, but this was getting ugly quick.

I often wondered when she did have sex with guys, did she take the leg off or did those poor bastards go home with splinters in their legs. Can you just imagine that you pay this whore for sex and she says, "Okay, but first let me take off my leg." Do you ask for a refund or just run like hell and go home to your wife and tell her how much you love her and how pretty her legs are. I wonder how many men in Baltimore today are telling the story about getting laid by a prostitute that had a wooden leg or are they just keeping that to themselves, what do you think?.

Needless to say, the judge and everyone in the courtroom were stunned and the judge, trying to keep his composure looked at me and said, "What the hell is she talking about." I had to explain the whole story in open court and although she did not seem to be embarrassed, as she stood there still holding up her dress to show the attachments for the leg, I sure the hell was.

The judge settled down and regained his composure and found her guilty for soliciting for prostitution and fined her one hundred dollars and court cost. I have lived with that story for quite a few years and now when we have police reunions or retirement parties, I am always asked to tell the story about pulling the prostitute's leg off. When I tell the story, those that are hearing it for the first time, just give me a look of disgust. When I get to the part about the leg, they just shake their heads. I know they have to believe me, who would come up with a story like that if it were not true and if they don't believe me and question my truthfulness, then I really don't have a leg to stand on…that was cruel…let's move on.

PROSTITUTE ROUNDUP

Just one more wild and crazy story about prostitutes, although I have a lot, not prostitutes, stories, so I will tell you just one more, I promise.

My partner, Joe, and I started out one night with the intentions of making a lockup around the War Memorial Plaza which was directly across from Baltimore City Hall. We had noticed for about two weeks that the prostitutes were using this area to pick up the "johns" who patrolled around the block until they made a deal with the prostitute. Our plan was for me to drive around the area in my personal car, which was a 1967 Chevrolet Camaro, two door coupe. I loved that car! My partner would follow close by in his personal car, which was a piece of shit station wagon. He would act as protection for me in case anything would go wrong.

The prostitutes back then were known to carry weapons, which ranged anywhere from razor blades and knives to guns. It was also known that some of the prostitutes were working with their boyfriends or pimps and their only real intentions were to get you alone with the prostitute in a car and come up on you and rob you. It was understood on the street that prostitutes knew that if they robbed a potential customer, the police would not be called and the customer would just go about his business, because he did not want his wife to find out he was out getting laid.

It was about 8:30 PM on a typical hot, humid, Baltimore summer night, and it was just getting dark. I made my first approach around the War Memorial Plaza and sure enough the place was loaded with prostitutes. I pulled my car over at Fayette and Gay Streets and in no time at all, I was approached by a prostitute who leaned in the car and said, "What can I do for you big boy?" We didn't even have sex yet and she was already calling me "big boy." I asked her how much and she said, "It depends on what you want." I should point out that to make a good legal arrest for prostitution, that would hold up in court, you needed to have the prostitute say what she would do and the price. The rule on the street back than was that if a prostitute approached a vice cop, you were getting locked up, whether you said all the right words or not. I told her that I only had twenty-five dollars and she said that would be fine and she got in the car. I would also point out that there was some explicit talk about exactly what she would do to me for the twenty-five dollars, but for the purpose of some halfway decent reading and also the possibility of my grandchildren reading this book one day, I will leave all that nasty shit out.

As I drove away, she wanted to direct me to a very dark lot on Gay Street near a vacant warehouse. I knew better to go there, because I did not know if my partner could pull his car in there without spooking this broad. I told her I had a better place and I drove around the block and drove right up the ramp to the police station. I knew this could be a dangerous move, because a lot of these prostitutes that worked the streets were tough and could handle themselves well and this one was a lot bigger than me. I was surprised that she did not try to bolt on me, when I told her I was a cop and she was under arrest. My partner was right behind me and at this point when I stopped at the top of the ramp, I showed her my badge and told her to just sit still and don't make any moves until I opened her door. I was again surprised that she did not try to get out of the car and run, but I tried to use my very convincing cop voice and I guess the Smith and Wesson I pulled out of an ankle holster made her think that running might not be the best course of action.

We took her in the police station, put her in a holding cell, and went back on the street, to try our luck again. Here is where it gets real interesting. I drove back to the War Memorial Plaza area and pulled my car to the same corner. I was there about two minutes when another prostitute came over to the vehicle. This one said the same lines as the first prostitute and I told her to get in and I did the same thing with her that I did with the first prostitute. When we put this girl in the holding cell with the other one, it was funny to hear them talk about the lockup. I heard one of them say, "That same son of bitch got me, that ain't fair!"

I went back to the same area and yes, the "pickins" were good and another prostitute came over to the vehicle. This one was a little smarter or at least it seemed so and she asked me if I had just been there and picked up a girl. I told her that I was there and said that the girl got out of the car before we could make a deal on how much I wanted to spend on her. She got in the car and we made a quick deal and I was driving her to the police station to meet her two other buddies. I remember that this prostitute was actually attractive and very well built. I could not help but notice that while sitting in my little Camaro, her legs were looking damn good. She talked a little better than the average prostitute. After the discussion about money and what she would do for me, we actually had a decent conversation on the way to the station. She told me she was in town from Boston and was trying to make some money and would then be heading back to Boston.

As I approached the ramp, I have to admit that I was thinking about letting this one go and continuing our discussion later. I could see my partner in my rear view mirror and I didn't know how he would think about letting her go. I was thinking fast and I figured we already had two in the box, so to speak and if I wanted to, I could let her go and drive back to the plaza and just get another one. If you think this is terrible for a cop to do, get a life and picture yourself as being a fairly good looking twenty-seven year old with a beautiful woman in your car and can offer her a deal that she can't refuse. Being a good cop, I did what a good cop would do and I drove past the station, and pulled over and told her that I was a cop. I told her that I was not going to arrest her for prostitution, but if she was going to be in town for a few days, I would like to hook up with her. I was surprised at what happened next. She started to cry and shake all over and I mean all over. I told her to calm down that she was fine, but by now my partner had pulled in back of me and came walking up to the window. He looked in and said, "What the hell is going on?" She started to cry and shake more. I got out of the car and took Joe to the side and told him that I was going to let this one go and he said, "You got to be kidding." I told him to go and take another look at her. He took a look and came over to me and said, "You got to do what you got to do brother, I'll meet you in the station."

I asked where she was staying and she said she was at the Quality Inn on Pratt Street. I started to drive her to her hotel and she continued to cry and told me she did not do this on a regular basis and she was in town with two other girls who had talked her into making some quick money. For some reason, I found myself believing this girl and as I pulled up to the hotel, she stopped crying. I could now see her more clearly and she was beautiful, not your typical run of the mill prostitute.

I started to preach to her about the dangerous life of prostitution and how she could get hurt or even killed in this city. She started to cry again and I told her that she had nothing to cry about, that I was giving her a chance to straighten things out and take her life in a better direction. I knew at this point that I could not turn back now and still lock her up. I also knew that I probably should not get involved with her and just chalk this event up as a good deed and something she might remember the rest of her life. I told her that I had to go and that what happened tonight was between she and I and it was personal. I told her that it would be in her best interest not to discuss it with anyone, at least anyone in Baltimore. She assured me that she would not tell anyone and she was heading back to Boston as soon as she could hook up with her girlfriends. I was thinking, that might be a problem, I may have already locked most of them up.

I drove back to the station and Joe was waiting on the ramp for me. I parked the car and walked over to him and before I could say anything, he said, "What the fuck were you thinking?" Instead of my usual statement of "Who me," I knew that he was mad and he had a right to be, but I was also thinking that knowing him, he would have done the same thing. After a few minutes of exchanging pleasantries which I can't repeat, we laughed it off and decided to continue our mission to clean the plaza of prostitutes. Joe told me to put my game face back on and let's get back to the plaza and see what was left on the meat rack.

We went with the same plan and I drove right up to the plaza and parked in a different spot and sure as hell, here comes one, struttin her shit. This one was bold, as she just got right in the car and said, "Ain't you the guy that was up here earlier and picked up one of the girls?" I always considered myself a fairly quick thinker and it usually pays off. I told her that I was really pissed off, because the girls that got in my car all got out after we could not come up with a decent price. This prostitute looked stunned and asked what I meant. I told her that the girls that I picked up had all turned me down after getting into my car. This prostitute was apparently desperate and said, "I'll take care of you honey" and looked relaxed as we drove away. While I was driving, she actually apologized for the other girls and said, "You won't regret getting me baby." Well, I drove her to the ramp of the police station and told her I was a cop and she actually laughed and said, "I can't believe I fell for your stupid bullshit."

My partner and I discussed if we should continue or switch rolls. After all, I was getting tired of being told I was going to have sex and then busting some attractive women. We decided to talk about it over a cup of coffee. We were walking down the "block" to a small coffee shop. Sure as shit, we were approached by two females who smiled and like I told you earlier, that was about all we needed. We stopped and talked to the ladies and before you know it, bingo, we were asked if we were looking for some fun. As we were talking to them, I was thinking, damn, a working man can't even take a break to get a cup of coffee. We had a discussion and I told them I had a hotel room close by and we would all go there. The ladies told us they were from out of town and I think I had heard this earlier. They said they did not know the area well. As we walked them toward the police station, one of them asked where we were going. I told them we were getting our car which was parked in a parking lot under the police station. I really did tell them that and I remember them laughing and giggling about parking a car under a police station. Joe and I laughed harder than they did, because if you think about it, it's pretty damn funny. As we approached the station house, I told the ladies that we were actually cops and they were under arrest for soliciting for prostitution.

Well, now we had six prostitutes in the holding cell in the station and the desk sergeant told us that we had to do something with them because he needed the room for other prisoners. We decided that because it was only about 10 PM, we would take time to write the charging documents on the ladies and go back out on the street. We decided to relax and get a few drinks.

After all, we had been working real hard. Don't you just love it when vice cops say they are working hard; most guys would give up their first newborn to do this job.

We ended the night, which was actually the early morning hours by the time we left the station. I went home and like any working man, I was really beat from a hard day's work…I know, you are now saying, "bullshit", to the hard day's work part. I got in the house about 4 AM and after reading some mail, I jumped into bed. I rolled over on my side and as I was trying to fall asleep, I was thinking of the prostitute that I let go. I was thinking, damn, if my wife is that deep in sleep, maybe I can make it down to the hotel and get a little bit and return before she wakes up. I actually could not sleep, but I knew how wives work and if I made a move for the door, she would bust out of that sleep, like a jack in the box.

I finally fell asleep with the thought of little prostitutes dancing in my head, no not sheep, prostitutes, that's the good part about dreams; you can make them what you want.

Switching To Guys – Guys Solicit Also

One night, we decided to switch it up a little and go after some gay guys. We decided to drive to the area around Park Avenue and Read Street which was a known area for homosexuals trying to pick up men or boys in their cars. The procedure at this location was that men and boys would stand on the corner of Park Avenue and Read Street and the gay guys would circle the block and pick out who they wanted. We decided to give it a try and because I was the youngest and the smallest, I had the better chance of being picked up by a gay guy. My partner was six feet, four inches tall and weighed about two hundred and thirty pounds, so he might not be the type of person a gay guy would want to pick up. I was five feet, eleven inches tall and weighed about one hundred and fifty pounds at the time.

I stood on the corner and as luck would have it, I was picked up within ten minutes. Our plan was that after I got in the car and the car drove off, my partner would pull his unmarked vehicle real close to the driver side door of the gay guy's car. I would than reach over and take the keys out of the ignition and announce that I was a cop. I had done this many times in the past and for some reason it was always a very touchy situation. It was dangerous, especially if the guy did not believe you were a cop. Remember, he is thinking that he is picking up a gay guy and when you reach for the keys, he might think he has a gay car thief. Also, just because these guys were gay, it did not mean they were small weak people. Most of the men we arrested were usually big guys and you never knew if they had weapons in the vehicle. I really didn't like this part of the job; it was something about sitting in a vehicle and talking to another man about sex. I would rather stick with the prostitutes, but you gotta do what you gotta do to be a good vice cop.

As a final note on this arrest, as we were booking this guy we asked what he did for a living and he said he was an emergency room doctor. I really don't remember the hospital he worked in, but this was very typical of the men arrested for picking up other men and boys. We had previously arrested on the same corner: a Marine, a priest, a banker, a school teacher, and many other "normal" occupations. Apparently these men lead seemingly normal lives during the day and troll the streets of Baltimore at night to pick up men. We made these types of arrests, because our captain put the pressure on us. He was getting complaints from the neighborhood associations about these guys hanging on their corners.

I actually felt a little uncomfortable when I would go to court with these arrests, because like with the female prostitutes, you had to testify to the exact language used by the gay guys when they picked you up. I don't know about you, but to stand in a packed courtroom, in front of a judge, states attorney, and most of your fellow police officers and testify that this pervert wanted to do certain things to my anatomy, just seemed a little embarrassing to me. I did it and apparently I did it well, because we made many arrests of gay guys soliciting for perverted sex acts while I worked vice.

I am not sure if they still arrest gay guys for soliciting these days. Hell, you can get in the Marines or other services if you are gay and probably join the police department also. I can't imagine being in a fox hole with a Marine and he is gay. I guess instead of hollering, "gung ho" he might be hollering, "gung hung" or something like that and sleeping on your back with one eye open would be wise.

NAKED IN THE GAY CLUB

I actually had another very weird situation involving gays, when my sergeant asked me to go into a gay nightclub in the city. The club was a known hangout for gay guys. The sergeant wanted to see what was going on and to check to see if alcohol was being sold there and to get solicited for a perverted sex act if possible. I was real hesitant about this assignment, because when we would watch this club, we saw some pretty big muscle dudes going into the place because it also had a workout facility in the club. I also knew that I would be going into the club without a gun and badge, because if I got in and said that I wanted to work out, it would not be possible to have my gun and badge.

I had no choice in this assignment and if anyone was going to get in and look like they belonged, it was me. The plan was to go in the club and after I got past the front desk, I was to walk around and observe as much as possible. My sergeant, Pete Bailey, was giving me some instructions and while he was talking, he and my partner could not keep from laughing. I knew they were enjoying this and for once, I was wishing that I was a bigger guy and didn't get all the shit jobs.

Pete said that he and Joe would wait outside in a car for about thirty minutes and if I did not come out by then, they would come in with some uniform officers. I told Pete that I was real hesitant about this and he assured me that nothing would happen and he and Joe would be in the place in about thirty minutes and what the hell could happen in thirty minutes.

I made sure I had nothing on me or in my wallet that would identify me as a cop and I was dressed with just jeans and a short sleeve shirt. I went into the lobby of the club and was stopped by this huge guy that was wearing this outfit that professional wrestlers wear. The outfit was the weirdest looking thing I have seen. I mean this guy was huge and had bulges all over his body, including his private parts, not that I was staring at his private parts.

I asked if I could come in and look around and see if I wanted to join the club in the future. I was asked a whole lot of questions about where I lived and what I did for a living. In situations like this, I had to use my correct address, because of my driver's license and I did not like to do that, because of possible retaliation. I told them that I was employed at the American Can Company in Baltimore County. I used that occupation, because I had a brother that worked there and if anyone ever went that far as to check my employment, they would get the verification that an Ellwood worked at the can company.

I went through this questioning process for about ten minutes and it seemed strange that it took so long and it made me more suspicious that something was probably happening in this club that they wanted to screen everyone thoroughly. After I answered all the questions, the part came that I will never forget and has been a joke over the years with me, Pete, and Joe. The huge guy that was at the door asked me to follow him and we walked down a long corridor and it had a lot of doors. I could not see anyone working out, like lifting weights and things like that. While we were walking, the big guy did not say much, until we got to the end of the corridor. He opened a door to a small dressing room and said, "This is where you can undress." Well, this kind of caught me off guard and I said, "Excuse me, what did you say?" He repeated it and said, "This is where you can undress." I said, "Undress for what?" He smiled and that really scared me. He said that if I wanted a tour, then I needed to be undressed and I asked him why he was not undressed and that was a big mistake. He went into a very small room and within seconds he came out and he had nothing on and I was now wondering if the thirty minutes had gone by and where in the hell were Pete and Joe. I had no alternative than to take off my clothes and go along with this guy. I came out of the small room and he directed me to follow him back up the hallway. He reached over and held my hand and now I'm freaked out. I could not do anything, as he was directing me and all I could think of was that Pete and Joe were going to bust down this door any minute and what the hell would I do with this guy.

As we walked along the hallway, he partially opened the doors to a few of the small rooms. In each room, it appeared to be two guys naked and doing things to each other that I care not to explain in this story. I got the feeling that we were going to come to a door and he would say something like, "we" can use this room and that bullshit was not going to happen, regardless of my assignment or how big this bastard was. No way in hell were we going to have a scene from Deliverance, with me playing the guy that squealed like a pig.

At this point, I knew in my mind that the thirty minutes had passed and I was pissed and was thinking if I live through this, I will get those two bastards back. I could just imagine that they were outside somewhere sitting in the car and laughing. I was talking to the guy, but I don't know what the hell I was saying. I can remember asking him where the exercise room was and he never answered, just sort of laughed. Now I am furious, because for some nasty reason I think Pete is playing with me, but he has no idea what the hell I am going through with this "Atlas looking" son of a bitch, who doesn't really say anything, just keeps smiling at me.

Just when I am about to tell this guy I am a cop, which he probably would not believe me anyway, the front door gets pushed open and in comes Pete, Joe, and about ten uniform cops. Well, I really can't describe what happened at this point, except that total chaos erupted. Naked men were running all over the place and that included me. We didn't know until later that evening, that there were secret exit doors in the building and the naked men were grabbing what clothes they could and running for these exits. I was running to catch up with the big "Atlas" guy, but the uniform cops did not know who I was and they chased me. Two of them caught me, threw me against the wall, and cuffed me. I was screaming to them that I was a cop and to get my clothes, but one of them said, "Shut the fuck up fag."

I stood cuffed and against the wall for a few minutes before Pete and Joe came around the corner and they both literally fell to the ground laughing. I was so pissed and I was screaming, "Get me out of these fuckin cuffs or I will kick your ass!" Pete came over and said, "Hey just calm down, it's kind of funny seeing you in your birthday suit." Even now the uniform officers did not know what the hell was going on, until Pete told them that I was a vice cop and working inside this place trying to make a case. The entire time he is talking to them, I am still cuffed and naked against the wall. Finally I had enough of this bullshit and said, "Pete if you don't get these fuckin cuffs off me and get my clothes, I am going to shoot your fat ass, as soon as I can get to a gun!" He could see that I was really upset and told the officers to take the cuffs off. I was then just standing there naked having a conversation with a young uniform officer who must be thinking; if this is what the vice squad does, I am staying in uniform for my whole career.

I went to the room where I had taken off my clothes and they were gone. Apparently one of the other naked guys took my clothes in his haste to get the hell out the secret door. I looked around for some clothes and found some, but after what I saw in those small rooms, I was not about to put on someone else's clothes. I did find a pair of shorts and a tee shirt that looked fairly germ free and I put them on until I got to the station and found a jumpsuit.

Even today, this many years later, I still get a queasy feeling thinking about walking around that club holding hands with that big guy. If you are wondering if any arrests were made, the owner of the club was charged with setting up and maintaining a disorderly house and operating a club without a license. The big guy and all the others got out the hidden doors.

A couple of weeks after this incident, I was riding around with Pete and he said, "Let me ask you something about that night in the gay club." I knew something was coming that would bring back the pissed off feeling that I still had for what he did to me that night. However, I wanted to know what he had on his mind, so I said, "Okay, what do you want to know?" He pulled the car to the side of the road and said, "I was wondering, you keep referring to that guy in the club, as the big guy. Just how big was he?" I had a soda in my hand and was about to throw it on him and made the motion, but he covered up and I could not help but to laugh and smack him in the head. He pulled off in the car and when things were a little quieter, I said, "I think if you would have waited another ten minutes before knocking down that door, I could probably answer that question" and then thoughts of the movie Deliverance came back to me.

Dancing With My Sergeant

This is a short story about you never know who sees you when you are out in public, so be prepared.

I was working in the Vice Unit and our captain, Jim Cadden, called us in one day and gave us a very unusual assignment. He said he thought he had, in his words, a "gay cop" working in the district and he wanted us to check it out. He went on to say that he had information that a cop in the district was frequenting a gay bar and he wanted us to go in that bar on the upcoming weekend and see if he was there. I won't name the cop, but at the time, I knew this guy pretty well and I was totally surprised at what the captain had said about him. We really did not have much say in the matter, as the captain was quite adamant that he wanted to know about this guy and if he was gay, he wanted to get him off the police force or at the least, out of his district.

Well, the following weekend, my sergeant, Pete Bailey, and I went into the gay nightclub, called the Downtown Club at about 10 PM and it was packed. You have to understand that when you go in a place like this, you have to act like everyone in the place, in this case, gay. If you do not act like everyone else, you will stand out and probably be made as a cop or definitely someone who does not belong. With my sergeant, that would not be a problem, as he was a real character and could pretty much play the part in any situation that would come along. We really did not think anything would materialize with this assignment, so we thought we would just go in the gay nightclub and hang out for awhile, have a few drinks, and take in the sights.

I can remember Pete telling me the night before, to come to work looking a little gay for the assignment. Well, I am not sure what the hell looking a little gay is supposed to look like. I wore what a lot of men were wearing back then: white slacks, white shoes, and a light blue shirt. As I was driving to work, I thought to myself that I really did look gay. When I got to work that night, Pete could not stop laughing at me and said, "I am starting to wonder about you." Well, he was no prince of fashion himself and he also looked a little gay, in his plaid polyester pants and his pink striped shirt. When we were walking out of the station going to our car, some of the uniform cops gave us the business. Pete just grabbed my hand and kissed me on the cheek and called them all jealous bastards and we just kept on struttin our shit. I laughed so hard, I almost dropped my purse.

When we went into the gay nightclub, there were flashing lights and a live band playing. The place was really jumping. We could hardly move through the crowd to the bar, where we definitely needed a couple of drinks. We got a drink and started to look around the place for the police officer that we were supposed to be looking for. It was almost impossible to see the other end of the club, but Pete thought he saw the guy. I asked Pete, "How in the hell are we going to make our way back there without him seeing us?" Pete said, "We will dance our way back" and he grabbed my arm and we started to dance.

The dance floor was crowded with all gay men and I really can't articulate some of what I saw, except to say that they were grabbing and holding onto each other's parts while they were dancing and making all kinds of gyrations and sounds. I noticed Pete watching the other dancers and I was thinking he was going to put some kind of move on me, to show the others that we belonged. It was bad enough dancing with my sergeant, but if he started any shit, like grabbing my ass or kissing me on the ear, I would have nailed his ass right there on the dance floor. I guess I could have screamed that he was molesting me or something; I assume gay guys get molested.

I mean they were all swapping spit, squeezing butts, running their fingers through each other's hair, and all sorts of nasty shit. Pete decided he would have some fun with this and he was grabbing me and pushing me across the floor. I was laughing so damn hard; I thought I would piss myself right in the middle of the floor. Well, as we danced closer to the other end to get a better look at this police officer, Pete swung me around and I bumped into two men dancing. I started to say excuse me, when I looked the guy in the face and saw that it was my family doctor. You have to understand that my family doctor did not know what I did for a living, because I did not go to him that often, he mostly treated my wife and the kids. Pete did not know it was my family doctor and I was trying to pull him in another direction and he was laughing and resisting me. I grabbed him by the shirt and said, "I got to get the hell out of here, that guy is my family doctor." Well, the doctor was also trying to pull his partner in another direction and it was at that point that I realized that he probably did recognize me.

We did get to see the guy we were supposed to be looking for and it was not a pretty sight. He was sitting in a booth and had this other guy sitting on his lap and they were kissing, laughing, and having a good time. I told Pete, "That's it, we did our job. Let's get the hell out of here, I'm getting a little sick of this place."

As a police officer, it was absolutely disgusting to me to see a fellow police officer acting like he was. I mean this might be a guy that I would depend on down the road to come to my aid or possibly save my life.

We danced our way toward the front door and left the place. I could not help but to think for the rest of the night how I would tell this story to my wife. She would usually ask how the shift went. Even though she knew that I worked in the Vice Unit, it would be tough going home and telling her that I saw our family doctor tonight. She would have to say, "Where?" I would then have to say, "Oh Pete and I were in a gay nightclub and we were dancing and that's when I saw our family doctor." I guess I would expect her to say, "Oh that's nice, the kids and I have an appointment with him next week. I will make sure to discuss it with him."

The guy we were in the nightclub looking for did stay on the police department for about six months more before he quit. I would see the guy going out on the street in uniform and always wondered whether he also saw us in the nightclub that night. When he finally quit the job and the story got out, most of the officers he worked with thought that there was something funny about the guy. They did say that when he was on the street, he did his job and was a good police officer.

We left the nightclub that night and went back to doing what we did best, locking up whores and perverts. I see Pete on a regular basis, now that we are both retired and he has gotten older and gained some weight, but he still has some good moves and always tells me that I still have a nice ass.

PUMMELED BY A PIMP

I have a short story about my most serious injury while on the job. I was working in the Vice Unit and I was down on the "block" looking for prostitutes. From prior stories, you know that the "block" was where the strip joints were. I was standing on the corner of Baltimore and Gay Streets. I was standing by myself; Pete and Joe were across the street watching me. I was approached by a black female prostitute and we had a brief discussion about sex. Although the conversation was brief, she came right out with it and asked if I was looking to get laid. I gave a signal to Pete and Joe that I was going to make the arrest. I put my hand on her shoulder and told her I was a cop. I told her that she was under arrest for soliciting for prostitution and I started to lead her away toward the Central District. Pete and Joe were crossing the street to walk with me to the district. I never saw it coming, but a black guy came running directly toward me. I first caught a glimpse out of my right eye, but I thought he was going to run past me. I did not see the direct hit on me, but Pete told me later that the guy hit me like a linebacker. Pete said he did not think the guy was coming toward me. He said that even if he thought the guy was heading toward me, he could not have stopped him. The black guy literally lifted me up on the run and he and I went through the window of Pines Drug Store. He must have been running extremely fast, because I really did not see or feel him until he hit me. Pete said that the guy struck me about chest high and we went through the window, with him on top of me.

Pete and Joe came running to assist me. They got me out of the window just as the top portion had fallen to the exact spot that I had landed inside the store. I was told later, that several bouncers that work on the "block" also came to my aid. As I lay on the sidewalk bleeding profusely from a very serious head wound, Pete and Joe made the arrest of the guy. Pete was doing the best he could to stop the bleeding, but it was pouring out like a sieve. I think I was conscious during this ordeal, but I was told that I was fading in and out. Pete called for assistance and told the police dispatcher an officer was seriously injured and needed an ambulance as fast as possible. I don't remember the ambulance ride, but I do remember being in the emergency room at Mercy Hospital. I remember getting a lot of attention and that usually happens when a police officer comes into the emergency room with a serious injury.

I knew I was in bad shape. I didn't find out until much later, that the Homicide Unit was called to the scene. I saw the outline of my body with chalk later and that was scary. I received about thirty-eight stitches in the back of my head and neck area. I had to have a blood transfusion because of the amount of blood I lost. In the emergency room, I remember the nurse saying, "Stay with us, stay awake, you're going to be fine." I was scared when she said, "Stay with us." I know what stay with us means. They were cutting off my jacket and actually moved me to a cleaner gurney; the blood was still pouring out. I heard the doctor say, "We need to start to sew this guy up quick." I think they gave me something for pain, but I could feel them working in the back of my head.

When you lose blood as fast as I did, I found out that sometimes your hands become deformed and very stiff. When I saw that, I was really worried. We joke about it now, but when I was on the table in that condition, Pete started to get a little goofy. You would think the guy would be sympathetic to an injured comrade. He was his usual self; kidding with the nurses and watching them stitch me up. He asked the doctor if my hands would come around and the doctor said they should be getting feeling in them real soon. Well, when Pete heard that, he started to grab my wallet. I tried to fight him off with my deformed hands. We were laughing and the doctor was not real happy with all this horseplay going on. He told Pete to get the hell out of the room. He said he was going to stop sewing me up if Pete didn't leave. I guess it sounds a little goofy to the average person that someone would be doing that to his friend in an emergency room. I didn't particular care for it either, but I guess Pete was trying to make me laugh. He did finally stay out of the room and the doctor proceeded to stitch me up.

It turned out the black guy was a pimp for the female I was trying to arrest. He told Pete that he thought I was messing with his girlfriend and that is why he threw me through the window. Hell, if he thought I was messing with his scantily clad whore girlfriend, is that any reason to throw someone through a window. I would hate to see what he would have done to me, if he was really pissed at me. Pete said he charged the guy with assault on me and resisting arrest. The female prostitute was charged with soliciting for prostitution.

The next morning I went to court and I was a sight to see. I had a turban bandage around my head and some blood was seeping through the turban. The case against this guy was called and I went to the table in front of the judge's bench. They brought this guy out from the cell area in the rear of the courtroom. I looked at him and I could not believe what I was seeing. This guy appeared to be in much worse shape than I was. They had to assist him up to the table. He had bandages all over his body and he could hardly walk. I was thinking, did he get all these injuries when he went through the window on top of me?

The judge proceeded and after the charges were read, he asked me what happened. I testified to the facts like I have already told you. When I was finished, the judge said, "Is the man standing next to you, the man who threw you through the window?" I looked straight at him and said, "Yes, your honor, that's him." I can tell you now that I knew it was the guy, but if I had to pick this guy out of a crowd, I could have never done it. I never saw him at all when he ran into me and put me through the window. I did know that he was immediately arrested at the scene, because Pete told me. The judge asked the guy what he had to say. He told the judge that he thought I was messing with his girlfriend. Before he could finish, the judge stopped him and said, "Is this the way you handle people that are messing with your prostitute girlfriend?" The judge told him that he did not want to hear anymore, but the guy told the judge he wanted to talk about what the cops did to him after they arrested him. He went on to say that several cops put him a car and took him down near the Baltimore harbor. He said, "They beat the shit out of me." They handcuffed me and were dipping me in the water. They were telling me that they hope the crabs bite my black ass." He told the judge that after that, they continued to beat him. He said that when he finally was put in the cell, the next shift coming on also beat him. The judge was a real decent guy and always took up for cops when someone resisted arrest or assaulted a cop. The judge told the guy that he had heard enough. The judge told him that when you take the law into your own hands, you need to be punished. He said, "When you injure a cop in this city and come before me, you are going to pay big time." He sentenced the guy to eighteen months in jail. He suspended one year of it and placed him on probation for three years.

As they were leading the guy away, the judge said, "By the way, I don't believe a word you said about cops beating you. I know all these men and they would not resort to violence like you did." Well, over the next few days and weeks, I found out that the judge was wrong; they did put a big time ass whipping on that guy. I really don't know what actually happened to the guy. I do know that when you mess with a cop in Baltimore and hurt him, you will get your ass kicked in a big way.

Looking back on it, I think that he knew I was a cop. His whore girlfriend approached me and solicited me for sex and that was her mission. He probably had to assume that she was being arrested, because I am sure that I had a badge in my hand. I am not sure if he wanted to put me through the window of the drug store; maybe, he just could not stop. He got what he deserved and I am proud of the guys who took him for a ride and introduced him to the crabs in the harbor. There should be signs posted in bad areas of the city that say, "If you fuck with a cop in Baltimore, you will get the ass beating of your life." Maybe they could put that on the benches that are in the bus stops, next to the sign that says, "Have a nice day in Charm City."

Here Come De Judge

One time in the Central District while still working vice, Pete was called into the captain's office and he asked Joe and me to go with him. The captain was usually a very mild mannered man, but this day he was a little upset. He was not mad at Pete or us, but he started off by saying, "What the hell is going on down on the block?" Pete looked at the two of us, then looked at the captain, and asked him what he was talking about. The captain said, "I am getting a lot of complaints from the city council about the open air prostitution happening on the block." The captain went on to say, "Pete, if you and your guys can't get things under control on the block, then I will find some cops that will." We knew that the prostitutes' numbers were growing, but we were actually doing a good job and had made numerous arrests on the block for soliciting. The captain said, "I have to attend a meeting with some city council members next week and I want to be able to tell them that we are cleaning up the problem on the block." Pete assured the captain that we would get on it and we would come off the day shift, to work nights until we have it under control.

We left the meeting and Pete asked us if we would not mind working some night work until we can assure the captain that things are under control on the block. I didn't mind, I actually enjoyed night work as compared to day work, even if it did take me away from my family. It was something about working vice at night in downtown Baltimore. We had the most active district in the city when it came to vice activities. I loved the idea of being in plainclothes and making arrests, whether it was for prostitution, alcohol violations, gambling, or just going into nightclubs and checking young people out for drinking under age.

Back in those days working vice, I had long hair and dressed in some of the most outrageous clothes you ever wanted to see. I look at photos of me, Pete, and Joe back then and it is hilarious to see how we looked, but you had to dress the part. Even though we dressed the part, I always thought that people knew I was a cop. I would leave my house for work and I can't imagine what my neighbors thought. I know some of them knew that I was a cop, because they had seen me in uniform, but a lot of them never knew what I did. I also had a car back then that fit right in with the type of work I was doing. The car was a SIMCA and I am sure you are thinking, what the hell is a SIMCA. The car was made in France and in the 60s; it was the most popular car in France. To make sure I fit in with undercover police work, I put large stick on daisies all over the car. I also had a Camaro, but the SIMCA was my choice for fitting in with the hippies and others of that era.

Well, we started back on night work on a Friday night. All that week, we were thinking of how we could make an impact on the block and let the prostitutes know that we meant business and if they wanted to hustle, they better find another district. We were in the office at about 9 PM and Pete came up with a plan that at first sounded a little crazy, but we researched some law books and decided to give it a go. Pete said that he found an old law on the books that pertained to prostitutes and it stated that arrests could be made for leading a lewd and dissolute course of life. The law actually stated that if prostitutes were observed in an area for a period of time and it was felt that they were soliciting for prostitution, they could be charged under this particular law. I was actually surprised that such a law existed, but it sounded good and made sense to me.

To be truthful, in some areas of downtown, the prostitutes over a period of time, knew the guys working in the vice unit and would move or sometimes run when they saw us coming. Pete decided that we would drive around down on the block and the surrounding side streets and when we saw a group of prostitutes, we would just grab them and lock them up. Well, it didn't take long for this plan to show results. We drove around and in a period of about two hours, we arrested seventeen prostitutes and they were shocked when they found out what the charge was. We had them all booked in the district and we were back out on the street by about 11 PM.

In those days, when things were either slow or we had already made enough arrests for the night, we would hook up with some guys in the drug unit and knock down a few drinks. On this night, we met up with Leon Tomlin, who was the sergeant in charge of the Drug Unit working the night shift. We also met with three of his men, Vernon Wilhelm, Augie Buchheit, and Larry Clark. We had met with these guys on other occasions when things were slow and drank a few drinks down on the block at certain places that loved cops. Later that night, we were all heading into the station to make some reports and probably just head home.

We were in the district and fooling around and someone, I think it was Leon, said, "It's early yet. Let's have some fun with those whores you guys locked up." I was not sure at first what he meant by having some fun with those whores, because if my memory serves me, they were not much to look at and having fun with them was not something I wanted to partake in. I am not sure where Leon got this idea, but he said, "Come in the courtroom and I'll tell you what we can do".

The courtroom was attached to the station house and easily accessed through a hallway. We went in the courtroom and we were all sitting around talking and all of sudden, Leon came out of the judge's office and had on the black robe. Now, if you remember, Leon was about six feet, five inches tall and weighed about two hundred and fifty pounds and was a very imposing image in that judge's robe. We were laughing at him and he said, "Here is how we are going to do this," and we listened as he went into this plan that somehow sounded pretty neat, the more he talked. Leon said, "Let's have some fun with these broads and then we can call it a night and get out of here." Leon directed this as if he was a Hollywood producer. He said, "I'll be the judge, Dick can be the state's attorney, Vernon can be the defense attorney, Augie can be the bailiff, and Larry can be the turnkey."

I think we were laughing so hard and I was thinking, no way in hell can we pull this off. Leon continued to direct the production and he took his place up in the judge's chair. Vernon and I stood at the trial table where the testimony took place. Augie stood up near the bench where Leon was and Larry was in the back where the women would be brought out of the cell area and into the courtroom.

Well, all the so called actors were in place, but we forgot one important thing. We needed the turnkey to get the ladies out of their cells and into the courtroom and nobody had even talked to the turnkey to see if he would go along with the fun. Well, we talked to the turnkey and he actually thought it was funny and said that he would go along with it. You really have to picture this: we had all the lights on in the courtroom, it was about a little after midnight, Leon is wearing the robe and looks real judge like and Vernon and I are at the trial table waiting for the defendants. It actually looked as real as it does when court is in session.

The seventeen women were awakened and told that they were going to be tried in "night court," which there was no such thing, but they didn't know. They were paraded out and told to sit in the benches in the front of the court and it was a sight to see. Half of them were awakened from a deep sleep and looked a little rough, most just looked their normal rough. As they sat in the benches, Larry the bailiff, said, "Hear ye hear ye, court is now in session and the Honorable Judge Leon is presiding, and all rise." All the women stood and Judge Leon came out and took his place in the judge's chair and said, "Good evening everyone, are we ready to try these guilty people." I was standing with Vernon and when he said that, we just busted out laughing, but when I looked at the women, they were not laughing and things were going good to this point. Judge Leon said, "Bring the first guilty whore up here and let's gets this show on the road." Augie grabbed the first girl in the front and told her to stand in front of the judge and she did. Judge Leon said, "Who is here to represent this bitch tonight?" Vernon answered up and said, "Your honor I am representing this young lady and we plead guilty as charged." Well, this girl looked at Vernon and said, "You ain't my fuckin lawyer and who the hell said you were." Judge Leon stood up and said real loud, "I want to remind all you ladies of the night, that there ain't gonna be no fuckin bad words used in my court, you got it." He went on to tell this girl that she is being found guilty of soliciting to get laid and the fine would be a hundred dollars. He told Augie the bailiff to, "Take the bitch away."

Well, I think you get the idea of what went on in that courtroom that night and we actually went through about ten of the ladies, before we decided that it was getting late and we needed to get the hell out of that courtroom and go home. It was probably the funniest stunt that I had ever been involved in the entire time I was on the job. When we were leaving the station house and going to our cars to go home, we were almost pissing our pants laughing.

The next morning we had to be back for the "real court" and this time it was only me testifying. Pete had gone home early that night, but he did come in for court. Court started at 9 AM and we knew that with that many arrests, we would probably have our case called first. The judge that was presiding that day was Judge Brocolina and he was actually a pretty decent judge, well respected by everyone. The judge came out and took his seat and the ladies were brought out from the cellblock and they were all lined up at the trial table, just to the left of Pete and I. The charges were read out and the judge asked us who would do the testifying and I told him that I would and gave him my name.

I testified that the ladies were all picked up and charged with leading a lewd and dissolute course of life and that we had observed them on the block soliciting men for prostitution over a period of time. The judge called one of the ladies up to the trial table and asked her how she wanted to plea to the charges and that's when all hell broke loose. When asked how she wanted plea, she said, "Your honor, we already been tried. What's going on?" The judge looked at the states attorney and he just held up his hands and said, "Your honor, I have no idea what she is talking about." The judge then said, "What do you mean you have already been tried and who tried you?" Pete was nudging me and whispered in my ear, "What the hell is going on?" and I could not tell him, but he was about to find out. The girl looked directly at me and said, "You tell him sir, you were in the courtroom last night when we was all tried and found guilty." I was about to give it all up, but I waited thinking that a miracle would happen. Maybe the court house roof would collapse and crush us all and at that time, that would have been better then what was about to take place. The judge leaned forward in his chair and said, "Officer Ellwood I am not sure what the hell is going on, but you better tell me something real quick." I started again to give it up, but I was interrupted by a couple of the other ladies who were now screaming to the judge, "We was tried last night by a big judge and he was calling us bitches and whores and he was a mean son of a bitch." One of them went on to say, as she pointed directly at me, "He was the states attorney last night" and that was the last straw for the judge as he said, "Officer Ellwood I want to talk to you in my chambers right now."

The judge got up from his chair and told everyone to just stay in their seats and he would be back in the courtroom in a minute. As I headed for the judge's office, I was trying to think how in the hell would I even explain what we did last night in his courtroom. What possible bull shit story would he believe and I could not think of anything. I went in and just stood there and the judge said, "Sit down and tell me what happened and it better be the truth." I paused for a moment and I thought, what could I possibly tell this man, after what he had already heard in the courtroom from the women. I decided the best course of action was to man up, take some responsibility and just blame it on Leon. No, I am kidding, I did not blame it on anyone, but I did know that the judge and Leon were pretty good friends, so I was thinking I would tell the truth and when he found out that Leon was there, maybe he would cut us some slack.

I told him the story and I kept telling him that it was just a joke and we assumed that the women knew we were only kidding with them. I tried to play it down some, but as I talked, he just shook his head. I stopped talking and he was still shaking his head and finally he said, "Are you telling me that Leon Tomlin put on my robe and went out on the bench and pretended he was a judge?" I kind of sheepishly shook my head a little and said, "Yeah I think that's what happened." He got up from his chair and leaned on the desk and said, "You think that's what happened, were you there or not and who else was involved?" I was thinking that so far in this conversation, he has not said anything about making sure I would get fired from the job, so that was good, so I commenced to tell him the story. When I ended the story, he actually laughed, but then he said, "How fuckin dumb can you guys be and if you were that bored, you should have gone on the street and pulled some other shit out there and not in my courtroom." He started back to the courtroom and turned to me and said, "What the hell am I supposed to do with all those hookers, now that they think they have already been tried?" He kind of stood there and I assumed he was waiting for an answer, so I said, "How about just finding them not guilty and telling them the trial last night was not really a trial." This sort of pissed him off and he said, "I have a better idea. Let's go out there and you explain to everyone that last night was a joke and they were really not tried." At this point, I figured fuck it, that sounds like a plan to me and I said, "Okay judge let's do it." He said that he would find them all not guilty and this incident was not over. He headed for the door and said, "I intend to talk to Leon and all the others that were involved last night and I am sure your captain would love to hear this story."

We went back in the courtroom and the judge said, "Ladies and gentlemen, Officer Ellwood wants to address the court concerning the charges against these seventeen ladies." I actually didn't know what I was going to say, but I wanted to make it short, so I said, "There seems to be a misunderstanding." I went on to say, "Last night me and some other officers played a little trick on these ladies. We pretended that we were trying them for their charges, when we were actually kidding and on behalf of everyone involved, I apologize." Well, there were a few gasps in the courtroom and the judge asked that there be order in the court and then he said, "I would like all seventeen ladies charged to come up to the trial table." As the ladies paraded up to the trial table, they gave me some well deserved nasty looks and I could do nothing except give them a little smile. The judge again apologized for the actions of a few police officers and told the ladies that it was not over. He said that he would be talking to those involved and would conduct his own investigation. The judge then told the ladies, "You are all not guilty and after you are processed, you may leave the building." After his statement, there was a big sigh of relief from the ladies as they were led back to the cell block to get their belongings.

Well, as you can imagine, you would think that this is the part of the story, where I tell you that I got fired, but thank God that did not happen. I left the courtroom and some reporters wanted me to talk to them about what we did. I might not be the brightest bulb on the tree, but I knew if I gave them anything to put in the paper, I am sure that meant employment suicide. I wanted to get the hell out of the building, but I was not fast enough and when I was trying, the shift lieutenant told me that the captain wanted to see me in his office.

I went in his office and he shut the door and he just sat there and smiled. He didn't say anything for a few minutes; he just kept changing the facial movements of the smile. He mixed in a little shaking of the head with the smiling and I just sat there and I didn't dare attempt to smile back. I knew that he was just thinking of the words he wanted to use. I figure, hell, I might as well get it over with and I said, "Captain, I know what you are thinking, so let me try to explain what happened." He stopped smiling and the face quickly went into a weird looking contortion, sort of like he was struck with Bells Palsy. I was not that lucky, because if that happened, the next thing would have been a stroke. I figured with a sudden stroke, I would be in position to give him mouth to mouth and save his life and all would be forgotten. I would be a hero and because of the stroke, he would not remember our conversation. I could lie and tell him later that he said, everything was okay and there would be no discipline handed out for what I did…don't that shit sound good, but none of that happened. He found a way to talk through the Bells Palsy look and said, "Can you do any fuckin thing without getting into trouble?" I started to think, maybe he has a point and maybe I really can't do much without getting into trouble. But this time it was not my idea for the little incident that we pulled, it was Leon's and the good thing was that everybody liked Leon. The captain said, "I think I know what happened, but tell me the reasoning behind why you all would do something as stupid as putting on a judge's robe and think that you would get away with it." He said, "Take your time, because I have been around a long time and this really interests me. I know that I will be in the Police Commissioner's office real soon discussing it." I actually thought he was being nice to me and I started off real slow and he jumped up and said, "Fuck it, I don't want to hear anything! What could you possibly say that would change what happened in that courtroom this morning? It's all on the record."

Now I'm scared, because he is up, walking around, looking out the window and the Bells Palsy came back. I got saved by the bell when the phone rang and that gave me a chance to take some deep breaths. He answered and while he was talking on the phone, he shook his fist at me. I completely understood that this was not good when the captain stands about three feet from you and shakes his fist at you. He hung up the phone and said, "Well, just as I expected, the commissioner wants me in his office right away." He was getting his jacket and I started to make my way to the door, when he said, "Where in the fuck do you think you are going?" and I said, "I thought we were done and I was going to go home." Big mistake, he came real close to me and said, "Don't you move from this office until I get back from seeing the commissioner" and he walked out the door.

I sat there gazing around the room and checking out all the nice certificates, awards, and photos he had in his office. I was thinking that I won't last long enough on the job to get anything like that. I got out of my chair and moved around; maybe I should just leave him a note saying I was sorry and that I was heading up to the state office building and get in the unemployment line. I was really getting fidgety and I could not sit in that office any longer. I walked out into the administrative area and was just wondering around, when I saw Leon Tomlin coming into the building. I didn't have to go after him because he spotted me and came over and had that great big smile on that great big body. For some reason, I felt a little better. Leon grabbed my arm and said, "Let's find some place to talk". We found an empty room and Leon shut the door and asked what was happening. I started to tell him and he said, "I know all about what happened in the courtroom this morning. What happened with your captain?" I told him that the captain was now in the Police Commissioner's office and he had told me to wait in his office until he got back and he was not very happy. Leon told me to just take it easy and he thinks everything will work out and he went on to say that he had already talked to Judge Brocolina.

Leon had a lot of friends in the department and I was glad that he came in looking for me, because he was the kind of guy that would not let you go down by yourself. Leon said, "I have already apologized to Broccolina and told him that I would take full responsibility for what happened." Leon said, "I don't think it is going to go any further, we might all get a slap on the wrist, but I don't think anybody is losing their jobs." I started to feel pretty good and Leon said, "Let's get a coffee and I will wait with you to see what your captain has to say" and now I am feeling real good, because the big guy is on my side and if necessary, we could fight our way out of the station.

The captain came back from his meeting with the commissioner and when he saw Leon, he was smiling. He greeted Leon and ignored me. At that point, I didn't care if he talked to me or not, just tell me I still have a job. We went in the captain's office and he shut the door behind him and flopped down in his chair and said, "You should have seen the commissioner's face when I was filling him in about what happened in that courtroom." I could not believe this was the same guy that had earlier survived Bells Palsy and an almost fatal stroke. He was laughing and now he is even looking at me and we are having a good old time. It was one of those weird situations when you know you got to laugh when he laughs, frown when he frowns, look serious when he does, and the main thing is to keep laughing. Leon told the captain that he had talked to Judge Brocolina and that the judge was okay and would not want to make any complaints against us. Wow, that was good to hear the word "us", because up to this point, it was all "me." I was feeling a lot better and the thought of the unemployment line was a thing of the past. I got a job and life is good again.

The captain told me that unless there were any formal complaints, he would just let it go. He did warn me in front of Leon that if anything like this happens in the future, I would be walking a foot post in Siberia. Before we left the captain's office, Leon again told the captain that he was responsible for the incident and that the others involved, just went along with the program and the whole thing was just a stupid incident.

Many years after this happened, I would always hear some guys talking about the time when some police officer put on the judge's robe and some other cops pretended they were attorneys and held a mock trial in the courtroom with some prostitutes. I have actually been standing around at parties and other police affairs and heard the story being told. I feel like I want to jump in and say, "Hey, that's me that you are talking about," but I don't. I am thrilled to know that in some form or other, the story still lives in the police department. I occasionally meet with retired cops and it always comes up and it is as funny today, as it was many years ago.

MASS ARRESTS - ALMOST MY DEMISE

This short story starts when I received some reliable information that a party was being held in a rented warehouse on Market Place in the Central District. The problem with the party was that they were selling tickets and advertising the sale of alcohol. The party would be held in a vacant warehouse.

I was asked by my sergeant, to go into the party and check it out. Well, I went in about 10 PM and I could not believe what I was seeing. I paid ten dollars at the door to get in the place and when I went up the stairs to the second floor I could hear the band. When I turned to come in the hall, I saw an estimated three hundred people dancing and hanging around the bars that were set up in different spots around the room.

The concern with this party was that whoever was running it did not have a liquor license and did not have a permit to charge for entering the building. I walked around and knew that if we were to make any arrests, we would need a lot of help. I left the party and was told that I could get back in with my hand already stamped. I met with Pete and my partner and we discussed what we were going to do. We decided that we would ask the city wide Narcotics Unit to assist us. We knew the men working in that unit, as we sometimes assisted them with investigations in our district. We called their sergeant, Leon Tomlin, who I have already told you was a good friend and worked similar hours that we did. We met with Leon and his unit and discussed how we would enter the party and who would we arrest. It was decided that Sergeant Tomlin and I would enter the party and the other cops would be available close by on the outside of the building. Leon had a police radio and although we would act as if we were not together, we would stay in close proximity for safety purposes and mainly to keep eye contact.

When we both went in the party, it seemed to me like the crowd had gotten even bigger. I would estimate that there were about three hundred or more people in the hall, maybe more. I could not believe that someone would hold a party this big and not try to get a legal license for the sale of alcohol. I wonder what they were thinking; nobody would notice an additional three hundred cars parked in a fairly isolated area. I went in the men's room to discuss with Leon what the next step would be. We decided that one of us had to get up on the stage and take the microphone from the band singer. We needed to make an announcement that we were the police and that everybody was under arrest. Well, as Leon was a sergeant and outranked me, I got the job of going on the stage and making the announcement. I must say that I was a little apprehensive about this, as it could get ugly quick. I didn't know if we could handle a crowd this big, but what the hell, it seemed like fun at the time and it would sure as hell pad the monthly stats.

The plan was for me to get the microphone and make the announcement and Leon would call the other cops waiting outside and they would be at the door when people would try to exit. As I approached the stage, I was thinking there is no way this is going to work, but being an optimist, I proceeded right for the stage. The band was very loud and the singer was jumping all over the stage. I did not know the song, but I was trying to time myself so that I would jump up on the stage as the song was ending. Well, I waited and then I figured the hell with it, there is only one way to do it and I jumped up on the stage and grabbed the microphone from the singer. Needless to say, he thought I was just a crazy drunk from the crowd and he tried to get the mike back from me.

I showed him my badge, but the music was so loud, he could not hear me telling him that I was a cop. I was trying to tell him, we were shutting down the party, as we struggled for the microphone. I think I finally convinced him, but the partygoers kept dancing. The crowd thought I was part of the entertainment, because the music never stopped. I won the struggle and announced over the microphone that we were the police department and at this time, I could see Leon and the uniform troops approaching the stage.

Well, I think it finally set in with the partygoers and they started to exit the building from every door and window in the place. The band stopped playing and I announced again that the party was over and everybody was under arrest. Well, that did it and they started running and screaming and things were getting out of control. We had cops on the doors and they were detaining as many partygoers as possible. When all the dust had settled, we had arrested one hundred and seventy-five people, which means a hell of a lot got out of the building. When I got to the police station, people were lined up and sitting in every spot in the station house. I can remember the shift lieutenant approaching me and saying, "What the hell are you doing and where in the hell are we going to put all these people?"

In the police station and with the assistance of several police officers, we worked all night and did the paper work on all the arrested people. We identified the people who actually set up and ran the party and they were charged with alcohol violations and operating an event without a license. The rest of the crowd that was arrested was charged with participating in a disorderly house, which we knew was a pretty weak charge. I want to point out that this was 1970 and there were some strange laws back then. I don't think if this occurred today, the one hundred and seventy-five people would have been arrested.

The court appearance in this case was the next day at 9 AM in the Central District Court. My partner and I worked all night and did not go home or get any sleep and we were really dragging. The word was out to the news media about this large arrest and the courtroom was filled with reporters. The judge presiding that day was the less than honorable, Judge Jerome Robinson. A little history on Judge Robinson is that he did not like cops and could be real nasty in the courtroom. He also had the nickname of "Flaky" and he got this nickname because his dandruff was all over his black robe. It was kind of incredible that he would sit on the bench day after day and not figure out that he had a hell of a dandruff problem. He was also known for being late for court and ending court whenever he wanted to, no matter how many cases were still to be heard. Well, when I saw that he was sitting, I knew I was in for a real bad day.

Our case was called first and the bailiff paraded all one hundred and seventy-five people into the courtroom from the cell block, which back than was connected to the courtroom. I was standing at the table in front of the judge's bench and my partner was next to me. I was going to testify as I was listed as the arresting officer on all the charging documents.

I had a large stack of the charging documents with me and placed them on the table. The state's attorney started the proceedings by reading the charges to the judge. Instead of asking each person how they plea to the charges, the judge said, "I will assume you are all pleading not guilty" and they all moaned to the affirmative. The state's attorney made a few comments about the charges and then I stated my name and starting to testify. I got about two minutes into the testimony and the judge abruptly stopped me. The judge leaned forward and said to me, "I can't believe you locked up all these people for being at a party." I started to say something and he said, "I really don't want to hear from you, I want the state's attorney to tell me why these charges were placed against these people." The state's attorney started to go into the fact that all the charges were legitimate and everyone charged did in fact violate the law in some form or another.

The judge looked at me and said, "Don't you think this is a waste of time? You could have been doing something else." I said, "Your honor I was only doing my job" and with that, he said, "Shut up." I then picked up all my paperwork from the table and was arranging it and I was really pissed. I fumbled a little with the paper and most of it fell on the courtroom floor. The judge stood up and looked at me and said "I guess you are upset with me and throwing your paperwork on the floor is really childish." I started to tell him that the paperwork slipped, when he said "Stand in the back of the courtroom until I decide what I am going to do with this mess." At this point I was really upset and I told the judge, "Sir, I am not standing in the back of the room. I am a police officer and I am standing at this table and I don't like the way you are talking to me." I was also thinking that the last time I was told to stand in the back of the room, was in Catholic grade school, when the nuns would make us stand in the back of the room when we were bad.

Well, being the wimpy old bastard and flaky son of a bitch that he was, he looked a little baffled. He was also at a loss for words. He pulled his flaky ass together, struggled to get his fat ass out of the chair and said, "This court is in recess" and he walked off the bench to his office.

Everybody in the courtroom was stunned and just stood around for awhile until the state's attorney told everyone to just stay seated and he would talk to the judge. A short time later, the judge came back out on the bench and without any further testimony from me or anyone that was charged, he said, "My decision on these charges is that all parties involved are not guilty and you are all free to leave the courtroom." I did not say anything, but the state's attorney said, "Your honor you have not heard all the testimony in these charges." The judge said "I made my decision and all the people charged in this case are allowed to leave the courtroom right now."

Well, I did not know it at that time, but when the judge went in his office, he had called my captain and obviously complained about my actions in the courtroom. When I left the courtroom, I was notified to go see my captain immediately. I went in the captain's office and he said, "Sit down, we need to talk." I did not do much talking, as the captain started by saying, "This situation is out of my control, you are being transferred because Judge Robinson called the police commissioner and complained about your actions in the courtroom." The captain said he was very sorry this was happening. He said he had no choice, because when the police commissioner called him he said there would be no discussion on the matter: Ellwood was to be transferred immediately. The captain was actually a very nice guy and was real upset with this bullshit. As I was leaving his office, he said he was sorry and that he knew that I had done nothing wrong and to hang in there. He also said to let the dust settle a little and he would do whatever he could for me in the future.

I later found out that Judge Jerome "Flaky" Robinson actually called Maryland Governor Marvin Mandel. Mandel and the judge were very close friends and former lawyer buddies and the governor had appointed Judge Robinson to serve on the bench.

I will end this short story with saying that what appeared to be a bad situation, actually turned out pretty good for me. Following this fiasco, I was transferred to the Northeast District. It was a good district and a lot closer to my home and I was put back in the Vice Unit. I did have occasions after this incident to take cases before "Flaky" Robinson and he acted as if nothing had happened or he was probably to senile to remember.

About one year after this incident, I got the word that "Flaky" had died. I know that you usually don't celebrate when people die, but I did. I can't help but think, here is a guy who when he had the robe on, thought he was God. He thought he could treat people like shit and now he was going to meet the real judge and I wonder how he would make out. I do know one thing that he does not have to worry about any longer is all those flakes all over his robe. I am sure that where he is, they will burn off… may his sorry "Flaky" ass rest in peace, case closed.

VICE IS NICE – POLICE CORRUPTION IS NOT

After my transfer for locking up a one hundred and seventy-five people, I was sent to the Northeast District. The captain of the district was Henry Diesel, a friend of my dad's. When my dad was on the job, he and Diesel worked together in the Traffic Unit and remained friends over the years. My dad retired in 1963, a couple of years before I came on the job. I know now that by him being on the job and well liked, he opened a few doors for me.

When I arrived at the Northeast District, I was assigned to the Vice Unit doing the same work I had been doing in the Central District Vice Unit, locking up prostitutes and investigating illegal gambling. I was actually surprised at my new assignment and everyone treated me great in my new district. I think that in the police department, when your fellow cops know that you got shit on and were transferred for just doing your job, they want to make sure you get treated with respect. They want you to know that they understand why you were moved and that it could happen to them.

In April of 1971, after settling into my new assignment in the Vice Unit, I was investigating a big gambling operation that was located in the district. It had the overall appearance of being a very large illegal numbers and horse race betting operation. I was getting close to writing a search and seizure warrant for the home that was the apparent headquarters. After several weeks of observations and information from a police informant, I had enough documentation to get the search and seizure warrant signed.

With the warrant signed, we raided an address on Walther Boulevard in northeast Baltimore which was an apartment complex. We knocked down the door, which we usually did on gambling raids, because the bad guys try to flush the paperwork down the toilet or destroy it some other way. I was actually surprised to find the bad guys this time, were two ladies who were operating the phones and taking bets in this apartment. We interviewed the ladies who were very upset and crying about being arrested. After the interview, they were taken to the district and charged. The method of operation for this unique organization was that the ladies would answer the phones and take the bets as they were called in. It was basically a credit operation, in that you could call in and if you were in good standing, you could place a bet over the phone and the amounts would be recorded. If the player had a large winnings that day, they could come to the apartment or meet someone on the street and be paid. If they wanted to, they could just let the winnings carry over and keep betting and collect the winnings whenever they wanted to.

While searching the apartment, we recovered approximately $10,000 in cash and all the books that documented the betting operation on a daily basis. The ladies, who were just small players in this operation, were interviewed and they refused to positively identify the backers of the operation. Within just minutes of the ladies arriving at the district, a well known Baltimore attorney arrived and informed us that he was representing them and they had nothing else to say to us. The ladies did not even know this attorney and it was obvious the attorney was sent by the backers of the gambling operation. This was one of the perks for the employees working in this illegal field.

Later that afternoon about 4 PM, my new sergeant, Tim Mc Shane and I were in the basement of the district in our office. We were finishing up with the paper work on this investigation and the criminal charges against the two ladies.

I got a call from the desk sergeant who said that a man was here to see me about the arrest. I met the man in the hallway and I could not believe how this guy was dressed. It was as if I was watching an old Humphrey Bogart movie or a scene from the Sopranos. He was a short white man with a tan. He was about five feet, six inches tall and he had on a pink suit. He was wearing a white hat, white shoes, and was smoking a cigar. I could not help but think later that if you were a bad guy and wanted to be a gangster, maybe you should not be so obvious with the way you dress. At first I thought this was some kind of a joke, as cops are always playing jokes on each other. The man put out his hand and introduced himself to me. He said, "Are you Ellwood?" I said, "Yes, what can I do for you?" He started by speaking real low and I could hardly hear him. He moved a little closer and said, "Can we talk about the gambling bust on Walther Avenue?" I said, "Well, who are you and what do you want to talk about?" He put his hand on my arm and directed me to the side of the hallway and said, "I was told that I can trust you." He said, "I have talked to people on the street and some other cops and they all told me that you would work with me on this problem."

I must point out at this time, that the FBI was working on corruption in the Baltimore Police Department and rumor had it that several cops were going to be indicted for taking bribes. The first thing that ran through my mind at this point was that this guy was setting me up and could be working for the FBI. I told him to tell me what he wanted and that I was busy. He said, "You know you got my books from the raid on that apartment. They have all my clients in them and if I lose those books, I probably will lose thousands of dollars." He said, "I don't really care about the ten thousand dollars in cash that you got from the apartment: that is small change compared to what is in those books you have." He went on to say, "Why don't you meet me somewhere tonight and we can discuss this a little more and not here in the basement of the police station." As I looked at him, I was thinking, well if you had the balls to come in here dressed like that and flat out try to bribe me, you are either working with the FBI or a brazen son of a bitch.

I had a lot running through my head at that time, but I was not sure if I had enough legally to lock him up at that moment for bribery, although I wanted to. I told him that I was not in charge of the Vice Unit, that I had a sergeant who was the only one who could make any decisions. He said, "That's fine, bring him with you tonight and we will work this out." Then he made the weirdest statement that my sergeant and I laughed about for years. He said, "Can we trust the sergeant?" I laughed when he said that and I knew my course of action would be to get this bastard eventually for bribing police officers. He handed me his card and said, "Call me later and we can decide where we will meet." I stood there with the card in my hand and my mouth open as he walked out of the building. When he got to the door, he looked back, smiled, and gave me the thumbs up sign. I was not sure what that meant. I was waiting any minute to see Tony Soprano waiting outside in a Cadillac for this little prick.

I went back in the office and called my sergeant, Tim Mc Shane, to the side and told him the story about what had just happened. He was shocked at what I told him and at first thought I was kidding. From the description of the guy and the conversation, he knew I would not be able to come up with such a story. He thought about it and had the same thoughts that I had about maybe they were trying to set us up for a bribery charge. We decided that we could not just ignore this guy. We decided we had to talk to the captain and get others involved before this character went off telling some made up story; like we approached him, instead of him approaching us.

The captain, after hearing the story, did not hesitate and called the local office of the FBI. He asked if an agent assigned to the Bribery Task Force could come to the district. We were later called back to the captain's office and met two FBI agents who were working on corruption in the police department. The captain shut the door and told the FBI agents to take over. The FBI agents introduced themselves and seemed like pretty nice guys. They were very FBI agent like: three piece dark suits, short hair cuts, and very careful with their words. The agents said that the captain had filled them in, but asked if I would go over the entire scenario starting from the raid on the apartment, up to the conversation in the basement of the police district. I told the story, being very careful not to leave anything out. I knew I would probably be telling this story many times in the future. I wanted to make sure that if we were being set up; they got our version and not the gangster guy's story.

After a couple hours talking with the FBI agents, the plan was that Tim and I would meet with this guy. We were told that anything we did would be monitored by the FBI agents from this point forward. I was to call him and ask that he meet with us at the Haven Lounge which was a night club in the Northwood Shopping Center near the police station. I called the number on the card and talked to the guy about meeting with him and he was very excited and said "That's great, you guys won't regret it." We decided to meet at about 8 PM in the lounge and he said he would be alone. I told him that the sergeant would be with me.

We walked into the Haven Lounge and it was very dark, but I could see this guy sitting in the rear, alone at a table in the corner. I must admit that my stomach was rumbling at this time, because we did not know what we were getting into. As we walked towards the back, I again had the thought about the Humphrey Bogart movie and maybe some gangster was going to jump out with a machine gun and mow us down. We walked back and sat at the table and he called the waitress over and said, "Give these guys what they want." We ordered a beer and I asked the guy what his name was. He told me his name was Romey which I already knew from the card he gave me earlier that day. I introduced the sergeant to Romey and he wasted no time telling us what he wanted. He leaned in to talk and he talked loud this time, as there was some music playing. He said, "I need them books that you took in the raid." He said, "If you get them books to me or at least copies of the books, it would be worth a lot of money to both of you." He went on to say, "I will give you each a thousand dollars to get those books. I will give you each five hundred up front now and five hundred when I get the books." He said, "I think I can trust you guys and you don't have to worry about me. I have been playing this game for a long time and everyone knows that my word is my bond." I was not the sergeant, but Romey directed all his talking to me and I felt real uneasy.

Well, as we were told by the FBI agents to go along with whatever he wanted: we agreed and we each took five hundred dollars from Romey. He was very excited and ordered more drinks. He started into some talk not related to getting the books, but mainly about how many important people he knew in the city. We stayed awhile and left the lounge and headed back to the station. On the way back, we were both thinking how open this guy was with two police officers he had never had contact with before. I convinced Tim that we were doing the right thing and it would be over soon, boy was I ever wrong.

We went in the station and we had the phone number for one of the FBI agents, so we called him to tell him what had happened and ask for further instructions. He told us, as it was getting late and he was sure we wanted to go home, we should record the serial numbers of the money. He told us to make a report which we should keep in our possession and hold onto the money until we meet with him. The agent said that in his opinion, everything was going great and that they had checked out Romey. He said they would brief us when we met and discuss the future plans. The agent said that when we do meet, it was probably not good to meet in the police station anymore. The agent said he would meet us at a restaurant out of the city, in Harford County on Belair Road, called the Blue Bell.

We met the next day with the FBI Agent and he was extremely pleased with what took place with Romey. I saw the same excitement with the agent that I had seen with Romey, but for far different reasons. He told us he had checked out Romey and gave us his last name, which was Bernstein. He said that he was a mid-level player in a very large gambling operation which had its headquarters in a bar in northwest Baltimore. The agent said that Romey liked to talk and lead people to believe that he was some sort of ringleader in a major gambling operation. He said that the FBI had been working on this operation for several years and this was the big break that they had been waiting for. He said that with bribery charges, gambling, and racketeering charges against Romey, he was sure they could bring down the entire operation.

We had lunch with the agents in the Blue Bell Restaurant, which was known for their seafood. To be perfectly honest with you, neither Tim nor I had much of an appetite, even if the FBI was paying. After our report on Romey, the agent started asking questions about our families and what we did in our spare time, which made us both feel uneasy. I guess he wanted to break the ice, but I was real careful discussing my family. I did tell him that my dad was a cop and my brother was a cop and he seemed impressed with that. He seemed real relaxed about this situation, but Tim and I were not. I assume because they were on a task force investigating corruption in the department, they were used to this stuff. I know it had to be obvious to them that Tim and I were very nervous about every meeting we had with them. I don't think that anyone that would have seen us together would think anything of it, except that the agents always had on nice suits and Tim and I were dressed casual. Maybe the agents should have dressed down to our level.

After some lunch, the agent told us to make copies of the books that

Romey needed and give him a call to set up another meeting. On the way back to the station from this meeting, I could tell that Tim was very upset and extremely nervous. I was in no way a pro at this, but I had worked in vice a little longer than Tim and had seen characters like Romey before. I went over the possibilities with Tim and told him that no matter how long this took and no matter what the FBI asked us to do, we would come out of this okay. I don't think Tim was convinced and I could tell that it played on his mind.

Tim was a giant of a man at six feet, seven and probably weighed at least two hundred and seventy pounds, but as big as he was, he was a mild mannered old country boy. Tim loved his family and talked about them all the time. He played the guitar and was active in his church and loved to go camping. I can honestly say that I had never heard Tim use any bad language. The most you would get out of him was, "ah shucks" or "dag gonnit." If he was real mad, you might get an "oh shit," but that was it. When Tim was assigned to the Vice Unit, I don't think he really wanted it. Tim loved to work in patrol and constantly told me how much he missed it. He missed his old buddies in the Eastern District and the seemingly normal working hours, compared to the vice hours.

The next day we called Romey and we set up a meeting at a bar in northwest Baltimore. We were not aware of it at the time, but we were meeting him at the same bar where the FBI had a wiretap. The bar was the headquarters for the gambling operation that the agent had told us about. In this bar, Romey, seemed right at home and he was introducing us to people and made no bones about it that we were cops. After a short time in the bar, Romey took us to a back room that looked just like something out of; you got it, the Humphrey Bogart movie or the Sopranos. There was a large card table and a small bar and you had to be buzzed in the door to get back there. Some of the characters that were in the back room, looked like they could break Tim and I into little pieces if they wanted to. Well maybe not Tim, but certainly me and I was glad that big Tim was with me. I think Romey saw that we were not comfortable in this room and said, "Let's sit down and get down to business."

We sat around the card table and he asked about the books and I gave him the package with the copied material, just like the FBI had told me to do. At first he seemed a little unhappy. He said he really wanted the original books. I told him that was not possible because they were marked as evidence and the best we could do was to make copies. He laughed and said, "I think I am paying too much money for copies, but I also know I have no choice." At this point, I was sort of pissed at the whole ordeal and was about to tell him, "Fuck you, we can call this whole thing off and you can have your fuckin money back." I stopped myself knowing that we were in this for the long haul. I did not need to get my Irish temper up and blow the whole thing. He took the package from me and handed me an envelope. I started to look in the envelope and he said, "Fellows, I think by now you can trust me, because I know I can sure trust you guys."

We had a drink or two with him and left the bar. While driving back to the station, Tim said he wished this whole thing had not happened and that he hopes it ends soon. He said he was not sleeping well at night and the whole thing was starting to affect him. I told him that I felt the same way and to hang in there, that we were doing the right thing. I told him that it would be over soon and I was just as upset by it as he was. I knew the kind of person Tim was and even though I did not like all the secret meetings and taking the money, I also knew that Tim relied on me as being the steady hand. Tim had worked his entire police career in uniform patrol and this was his first taste of vice work. To have this happen was certainly something he did not expect. I don't give a damn how long I had worked in vice, I sure as hell did not derive any pleasure out of all this secret bullshit either.

Well, a couple of weeks went by and we did not hear anything from the FBI agents. Tim and I were getting a little antsy about what was happening. We finally got a call to come to the captain's office. We were told that we would be meeting with the FBI agents and our Intelligence Unit from the police department. We went to the meeting and the FBI agents were there and a lieutenant from the Intelligence Unit, Donald Wilson was there. We both knew this lieutenant and he had a reputation in the department of being a hatchet man. He was the man that the police commissioner used to go after people that were thought to be involved in nefarious activity. The lieutenant welcomed us and shook our hands and said "I am real proud of you guys." I could not help but think, he did not mean it one bit, because he had a shit eating grin on his face. The word in the department was that he would sink your ass in a New York minute or faster if he could, just to make points with the police commissioner.

We had no choice, but to play along with him, just smile, say thanks, and pretend we liked him. We were sure he was doing the same thing with us. I felt real uncomfortable with this lieutenant in the meeting; he just sat there and smiled at us the entire time. I knew that was not good. It was the kind of smile that says, I'll be watching you bastards and the minute you fuck up, I will be on your ass like stink on shit. The FBI agent did most of the talking and my mind was wandering and I don't think I heard anything he was saying. He then got to the part that did get my attention. He said they had an FBI informant inside the gambling operation that Romey was involved with. He said that the informant had told them that Tim and I had taken money in the past from known gamblers. I could see that Tim was getting a little rattled and I was hoping he would not say anything that he would regret. His face was getting beet red and I was thinking that any minute he was going to launch his huge body on the agents and the shit for brains lieutenant.

After the agent made that statement, I knew it was time to say something because there was silence in the room and all eyes were on us. I knew that whatever I said, it had to be good and it also had to be very convincing. I stood up, took a deep breath, and mustered all the nerve I could. I said, "Gentlemen, what else do you think a degenerate asshole like Romey would say to his friends or informants or whatever the hell you want to call them. He is a "wanna be" gangster and will say anything to impress his peers." I went on to say, "I want to assure you all that since being a member of the police department, I have never taken any money from anybody and I am absolutely confident that Tim has not taken any money either." I continued, "If you all want to get me for taking a cup of coffee, or a meal, or a gallon of milk, when I was in uniform, then you can sure as hell can get me." I was getting louder and said, "I don't speak for Tim, but I have known him for quite awhile and his reputation is impeccable and his service to the police department has been nothing but outstanding." I also went on to say, "I am shocked that this would be addressed, if it is coming from a no good asshole hoodlum, like Romey." I looked right at the lieutenant and said, "If you have any proof about this outrageous statement, I want to hear it right now and I am not leaving the room, until this is settled."

Well, I must have said the right thing, as the room was silent for a few minutes. Lieutenant Wilson was still smiling, but he did look a little uncomfortable in his chair and that was a good thing. As things were a little quiet in the room, I spoke up again and said, "What exactly are they saying about Tim and I and who was supposed to have given us money in the past?" Before the FBI agent or the lieutenant could say anything, the captain spoke up and said, "Gentlemen, I just want you all to know that I know these two men personally and they have been excellent police officers and their character and honesty has never been questioned in the past by anyone in the department." He was getting a little loud and went on to say that he knew my father and they had worked together in the past. He said that I had come from a family with a great history and reputation in the Baltimore Police Department, going back to the early nineteen hundreds.

At that point, the agent spoke up and said, "Guys, don't take what I said wrong. I am only reporting what is coming back to us from the informant and it does not mean it is true." He said, "I want to get it out in the open before we continue with this very serious bribery investigation." He said, looking directly at me and Tim, "We have checked you guys out pretty good and we do not believe anything this informant is saying." He went on to say, "We just want to be upfront with you guys, so there are no surprises down the road. We believe that you are both honest and loyal members of the police department or we would not be having this conversation today." He ended by saying, "When we do take this guy down, he is going to want to take anyone he can with him and we want to be prepared for anything that comes up."

Well, after the meeting, Tim and I got in the car and just took a long ride and for several minutes not a word was spoken by either one of us. We stopped for coffee and for awhile it seemed like we were fumbling over our words, not really knowing what to say that could put each other at ease. I could see Tim was upset and taking this whole ordeal, especially the latest episode in the captain's office, not too well. I was not older or senior in rank to Tim, but I knew how he was feeling and I tried to say something that would hopefully pump him up. I told him that we are still doing the right thing and no matter what happens down the road, we have nothing to worry about. I said, "Let's just keep doing our job and try to concentrate on other things at work and in our personal lives instead of this stupid ass bribery case." Tim smiled and agreed with me. As we got up to leave, I told him to pay for the coffee with all the fuckin money he has been taken from the gamblers. At first he gave me a look that could kill and then he pushed me out the door and we laughed like hell all the way back to the station. We both needed a good laugh.

Well, about four months went by and we were finally notified that criminal charges had been placed against Romey. We were told that others would be charged and a trial date would be set soon. It was good news for both of us, as we wanted this to go to trial and be over with. We wanted to see Romey's gangster ass behind bars, where he could wear that pink suit and fight off the inmates who try to get a piece of that fat ass.

About one month or so prior to the trial, I got a call from State's Attorney Bernie Coleman. I had known Bernie for years as a prosecutor in the Central District and we had knocked down a few beers on occasion. I considered him a very good friend. When he called, I could tell something was up, because he did not ask how my family was, or talk about playing softball, or eating crabs, or talk like we had always talked. He said, "Dick I need to ask you something and I want the truth. I know I will get it from you, because of our friendship and I would expect nothing but the truth from you." He went on to say that he probably would get in trouble if anyone knew he was making this call. I said, "Bernie, we have known each other for a long time and you know you can ask me anything and it will be between you and me." He said, "Have you taken bribes while in the police department?" I thought I would think about it and give him a detailed answer, but I decided to make it quick and I said, "Hell no." My mind was racing and I knew that this had to be coming up as a result of the bribery trial that was now scheduled for criminal court. He said, "You don't have to say anything else, I believe you and I am sorry I had to even ask you." I asked what was up and Bernie said he really could not go into it any further. He said that after the bribery trial of Mr. Bernstein, we would have a beer and he would let me know why he asked the question. Bernie then asked how my family was and how things were with the softball team. I knew that things were okay with us and that was a good thing.

Well, I am going to end this short story and just tell you what happened at the trial. I testified, because I had more experience on the stand than Tim and that was just fine with Tim. After all the preliminary motions took place, I was finally on the stand and sworn in. Romey was represented at the trial by one of the best lawyers in the city, Allan Merrill. After I was asked about my background and my experience in law enforcement by the state's attorney, we got into the particulars of the bribery charges. I then faced the cross examination by Mr. Merrill, which I knew would be very aggressive. I also assumed that he probably had something up his sleeve, because he was known for his courtroom antics and always played to the jury. He dressed like he was on the cover of GQ and I am sure he got lots of money from the gamblers he represented. I had a lot of respect for him, even if he did represent gamblers. I knew I had to be on top of my game in my testimony on this trial.

He started off friendly, as he usually does and then came the bomb, as he said, "Detective Ellwood, isn't it a fact that besides allegedly taking money from my client, haven't you also taken money from other known gamblers?" He was playing to the jury when he asked the question and never looked at me. I turned and faced him, just as he was walking back to the trial table. I leaned forward in the chair and said "No sir, I have never taken money from anyone while a police officer." He then said, "What if I told you I have a person who said he paid you money not to arrest him for running a gambling operation." I knew these questions were coming and I was prepared, but this time the state's attorney jumped up and objected. The judge sustained the objection and told Mr. Merrill to go in another direction with his questions. Mr. Merrill told the judge that the questions would be very relevant to the charges against his client. Before the judge could say anything, Mr. Merrill looked at me and said, "Please answer the question." Before the judge said anything, I jumped at the question and said, "If you have someone who said they gave me money, bring them into this court and have them say it under oath, because they are lying bastards." The judge finally jumped in and told me to watch my language in his court. He also told Mr. Merrill that he needed to proceed with defending his client. The judge seemed to be getting upset and told Mr. Merrill, "Move on and do not continue to question this police officer's integrity." The judge told Mr. Merrill that, "If this police officer did anything wrong, there are units within the police department that investigate those types of allegations." The judge pointed his finger at Mr. Merrill and said, "I don't want to hear any more questions along those lines."

I finished my testimony and later the jury went out to deliberate and we sat in the hallway of the courthouse for awhile. Mr. Merrill approached me and said, "I hope you are not offended by my questions." I started to say something nasty, but I remembered that the judge had told everyone involved in the trial that they should not have any discussion about the trial until the jury makes their decision. I stood up and said, "Mr. Merrill I don't know if you heard him, but the judge told everyone not to talk about the trial." He smiled and walked away and I knew that no matter what the outcome of this trial, I would most likely be facing him again in the future. I wanted to keep things on a professional level, as much as possible.

We were all called back into the courtroom about 4 PM after the jury deliberated for about two hours. I wanted a guilty verdict on this guy for a lot of reasons, most of which were personal and not professional. I wanted it because Romey's stupidity had put us through so much agony. I was thinking about all the days that Tim and I had kept secret notes and all the meetings with the FBI. I also thought about what Romey must have been telling all his cronies about the two cops that he paid off. I know that even though we did the right thing, talk like that gets around town and gives cops a bad rap. I could not help but think if the jury believed Mr. Merrill's statement about me taking money from gamblers, I hoped not. This was a Baltimore jury and lots of people in Baltimore did not like cops.

I shook Tim's hand before we went into the courtroom. Tim said, "No matter what happens, we did the right thing. Regardless of the verdict, I appreciate you keeping me focused while this was going on and hopefully I can get some sleep tonight"

The judge came out to the bench and the jury followed just behind him. They all took their seats. The judge said, "Before I ask the jury for their verdict, I want to thank everyone involved in this trial." The judge then asked the jury foreman, if they had reached a verdict. The jury foreman stood up and said, "Yes, your honor we have." Instead of the jury foreman reading the verdict, he passed it to the judge. The judge thanked the jury and opened the envelope and with his glasses way down on his nose, he asked Romey to stand. The judge looked directly at Romey and simply said, "Sir, the jury has found you guilty on all charges." The judge asked Mr. Merrill if he had anything to say and he said, "Your honor, we will be appealing this verdict. I would request that my client be allowed to continue on bail until the appeal." The judge denied the bail request and told Mr. Merrill that Romey had to go to jail and that a new bail hearing date would be set. The judge told Romey that his actions were despicable and a slap in the face to all the good and hard working police officers in Baltimore. The judge told Romey that he would have to go to jail until he received some paperwork from the Parole and Probation Department and then he would be called back to court for the official sentence. As the bailiff was putting handcuffs on Romey, the judge looked out toward me and Tim and said, "Gentlemen, you did an excellent job and you should be commended for your integrity and honesty. The Baltimore Police Department should be very proud of both of you." We both stood up and thanked the judge and left the courtroom. It was finally over.

Just as we were leaving the courthouse to go get a much needed drink, I saw Mr. Merrill coming down the courthouse steps. He looked over and said, "Congratulations fellows." I guess I should have let it go, but I wanted to say something to him. I walked over to him and said, "Mr. Merrill now that it is over, I can talk to you. I want to let you know that I come from a very proud family of good decent cops." I was being careful with my words and went on to say, "I was not offended by your line of questioning in the trial. I know you probably agree that your client is a scumbag, low life, creep, who would lie about anyone to get ahead or to save his sorry ass." Mr. Merrill smiled and tugged at his Stetson hat and walked away. Tim and I left and went to the bar and the drinks were especially good that day. Tim slept like a baby that night.

Promoted To Detective – 1973

In the spring of 1973, I got a call from Captain Jim Cadden, who was the Commanding Officer of the Homicide and Robbery Units in the Criminal Investigation Division. Captain Cadden grew up in the same Irish neighborhood that I had in east Baltimore and we were familiar with each other's families. He asked me if I wanted to come downtown and work in the Robbery Unit, with the intentions of eventually moving over to the Homicide Unit. I could not believe he was actually making the call, instead of one of his supervisors. This guy was not only a captain, but an absolute legend in the police department. He had risen through the ranks and worked in the Homicide Unit at every rank leading up to captain. After he asked me, he said, "You can think it over and call me back." I said, without any hesitation, "Captain, there is no thinking it over, I want to work in detectives, especially the Homicide Unit more than any unit in the police department." He said, "Do you want to check with your wife, because it is a big commitment and the hours might be long and tough on your family life." I said, "Captain, I don't have to check with anyone, just tell me when I report." Captain Cadden said he would first talk to the captain in the Northeast District where I was working at the time. I knew this would not be a problem, because the captain of the Northeast District was a great guy and would not stop me from advancing in the department.

I reported to the Robbery Unit on a Monday in April 1973. I was scared to death as I walked into the unit office and started to get all the stares from the veteran detectives. I can remember walking into the office and it was about 7 AM and no one was there except Sergeant Lou Davis. I walked around the small office and was looking out the window, trying to look like I belonged. I thought of leaving and coming back in time for roll call, which was held at 8 AM. Sergeant Davis came out of a very small office and introduced himself to me. He started to give me a breakdown of the unit and especially the supervisors. He told me that I would be working for Sergeant Herman Ingram and the lieutenant in charge of the unit was "Potts" Callahan. I will tell you a little more about the lieutenant later. I never did get to know his real first name; it was just "Potts" to everyone. Sergeant Davis showed me a desk that I could use, so I sat there and pretended I was looking through the desk, not sure what the hell I was looking for, because it was empty and real dirty.

The robbery detectives started to come in for work and as they did, Sergeant Davis introduced me to them. Some of them actually spoke to me and the others just made a grumpy noise and walked away; remember it was Monday morning. As it got close to the 8 AM roll call, I was really getting nervous. I was told that roll call was held in the Homicide Unit which was directly next door to the Robbery Unit. There were no chairs to sit on like in patrol districts, so everyone just stood around. A homicide lieutenant starting reading roll call and as he read each name, the detectives answered up to their names. Some said "Here sir" and some, the same ones that made grumpy sounds to me earlier, just made a grumpy sound when their names were called. I was thinking that these grumpy guys would be a problem, but some of them proved me wrong. The lieutenant was finishing up roll call, when the captain came into the room. When the captain got in front of the group, things got real quiet, even the grumpy guys perked up. As I told you earlier, Captain Cadden was highly respected by everyone in the department. He started to talk about the number of murders for the year in the city. It appeared that he was finished, when he said, "I want to introduce you all to a new member of the Robbery Unit." Well, I could have crawled under a desk at that point and I could feel the little sweat balls forming on my back. The room was small and crowded; I don't think he even saw me. He said, "Richard, where the hell are you?" When he said that, I could have died. Right away I got stares from the guys, like who the hell is this guy that the captain is calling him by his first name. I raised my hand and said "Back here sir" and I was so nervous, I think my voice gave away and I must have sounded like Gomer Pyle. Well, it was not over yet, the captain asked me to come up in the front so everyone could see me. I walked to the front and the captain put his hand out and we shook hands. He told the group that he knew my dad and he said, "If Richard can become half the cop that his father was, then he will fit right in with the Robbery Unit." I sheepishly thanked the captain and told him that I was excited to be in such a high profile unit and that I would give it my best effort.

I took a little good natured ribbing after the first roll call. Some detectives referred to me as the "Captain's boy", but it was all good, it kind of broke the ice. I got the feeling that they could see that the kidding was fine with me and I actually enjoyed it. I found out quick that if you could not take it and also dish it out a little, you would not be accepted in the unit.

Well, I said I would get back to the story about the lieutenant in the Robbery Unit who I only knew as "Potts." After that first roll call, most detectives were heading back to their desk or going out on the street or preparing for court, and that's when I heard a commotion in the hallway. People were running around and I heard someone say, call an ambulance. It seems that "Potts" had fallen down the steps and was lying at the bottom. You could hear him moaning like he was in tremendous pain. He was carted away to the hospital, never to be seen by me again. The story goes that he slipped on a paper clip and fell down the steps. At first I was thinking, this poor man fell down all those steps and was probably seriously hurt. But the story that was told to me after I had a few months in the unit was not quite the sad story I believed happened. I didn't know him personally and actually never formally met him. I knew he had about thirty years on the job and was thinking about retiring. He allegedly slipped on a paper clip and had witnesses to that effect and he used those witnesses at his medical retirement hearing. He got a full medical retirement which was sixty-six and two-thirds of his salary, tax free for the rest of his life. I never got to work for "Potts", but from what I understand, he moved to Florida after the "accident" and lived a pretty good life, which included a lot of golf and fishing. Some people say that "Potts" was holding that paper clip in his hand, with a little smile on his face as they put him in the ambulance. I am sure that paper clip is attached to his disability retirement papers and framed somewhere down in sunny Florida.

I was thrilled to be in the Robbery Unit, but my real goal was to be in the Homicide Unit. Sometimes I would just walk through the Homicide Unit and watch the detectives at work. I could not help but notice how intense they seemed to be. I also noticed a huge placard on the bulletin board in the homicide office that read; "No greater honor can be bestowed upon a human being, then to investigate the death of another human being." I will never forget that and I don't know who wrote it, although many of us think it was Captain Cadden, but he would never admit it. I would find those words very encouraging to me many times in the future when I finally did get to the Homicide Unit.

Well, as I got settled into working robberies and we sure as hell had a lot of them in the early seventies. I had some real good arrests and was getting noticed by the supervisors and the other detectives in the unit. I got called into Dick Francis's office. He was the new lieutenant in charge of the Robbery Unit. I figured he was going to tell me I was doing a good job, but you never know for sure. He was an imposing sort of person. He kidded a lot with the men, but when you tried to kid back with him, he was sort of funny about it. It was as if he wanted to say, I am the lieutenant and I will do all the kidding. Well, when I went in the office, he said, "Sit down, star." I sat down and said, "What's star supposed to mean?" He said, "Well, you have not been here that long and already you are making a name for yourself." Before I could say anything, he said, "Don't take this wrong, but you are making some of the older detectives in the unit look bad." Again, before I could say anything, he laughed and said, "I personally enjoy watching it and the entire buzz in the unit about you." He stood up and walked around from his desk. I was not sure what he was going to do. He walked by me and shut the door and sat in a chair next to me. He said, "I do have something to tell you, but I like to shut the door, so that everyone in the office wonders what the hell is going on." I still had not said anything and every time I thought of saying something, it seemed as if he just jumped in and beat me to it. Finally, he said, "How do you like working in the Robbery Unit so far?" Well, this was my chance to talk and all I said was, "I like it a lot." I could not really think of anything else to say. He said, "Well I like having you in the unit. I am going to ask you to do something for the unit and the department." All of sudden he seemed very serious and leaned forward in his chair toward me and said, "I want you to take an assignment that might be a once in a lifetime opportunity for you."

At this point he got up and walked back behind his desk and lit up a cigarette, at the same time putting his feet on the desk. I did not say anything, because it did not appear that he was finished talking. He blew some smoke my way and said, "Well, are you going to say anything or just sit there?" I said, "I guess I can't say anything until I hear what the opportunity is going to be." He laughed and said, "I am asking you if you would like to be detailed to the FBI Bank Robbery Task Force." Well, he sure as hell got my attention. I knew about this task force and they were an elite unit of FBI agents in Maryland working on bank robberies along with a few detectives. I also knew that Baltimore in 1973 was experiencing the highest number of bank robberies in recent years and the mayor was pressing the police commissioner to do something about it. The lieutenant looked like he was waiting for an answer and I jumped on it and said, "I would love to work in that task force." He reached across the desk and shook my hand and said, "You got it, star." He said, "I will tell your sergeant and there is no need for you to discuss this with anyone else, just report to the FBI headquarters in Woodlawn on Monday morning, they already know you are coming", which meant he knew my answer before he even asked.

As I now look back on working on that task force, I can tell you it was one of the best experiences I had as a cop. The city was averaging about two or three bank robberies a day. I remember one day, we had five bank robberies and the police commissioner was called on the carpet by the mayor and got his ass busted and in turn he busted some ass back in the department.

I have a lot of stories about the bank robberies that I worked on, but I want to tell you about one that stands out and I think is quite an incredible story. In July of 1973, we had a bank robbery at the Maryland National Bank located at Belair Road and White Avenue in the northeast section of the city. When we had a bank robbery, anyone available in the FBI Task Force had to respond to the bank. Well, on this day, I was actually very close to the bank and was the first in the task force to arrive at the bank. I went inside and talked to the uniform officer taking the report. The officer told me that as many as four men were involved in the holdup of the bank. He said that they all wore masks and the masks were animal faces; one was a pig, one was a horse, and the other two could possibly have been pig faces also. The story from the tellers was that the group entered the bank and one guy leaped over the counter and scooped up all the money and they were out the door in less than five minutes. A car was waiting outside the bank for the others and they made their escape north on Belair Road. It was later determined that they got about sixty-five thousand dollars from the robbery which was quite a haul compared to the average robbery of a bank that was netting the robbers about ten thousand dollars in those days. We had a policy in those days that we would not tell the news media exactly how much money was taken, because it would only encourage other bad guys to give it a try.

We did all the usual things on this bank robbery that we did in the task force, except to show some photos of known bank robbers, as that would be useless in this case. We probably stayed on the scene for about three or four hours and then went back to the task force office. This is the part of the story that gets a little crazy and it is still unbelievable to me today. I was in the task force office and I got a call from a person who said they knew who did the Maryland National Bank robbery. I was not too excited, as we got a lot of calls from people just after bank robberies, mostly to see if there is a reward and lots of time, the information they had was bogus. This call seemed a little different, because the caller said he knew me from the days I worked in the Vice Unit. I still did not feel he knew anything about the bank robbery, until he said something that had haunted me for a couple of years. He said, "I am the guy who hit you in the face with a beer bottle two years ago in the Rocket Lounge on Harford Road." Well, I almost fell off the chair and he now had my full attention. He went on to say, "Do you remember getting hit with the bottle?" I laughed and said, "I don't think you forget about getting hit in the face with a beer bottle." He said, "Hitting you with the bottle has been bothering me for quite awhile and I want to make it up to you. I know who did the bank robbery at Belair Road and White Avenue." At this point, I wanted to reach through the phone and choke the shit out of this guy. I knew

I had to remain calm because I had healed from the cuts on my face and my job now was to solve bank robberies.

Before I go any further, I will tell you that I did get hit in the face with a beer bottle at the Rocket Lounge while working in the Vice Unit. I was working in the unit and my partner and I had entered the Rocket Lounge and after seeing some people who appeared to be under age, we started to check cards. Well, about half way down the bar, I did not see it coming, but someone in the back of the bar threw a beer bottle and hit me in the lower part of my face face, around the chin. I don't know how I was not knocked out, except we later figured that the bottle probably glanced off my face and it was not a direct hit. I think that if the bottle would have hit me directly in the face around the eyes, I might not be writing this story today. At the time it happened, whoever threw the bottle got away out the back door and no one in the bar would identify him. I remember being treated at Union Memorial Hospital and got seventeen stitches to close a gash on my lip and chin area.

Well, with all this new anger running through me about this guy on the phone, I wanted to meet him and kick his ass. I also wanted to get the information from him about the bank robbery and he seemed like he knew about it. After all, my chin healed up and as they say, time heals all wounds or at least that's what they say. I knew I had to keep my anger under control, so I kept talking to the guy and it was not long before I was convinced that he knew what he was talking about. He described the masks used by the bank robbers, he described the guns they used, and he knew approximately how much money they got from the bank. After I convinced him that I would not do anything to him for hitting me with the bottle, he said he would meet me and only me. I agreed and we decided to meet at a house that was about one block from the Rocket Lounge in northeast Baltimore and about two miles from the bank that was robbed.

When I was on the phone, no one in the task force office knew what the conversation was between me and the caller. I got off the phone and I just sat there, still not believing what had happened. I had no doubt I would meet the guy and get any information he had, but down deep inside I also wanted to meet him to see what he looked like. I was thinking that after he gave me some information, then I would kick his ass, because that part about time heals all wounds is bullshit.

I guess the FBI agents knew something was up and asked me if the call I took was any good. Well, I told them the story and they could not believe it and they were asking about the night I got hit with the bottle. They wanted to know how come we did not catch the guy back then. I am not sure if they actually believed me at first. I don't know why they would not believe it: who the hell could make up a story like that. I had the scars to prove it. The only part the agent in charge did not like was that I wanted to meet this guy by myself. He did ask me for the address where I was meeting the guy and did give me the okay to meet him by myself with a few agents close by.

The bank was held up at about 1 PM and I had agreed to meet the caller at about 7 PM, the same day. This would give me plenty of daylight, just in case this was bullshit and the guy had something else in mind. I left the office and drove out to the location and passed the Rocket Lounge on the way. I was thinking about the night I got hit in the face. I could now see how this guy could get away out the back door of the bar and directly to his house. I was also thinking, why did I agree to meet him by myself, since he had already given me one scar. Did he want to finish me off? I guess you do some crazy things when you're a cop, especially when you are hungry for information about one of the biggest bank robberies that the task force had handled.

I pulled up to the house and walked up to a porch. I did not have to bang on the door, as a young white male opened the door and said, "I assume you are Detective Ellwood." I walked into the house and this guy seemed real shaky and before I could say anything, he said, "I am really sorry about throwing the beer bottle that night." He went on to say, he had been drinking and really did not mean to hit anyone and thought the bottle would just hit the wall. I said, "That's over with, I am here to talk about the bank robbery, just as we discussed on the phone." He wasted no time and took me to another room and showed me a bag with masks in it and another bag with three guns in it. He said, "These are the masks and guns they used." I asked about the money and he said, "I don't know where the money is. They dropped off the masks and guns about one hour before I called you." I then asked the big question, "Who are these guys?" He said, "I will tell you, but is there some way you can to keep me out of this." He went on to say, "If they find out I am talking to you, they will kill me." To be very truthful, I really did not give a shit if he got killed or not, but I had to play along to get the names of the bank robbers. He walked in circles in the room for awhile and then said, "Okay, one of them is my brother and the other two are guys my brother hangs with." I told him that four people were involved in the bank robbery and he said he only knew about the three that he told me about. He told me his brother lives in the same house he does and he did not know where the other two lived. I knew this information was too good to be true. I needed to make a call to the FBI to see how they wanted to proceed with this guy. I called and talked to the agent in charge and I started to tell him what I had and he said, "Just hang loose, someone will be there real soon." He hung up and I was thinking, he did not even ask for the address. I had no sooner hung up the phone, and then there was a rap on the door. When the door was opened, there were three of the agents from the task force. I said, "How did you get here so fast?" They told me they were parked across the street the whole time. I guess I should have figured that the agent in charge was not going to let me go to the house by myself. I found out later that they followed me in a van to the house. They were in the area the entire time and at first I was pissed, but after I thought about it for awhile, it was the right thing to do for my safety and I was thankful.

We decided that we would take the bags with the masks and the guns into the FBI field office. I got some more contact information from this guy. He told me his name was Donny Kidwell and his older brother was Teddy. I left the house and told Donny that I would contact him and I also gave him my phone number in case he needed to reach me. I told him that now that he was cooperating with us, that it was in his best interest that he did not discuss this with anyone. He assured me that he would not talk to anyone about this and told me that if his brother and his friends found out what he was doing, they would kill him.

We worked on the case until midnight and decided we would come back in at about 9 AM the next day and continue to plan our actions when we were a little sharper and had some much needed rest. The next morning when I got to the FBI field office, a meeting was already in progress. They acted as if I was late, but then I was thinking, maybe they started the meeting without me for a reason. There were a few faces at this meeting that I had not seen before. I got a coffee and sat at the table. The agent in charge introduced me to the new faces. One of the guys was a ballistics expert from the FBI Crime Laboratory in Quantico, Virginia. The agent started to talk and said directly to me, "We have been talking before you got here and this is what we are thinking. Let me know how you feel about it." He went on to say, "We are going to file down the firing pins on the guns we recovered and put them back in the bags along with the masks." He said, "We are going get you to give them back to Donny and have him put them in the apartment where he found them." He continued by saying, "We are going to work with Donny and hopefully he might be able to tell us when these guys plan to do another bank robbery." The agent stopped talking and looked at me with a smile on his face. I could only smile back and then I said, "You have got to be kidding me." He assured me he was not kidding and I could now tell this by his voice and demeanor. He went on to say, "If it all goes well, we will take this gang down the next time they do a bank and if we do it right no one will get hurt." After he said he was not kidding, I actually started to think as stupid as it sounds, it might work. I was the low man on the totem pole in the task force and regardless of what I thought, they were moving forward with the plan.

I can tell you that the FBI works quickly and most of the time, they don't ask your approval: they just go ahead and do it. After the morning meeting, I was told that the FBI ballistics man had already filed down the firing pins on the guns. This meant they were not asking for my approval on a damn thing, which again pissed me off, but I kept it to myself. I was asked to meet with Donny and give him the bags and ask him to put them where he had found them. I was also told to have no other discussion with him, especially about filing down the firing pins on the guns. I knew he would have some questions and I was told it was okay to tell him that we were putting the guns and masks back and he was to try to find out when they were going to do another bank job.

About two days after Donny put the bag with the guns and masks back in the apartment, I got a call from him. He was starting to get excited about working with me and being an informant. I don't think he understood the consequence if the gang found out what he was doing. He told me his brother and the others were talking about doing a bank job at the Union Trust Bank on Ritchie Highway in Glen Bernie, Maryland. He only knew that they talked about doing it next week. He did not have the day or the time, but he did tell me that they had picked up the masks and the guns from the apartment. I am not really sure even now, what the real motive was for Donny to work with us. Was he that mad with his brother or was the excitement of working with cops his motive or did he actually want to pay me back for the scar he put on my face?

We had an emergency meeting at the FBI office. The brainstorming was getting hot and heavy and it seemed like each time we had a meeting, there were more agents. We also had a few high ranking members of the Baltimore Police Department involved. I think the FBI wanted to get others involved, in case things went wrong. They would then have someone to blame, which was par for the FBI. I enjoyed working with the FBI, but they had the reputation of always wanting to receive information, but hardly ever providing it.

The FBI, by the process of elimination, had identified the probable bank location in Glen Bernie. They already had blueprints drawn up and a huge drawing of the area that was tacked up on the task force wall. I know to get things done like this, it was great that the FBI was involved, because if we went through the city police department, it would have taken an act of God to get anything done. The agent in charge started the meeting and told the group that this is something they had never tried before. I was thinking, wow, I am either in on the ground floor of a breakthrough technique or this whole thing might blow up. I also thought that some of us in the room may be walking foot patrol on the North Pole and as I was the only one in the room with a uniform, that would be me.

The plan was to have law enforcement people in the bank as tellers. We would also have cops as customers and we would have a police helicopter above the bank. There would be a slew of FBI agents and cops stationed all over the outside area of the bank. The plan was to let the gang come into the bank and announce the robbery. The agent smiled and said, "If all goes well, we will simply make the arrest." Well, when the agent got done talking, everyone just sat there and the agent had to say, "Are there any questions?"

Some of the people attending for the first time just sat there with their mouth open and their jaws dropped down to their chest. Well, hell yes, there are some questions, I know I had some. No one spoke up. I looked around the room and people appeared either stunned or they didn't give a shit. I could not sit there any longer, so I stood up and raised my hand. The agent pointed to me and I said, "I got a couple of good questions." I don't think the agent in charge appreciated the way I said it, because he gave me that FBI better than thou look. The one that says, I am a FBI agent and you are just a mere low life uneducated city cop. Well, I knew I had to ask the questions, because it seemed like common sense to me. As I looked around the room, I really did not recognize a lot of common sense people. I was thinking, I have to save the day, because if there was one thing I had and probably got it from my dad, was common sense. I now had the floor, so I stood up and felt confident about my questions. I wanted good answers, because in this whole ordeal, I was the one that cultivated Donny as an informant. I did not want to see him get hurt. I was also thinking that if things went bad, I would definitely not get to the Homicide Unit. I asked my first question, "What if the bad guys have changed guns and when they hold up the bank, they have guns with real firing pins?" Well, I was waiting for the agents to laugh, but no one laughed and it appeared that I had hit a nerve with a pretty good common sense question. The agent in charge looked at me and said, "Can you go into more detail on what you are talking about?" I was thinking, you got to be fuckin kidding me if you don't understand what I just said. I might be the mere low life city cop, but if you can't comprehend what I just said, than you must have slept through college and the FBI Academy. There should be a course in the FBI Academy for common sense or maybe there is a common sense drug that can be injected into new recruits. I stood up again and moved a little closer to the front of the room. This time I knew that I had to speak up and be perfectly clear. I knew that down the road if this fiasco went bad, some agent would say, why didn't we think of that before we went to the bank. In police work when it comes to taking the heat on something that goes bad, the bosses never reach down between their legs and grab a hold of their manhood. They would rather see careers ruined than to speak up and take responsibility. I started to explain, that although the plan sounded great, we had to take into account that when they came to rob the bank, they might actually have changed guns. If they changed guns, they would not have the guns with the firing pins filed down. I went on to say, "What if they rob the bank and we start to take them down and they decide to shoot it out. Do we just wait to see if the guns don't fire, or do we open fire on them and just mow down a bunch of guys that have guns that aren't worth a damn?" I said, "If this goes bad and someone gets hurt or killed, can you imagine how it will read in the newspapers." I knew at this point I had hit a button with the bosses in the room and silence set in and now all eyes were on me. The lieutenant in charge of the Robbery Unit spoke up first and said, "Who actually gave the final okay on this plan to file down the firing pins?" He looked at me for an answer. Well, I could see where this was going and it would not be pretty. I had made up my mind that before I left the room, I was getting answers to my questions. I looked at the agent in charge and nodded to him that the ball was now in his court. It was like we were getting ready for a volleyball game and were choosing up sides. I could actually see some jockeying and people moving around the room and contemplating what side they would go with. As all this movement was taking place, one of the agents who I actually had a lot of respect for, Tom O'Neil, spoke up and said, "Let's all take a deep breath, relax, and think this through." He said, "The facts are that we have already filed down the firing pins and given the guns back to the bad guys." He said, "That order was okayed by the agent in charge of the local office." He stood up and walked to the front of the room and said, "We now feel with certainty that we know where their next bank job is going to take place. The thing we need to work out is how we take this gang down when they come into the bank and nobody gets hurt on either side, the good guys or the bad guys." I could feel that a little calm was now coming over the meeting and that was a good thing and everybody took their seats. Some at the meeting said they had to go and the agent in charge, made it real clear to those that were leaving that they were not to talk to anyone about this plan and if they did, lives were in jeopardy. He also emphasized that not only would lives be in danger, but a lot of careers would go down the drain also.

When some of the bosses left, we actually started trying to figure out what we would do. We had a smaller group now and with smaller groups, things get done faster. While we were working on our plan, it was obvious that the gang was probably working on their plan to hold up the bank in Glen Bernie. I guess it boiled down to whose plan would prevail. The agent in charge said we would put the final plan on hold. He asked me to call the informant and see what he had heard about the movement of the gang. I called Donny and he said that he had heard them talking about the bank job and it was still on, but he still did not know the date and time. He said that the guns were gone from the apartment and that his brother, Teddy, seemed to be getting a little nervous about being part of the bank robbery gang.

It was decided that we needed to just pick up one of the members of the gang and fabricate a charge to get him in the building to talk to him. We decided that Teddy was a good candidate to be picked up and someone we thought would talk, especially since his brother said he was getting nervous. I went with two FBI agents out to where Teddy lived and we just sat on the location until we saw him going to his car. The agents pulled up to Teddy, jumped out of the car, and literally threw him against the car. The agent told Teddy he was under arrest and you could see he was upset.

A smart move on our part was to not say anything to Teddy on the drive to the FBI office. You could tell he was really nervous and kept asking what this was all about. On the way to the field office, he kept saying that he did not do anything. He said he wanted a lawyer and that's when I asked him, "If you didn't do anything, what the hell do you want a lawyer for?" At the FBI office, we put Teddy in a room and let him sit for about an hour. Sitting alone in a police facility was always a good tactic. Just think, you get picked up by the FBI and they don't tell you why, but just put you in a room. Can you imagine what was going through his mind? We could see in the room and he could not see out. We watched him as he paced back and forth in this very small room. A couple of times he banged on the door and screamed that he wanted to talk to someone and we just ignored him. The plan was to go in the room eventually and tell him we knew all about the bank robbery and if he worked with us, we would cut him a deal after the rest of the gang was locked up. I went in the room with an agent and Teddy appeared to be much calmer. We offered him some coffee or a cigarette and he refused both. We started to talk to him and did not waste any time. We got right to the point.

I told him that we knew he did the bank job. We lied and told him that we also knew who the other guys were. At first he said he was not involved in any bank robberies, but when we told him that we knew the other members, he got real quiet. He absolutely shocked us all when he asked what kind of deal he would get if he cooperated. The FBI agent said he would have to talk to the United States Attorney for the District of Maryland before he could promise anything. Teddy said he wanted to get released from our custody and think about it. The agent got a little loud with Teddy and told him that he either takes the deal now or you go over to city jail and sit there as a federal witness. I knew this was total bullshit. We probably could not hold him in jail, but with the reputation of the Baltimore City Jail, all you had to do sometimes was to mention the jail and suspects would confess to the Lincoln assignation.

Teddy got up, paced around in the room, and then said, "I guess I really don't have much of a choice." He very reluctantly agreed to work with us if we absolutely promised to protect him. The agent sat down with Teddy and told him that if he worked with us he would be released. He told him that if at any time while on the street, he crossed us and did not follow through with the deal, he would be arrested. The agent told Teddy that the FBI would recommend a stiff sentence if he did not work with us. Teddy was now between a rock and a hard place. He was sweating profusely and he agreed to work with us.

We drove him back up to his home and let him out of the car about two blocks from the apartment. On the ride back, Teddy kept telling us that if the others found out that he was helping us, he would be a dead man. We assured him that we would do everything in our power to protect him. Down deep inside, we knew that in the world that Teddy lived, snitching was probably a death sentence. We also knew we were up against the clock on this case. We did not know the exact day that they were going to rob the bank in Glen Bernie.

The day after we released Teddy, the FBI agent got a call from him and he told them that the gang was acting a little strange. He said they might not do the bank in Glen Bernie and might change their location. The agent told Ted, that it is extremely important that he stay involved with them as much as possible and find out what bank they were going to rob.

We had another short meeting and the FBI agents were worrying about Teddy. The agent in charge asked me to call his brother to see what was happening, but not to mention the deal we had made with Teddy. I called Donny and he said that he had not heard anything and that his brother was acting very strange lately. Donny said that he had never seen him like this before. I asked what he meant and he said he thinks Teddy wants to get away from the gang, but doesn't know how to do it. I told Donny to stay in touch with Teddy and if anything strange or unusual was taking place, to give me a call.

I think it was a couple of days later when I got a call at home from the FBI agent in charge. He told me to meet him and the others at the FBI office in Woodlawn. I knew something was up, because after he told me about the meeting, he just hung up the phone. I thought that was very unusual because we had become very good friends. We usually talked about our families, the Oriole game, or just cop talk. The other thing strange about the meeting, was that he called me at midnight and said to be in the office at about 3:00 AM and that only means that something real important had gone down.

I got to the FBI office at about 3:10 AM and the only people there were the agent in charge and another city detective. I started to get a coffee and the agent said, "We got some real bad news and you better sit down to take this." I continued to get the coffee and he continued to talk. I pretended that no matter what he had to say, I would not be shocked, after all this was police work. What the hell could be that shocking? Well, I was wrong; the agent sat on the edge of a table and said, "Teddy is dead." At first I did not quite pick up what he said, I guess because it kind of rhymes, "Ted is dead." Then he said it again and I heard it loud and clear, "Teddy is dead." I really didn't need to take a seat at this point, because I actually fell back into a seat and said, "What the hell are you talking about?" He said it again, "Teddy is dead." I got frustrated with his frankness and said, "I heard that part, but what the hell happened to him." He said that Teddy's girlfriend said that two guys came to the apartment and acted real friendly. They told Teddy that they wanted him to take a ride with them. She said that Teddy told her that everything was alright, but she knew something was up. She said Teddy was sort of swelling up with tears as he left the apartment with the two men. She said he kissed her on the way out and said, "I will always love you." The agent said that about three hours later a police officer was taking a leak in a park in Baltimore County and saw a Cadillac parked in the lot with a door open. When the officer checked it out, he found the keys in the ignition. He further checked the vehicle and opened the trunk. That's when he found Teddy's body in the trunk with several bullet wounds and one directly in the back of the head.

As the agent was talking, more people started to show up at the office and they could tell from the mood in the room, that something was wrong. After finally telling everyone as they arrived, the agent said, "We need to regroup and get down to some serious discussions on what we need to do." It was decided that another meeting would take place with all the bosses from the police department and the FBI. This time we would have to include cops from Baltimore County. The county needed to be invited, because they had a homicide investigation on their hands and we might know who did it.

It was about 8 AM when we had everyone in the room that needed to be there and the mood was very somber. The FBI agent went over the entire story from the very beginning. This was mainly for the benefit of the Baltimore County cops who were hearing this story for the first time. Some of the people in the room, especially the new invitees sat there and had a look of disbelief on their faces. We even had the colonel in charge of the Detective Division at the meeting. This guy had about thirty-eight years on the job and I was surprised that he did not seem that upset when he heard the entire story. He did say in very strong language, "We need to make sure everything is on the up and up with this investigation or heads will roll." When he said that heads would roll, I could picture the first head to go would be mine. I was the junior man on this task force. I actually did not have any good thoughts on how we would bounce back from this or how we could proceed. I knew that the agents did not want anything like this on their record and they would do whatever had to be done, to make it right. I also knew that everyone on the task force, along with the county homicide detectives would put it all together. I know that we had all figured out that the two men who came to Teddy's apartment were the other members of the gang and apparently they had found out that Teddy was a snitch. I think the only people in the room that were a little happy, were the county homicide detectives, as they now had suspects for their murder.

The new plan put together by the agent in charge was to pick up Teddy's girlfriend as soon as possible. We needed to pick up Teddy's brother Donny and stake out the last known addresses of the two other members of the gang. We needed to put a detail of men down at the bank in Glen Bernie, in case they decided to go through with the holdup. We would make sure the bullets were recovered from Teddy's body at the autopsy. The bullets needed immediate ballistics work to determine if the caliber matched any of the guns that were returned to the gang. We most definitely needed to make sure nothing was released to the press before all these things could be done.

That day was a work around the clock day. Nobody went home and nobody wanted to go home. We were in the most serious mood that I had seen this group in since we started. Even though Teddy was a gangster, he was working with us and we wanted to make sure the right thing was done for him. We had promised him that he would be alright. Although we probably could not have prevented his death, we had a sense that we wanted to find his killers; we owed it to Teddy.

It was very obvious to all of us that the others in the gang, must have got word that Teddy was working with us. It is also possible that they just saw him as a weak link and wanted to eliminate him. I know it sounds like a mob movie, but I am sure that when Teddy left with those two guys from his apartment, he knew he was not coming back. It kind of reminds me of the Donnie Brasco movie when Sonny Black, played by Al Pacino is sitting in his apartment and gets a call to take a ride with some mobsters. He sits in his favorite chair, smoking his last cigarette, and having a drink. He then he takes his watch, wallet, ring, and a necklace and puts them in a drawer. He leaves the drawer half open, so that these things will be found. He then kisses his girlfriend on the forehead. He tells her not to wait up for him and says, "I love you" and walks out the door to meet the mobsters who he knows are going to kill him. In the story, he is killed because he introduced Donnie Brasco to the mob and Donnie was an undercover FBI agent.

I don't think continuing much further with this story would be very interesting to you, so I will end it with telling you the final outcome. We eventually picked up the other members of the bank robbery gang. They all had prior felony records, which included armed robberies. We worked around the clock for a couple of days. We wrote search warrants for their homes and recovered two of the guns that had been returned to them. The firing pins still filed down. We convinced Teddy's girlfriend to testify against the men who came to the apartment. She was provided witness protection up until the time they were sentenced to federal prison. We put Teddy's brother in protective custody also until the trial. For a period of time, there was a lot of friction between the federal prosecutors and Donny. I guess that was understandable, after all, he knew that in some unforeseen way he had contributed to his brother's death.

The bad guys were all charged in federal court with the bank robbery and felons in possession of handguns. They were also charged in Baltimore County with the homicide of Teddy. The good news is that they all got life sentences without the possibility of parole. Donny left the state with the assistance of the FBI, although it was not a witness protection program. I think the government just wanted to help him with the expenses of leaving. They owed him that much. Teddy's girlfriend did not want protection and I assume she still lives in Baltimore.

I continued working in the FBI Bank Robbery Unit for about one year after this all happened. I can assure you there was never any investigation that would come close to this one. I remained friends with the FBI agents and we attended many cop functions over the years. I can tell you that when others were grandstanding and telling cop stories at police functions, none of us thought it appropriate to tell this story out of respect for Teddy: this is the first time. I only tell the story now, because the FBI agents are all retired or too damn old to remember it. Probably the other reason I am now telling the story, is because it is good reading and how the hell are you going to sell a book, unless you put all the good stuff in it.

PABST BLUE RIBBON HOLDUP MAN

Well, I was going to move on to my stories about my homicide days, but I have another short story about working in the Robbery Unit. In 1974, we were having a lot of armed robberies in the northeast part of the city, especially on the Harford and Belair Road sections. The way this armed holdup guy would operate was amazing and kind of funny at first, but after about six armed robberies, it ceased to be funny anymore. The guy would go in a bar and order a Pabst Blue Ribbon Beer, which was a mainstay in Baltimore bars back then. He would sip the beer and have some casual conversation with the bartenders, usually females. When the moment seemed right, he produced a gun and told the bartender it was a holdup. It did not matter to this guy how many people were in the bar at the time. He always ordered a Pabst Blue Ribbon Beer and then announced quietly and politely it was a holdup. He never got excited and never talked loud and only announced it being a holdup to the bartender. He would get what money he could get from the cash register and calmly walk out of the bar, usually after finishing his beer. He never wore a mask and always was alone. Everybody that got robbed would always talk about how nice the guy was. They always described the same person; the only difference was the color of his hair.

One night he went into the Red Rooster Lounge on Moravia Park Drive and sat at the bar. The bar was quite large and had several pool tables. The bar was usually very busy with patrons shooting pool and sitting around the bar. This guy comes in and sits at the bar and yes, he gets a Pabst Blue Ribbon

Beer. The bartender and the bad guy struck up a friendly conversation and part of the conversation was about how much money she earned tending bar. He also asked her how well she did with tips. The bartender went on to tell the robber that she was a single mom and worked at the bar to support her two children. She told him that although the hours were tough on her and the money was not that great, she enjoyed it very much. On this particular night, I guess because of the long conversation, he had two beers and placed a twenty dollar bill on the counter. The bartender had not taken out for the beers yet, when the holdup man pulled out his gun and told the bartender that it was a holdup. The bartender was completely shocked. He told her to get all the money from the cash register and she did what he said and gave it to him. He sat and was finishing his beer, when a pool shooter came to the bar and asked the bartender for change for the pool table. The bartender was very nervous and told the customer that she did not have any change. Not having change would seem very strange for a crowded bar with several pool tables and other coin operated machines. Before the pool shooter could walk away, the bad guy told him that he had change. The bad guy pulled money from a bag and gave the pool shooter change.

The holdup man started to get up to leave. He could see that the female bartender was crying and asked her what was wrong, as if he did not know. She told him that she would have to answer to the owner about the robbery. She said that she would probably have to come up with the money and maybe even lose her job. She also told him that her tip money for the day was in with the money she gave him. The robber told her that he would give the bag of money back if she would stop crying. He asked her not say anything and not to pull any alarms when he left the bar. She agreed and he gave the money back and started to walk out of the bar. When he got to the door, he stopped and walked back to the bar. He sat down and said, "I'm sorry, but I need that money more than you." He told her to put it all back in the bag and she did. He then thanked her and walked up the steps and out of the bar, just as casual as ever.

Now comes the strange part of the story, if not very strange already. I forgot to tell you that when he did the armed holdups, his method of operation was the same, except for the fact that he had different color hair on each holdup. When the robberies first started, we did not think it was the same person, except for the Pabst Blue Ribbon Beer part. The victims would always describe a different color of hair, but basically the same physical description and mannerisms.

I was assigned to these robberies and I got the same story when I interviewed each victim. Most of the victims said that the guy looked very familiar to them and everyone said he was a nice guy. I did everything that you are supposed to do on these types of robberies. I showed photographs and had a composite drawing done by the police artist. It was tough to do a good composite drawing because of the change in hair color.

I was getting nowhere on these cases, until one night I was out with the guys and having a few beers myself, not Pabst Blue Ribbon. I am pretty sure I was single at the time or at least for this story I was. I met this lady in a nightclub on Harford Road. I actually knew her ex-husband, who was a cop. We were talking and drinking a few beers. By trade, I knew that she worked in a hair salon on Belair Road and had been a hair stylist for quite a few years. As the night wore on, we were getting pretty friendly and this is when she laid a bombshell right in my lap. She started by asking me if she told me something, would I keep it between the two of us. I told her I would and she said that she was getting friendly with a guy that she met in a bar. She said that every week he comes to her house and she changes his hair color for him. Well, you can imagine, I almost fell off the bar stool. I immediately cleared my head from all the drinking. She went on to say he was a real nice guy and she just found it strange that he would change his hair color all the time. I tried to stay cool, but I could not keep from asking questions about this guy, because I knew what I was onto. I continued to let her talk about him, hoping she would say that she has been to his home or in his car or something that would lead me to this guy. I tried to stay calm and ask stupid questions; like, do you think the guy is gay, at which she jumped in and said she was very sure he was not gay. It was getting late and I could not think of any other way to work this lead, so I asked her if she really trusted this guy and she hesitated. I figured this is my opportunity to set the table, so I said, "There are some real crazies out there and you need to be careful." I knew I got her attention with that and she said, "Just to be safe, when he calls me the next time or comes over my apartment, I will get his full name and try to find out where he lives." I told her to call me as soon as she talked to him and I would check him out and she seemed okay with that. Well, the night ended and I will leave it at that, which means I can't go into what a cop has to do some time to get information. It's all for the fight against the forces of evil and if you believe that shit, I have some swamp land for sale in Florida. I think it all comes with loving the job and if you love your job, you will do whatever it takes to be successful, so I did.

I only shared this information with my partner in the Robbery Unit and did not put anything on paper in the investigation folder. About a week later, I got a call from Gina, that's her name in case I forgot to mention it. She asked if I could meet her for a drink and of course I said yes. Along with being a source of information, she was a good looking lady. She had already been involved with one cop, so why not one more. I met her and she said she had some information on the guy she was seeing. She said she told him that she would not do his hair any longer and he got very upset with her. She said he got real angry and she said she saw a side of him that she did not like and was now scared of him. I asked her if she got his name or any other information. She said his name was Freddie and she actually had an address. I asked how she got the address and she said that she picked him up one night in her car. She said they went drinking and then they went to his apartment. I asked her what Freddie was drinking and she said, "Beer." I am sure you know what the next question was, yes it was, "What kind of beer does he drink?"

It was like feeding a poker machine and winning each time with this girl. I liked her, but my main objective was to get this guy, we could work on me liking her later. She looked at me funny and said, "What the hell does that have to do with anything?" I was thinking to myself, it is jackpot time on the poker machine. She said, "He drinks Pabst Blue Ribbon" and my evil mind could only silently think, "Thank you, thank you and thank you." I am sure she was now getting a little inquisitive about me asking all these questions. I backed off a little and had some general conversation with her. I think she knew, from her past experiences with a cop, that I would not let anything happen to her.

I drove with her and she pointed out where Freddie lived and knew what apartment he had. She asked what to do if he keeps calling and I told her that it was probably in her best interest not to see this guy until I checked him out. I was not sure she would do what I said, because it seemed from our conversation that this guy sort of intrigued her, although she also appeared to be a little leery of him after all of my questions.

Well, two more bar holdups happened with the same method of operation. Finally, the big break came one day when the Equitable Trust Bank at Belair Road and Frankfurt Avenue got robbed. The bank teller gave the holdup man a dye pack in the bag along with some money. A dye pack is designed to explode a few minutes after it is pulled from the cash drawer by the teller. It displaces red dye that goes everywhere; I mean it goes everywhere. The witnesses to the bank robbery said that the holdup man got in a red car and when he did, apparently the dye pack exploded. One witness said they saw heavy red smoke coming from the car as it drove away. I was in the area and responded to the bank to assist if needed. I just happened to be the first robbery detective on the scene and went in the bank to talk to the teller. I wanted to get a description of the holdup man to broadcast over the police radio. I talked to the teller that was robbed and she said the holdup man was a white male, about six feet tall and had strange looking blonde hair. I know this all sounds too good to be true, especially the strange looking blonde hair. I just happened to have a picture of Freddie with me. I showed it to the teller and she screamed and almost passed out and said, "That's him." Well, that would have been two of us almost passing out, because my heart was beating big time and I felt like I had hit the lotto. I now knew that from the direction that the bank robber was traveling in his car and knowing that it was Freddie, he was probably heading back to his apartment and guess what, I know where that is.

I went out to my unmarked police car and asked a uniform patrol cop to follow me. I knew the uniform cop and told him, "We are about to catch a bank robber." I don't know if he believed me or not, but he followed me and I headed straight for Freddie's apartment. His apartment was not far from the bank. I assume he figured the bank was a good target. It was close to home and he was probably tired of holding up bars.

When I got to the apartment, I took the uniform officer with me and rapped on the door. I also had called for another uniform car to cover the rear of the apartments, in case he went out the back way. I got an answer from inside the apartment and it was a female voice. I told her that we were the police and she should open the door. She opened the door and we went in with guns drawn, because Freddie had a gun at the bank. She told us she had spent the night with Freddie and that she did not know where he was. From the looks of the apartment, they sure had a good time. She told us that he left the apartment early in the morning when she was sleeping. She said she did not know where he went. We asked if we could look around the apartment and she said she did not care. We looked around and did not find anything interesting. We left the apartment and I gave the female my phone number. I got her name and address and asked her to call me if she wanted to talk about anything.

I went back to the bank and I was not there more than ten minutes when my phone rang and it was the female from Freddie's apartment and she was crying. I asked what was wrong and she said, "I know I am going to get in trouble, but he made me do it." I said, "Who made you do what?" She said that Freddie was in the apartment when we were there and was up in the ceiling of a closet and had a gun. She said she did not say anything to us, because she was afraid of what Freddie would do with the gun. She said that after we left the apartment, he also left and told her that he was going to Atlantic City. Freddie told her not to talk to the police about anything. She told us she did not know where his car was. She said that he was getting a ride to the Trailways Bus Station downtown to take the bus to Atlantic City. She continued to cry hysterically and kept saying how much trouble she was in and she was on probation. I assured her that she did the right thing. I told her to stay in the apartment and someone would be over to pick her up and take her down to the Robbery Unit.

I hooked up with another detective from the Robbery Unit and we drove down to the Trailways Bus Terminal on Fayette Street in the city. It was about noon time and we checked with the ticket office and a bus was leaving for Atlantic City at 1:30 PM and so far twenty-two people had purchased tickets. I showed the ticket person the photo of Freddie and he said he was not sure if he sold him a ticket or not. We told the security officers at the bus terminal what we were doing and we took a seat in the terminal with others waiting for a bus. It was about 1:15 PM and sure enough here comes Freddie with a black carrying bag and drinking a soda. He was bopping along like nothing in the world could be bothering him. We knew we had to take him down quickly, because he probably still had the gun he used in the bank robbery. We also knew that if he got on the bus, we would be at a disadvantage. We decided that when the boarding of the bus started, we would just rush him. The plan was that one would take the bag and the other would take Freddie. I would like to say at this point that something dramatic happened, but it did not and it went off perfect. My partner grabbed the bag right off his shoulder and I grabbed Freddie and he did not resist. He actually kind of laughed and said something like, "I was expecting you, that bitch told you, didn't she."

We took Freddie down to the Robbery Unit and started taking a statement and as you can imagine, once he decided to talk, the statement became a book. We made a deal with Freddie, that if he told us about all his bar robberies, bank robberies, and any other robberies, we would ask the Baltimore State's Attorney's office for a break in the sentencing if and when he was found guilty.

We actually became friendly with Freddie, as he was in the Robbery Unit for about ten hours. We talked about things like where he went to school in Baltimore and where he grew up. We talked about family and also about some of the women he dated. We did discuss his hair color changing for each robbery. He was actually trying to protect Gina and said she was a sweet girl and did not know anything about what he was doing. He really did not want to talk about her, but made an interesting statement when he said, "She's as dumb as a doorknob." He said that the girl that was at the apartment when we were there has been a main squeeze of his since high school. He said she did not know what he was up to; I guess he wanted to protect her also. He didn't really find out until the trial, that his main squeeze gave us a statement. She was on probation for drug charges and told us she did know that Freddie was doing holdups.

When we were taking the statement from Freddie about the bars he held up, he would say, I walked in and ordered a beer. I would ask what kind and he proudly said, "The best beer in Baltimore, Pabst Blue Ribbon." When I told Freddie that we in the Robbery Unit had nicknamed him the "Pabst Blue Ribbon Bandit," he laughed and said, "Man, that's cool."

Well, to end this short story about the Pabst Blue Ribbon Bandit, Freddie went to court. Even with the state's attorney asking the judge for a little leniency, Freddie got twenty years with five years suspended. I did testify that Freddie was very cooperative, but the judge pointed out that he used a gun in all his robberies and for that, he was sending him away for a long time. At the trial, it was very unusual to see Freddie smiling at everyone and waving to some family. To him, it seemed like a passage in his life and he was caught and it was no big deal. Even when the judge sentenced Freddie, he thanked the judge. In his mind, he was a hero and a star and I really believe that when he did the robberies and changed his hair color, it was probably like putting on makeup for the big show. When he was being taken from the courtroom, he made a point to look back at me. He gave me a smile and said, "Go get them bad guys."

I did hear from Freddie when he was in prison. He wrote to me later when I was in the Homicide Unit. He told me that he took up cutting hair in prison and was doing just fine. He signed all his letters, Pabst Blue Ribbon Bandit. You gotta like a guy like Freddie, even if he is a bad guy.

HOMICIDE UNIT – LET THE GAMES BEGIN

Finally, in late 1974, I got the phone call I was waiting for since I had joined the police department. I got a call from Captain Jim Cadden and all he said was, "Are you ready?" I guess I was both excited and nervous and I said, "Am I ready for what?" The captain said, "You dumb shit, are you ready to come to the Homicide Unit and be a real cop?" Well, as you can expect, I could hardly answer him and finally when I got it together, I said, "Yes sir, I am really ready." He told me to report the very next day. I was already in the Robbery Unit and both units had roll call together each morning in the same room. I can't tell you enough, what it meant to be selected to go to the Homicide Unit. I can assure you that if you were not a good investigator, you did not get in the Homicide Unit. It also brought with it, much prestige among your peers, as everyone in the Homicide Unit was looked up to as the cream of the crop.

I can tell you that the night before reporting to the Homicide Unit, I hardly slept. I was probably getting ready for work a couple of hours prior to when I normally got ready. I made sure the shirt was one of my best. I had a new suit that I had just bought for special occasions and this was sure as hell a special occasion. In the Homicide Unit, it was like a detective fashion show each day. You might not think that men look at what other men are wearing, but they did in the Homicide Unit. We had the extreme dressers, who wore Joseph Bank or Eddie Jacob suits. Then we had guys like me that wore Macy's or Hecht Company suits. There was a small element of guys who really didn't give a damn what they wore and we called them the polyester princes. I don't mean to make fun of anyone, because the clothes really did not make the detective. It was his ability and tenacity to get the job done, but looking good helped.

I walked into roll call and most people did not know that I was moving over from the Robbery Unit to the Homicide Unit. Well, that did not last long, as the shift lieutenant, Frank Elder started roll call by telling everyone that Dick Ellwood was now in the Homicide Unit. I looked around and there were some nods of approval, except for my robbery sergeant. He apparently had not been told by the captain that I was going to homicide. He was obviously offended that he was not made aware of the change. He gave me the bad eye and after roll call, called me a traitor; no congratulations, just traitor. I did not say anything to him, I was just happy to be away from him and in the spot that I had dreamed of being since coming on the department.

I can remember that my first thought after roll call was to call my dad. I think I have probably mentioned numerous times already that he was a cop and worked thirty-two years on the job. I called him and I said, "I got some great news" and he said, "I know, you are in the Homicide Unit." I asked him how he knew and kidding me, he said, "Hey, you forget that I was a pretty damn good cop myself and I have ways of finding things out." We laughed about it and he gave me the same good advice he had always given me, "Work hard and you will be recognized."

At the time I got assigned to homicide, I also had a brother that was already in the unit. I think that John and I were the only brother's act that worked in the Homicide Unit at the same time. There were brothers that had each been in the Homicide Unit at different times, but we were the first to be there at the same time. It turned out to be interesting, working in the same unit with your brother. He was actually my younger brother, but having more time in the Homicide Unit than me, made him the senior man. I was the new man on the block. We had some good times in the unit, until he got promoted and was sent back to uniform patrol. I can remember going out on investigations with him. We would interview people and I would say, "Hello, I'm Detective Ellwood." Then my brother would say, "Hello, my name is Detective Ellwood also." Most of the time people did not even say anything, but I can remember one time we did it and this guy thought we were messing with him and slammed the door on us. We knocked again and when he came to the door, he said, "When you two are ready to be serious, we can talk." I asked what the problem was and he said, "You both said you were Detective Ellwood and if I am going to talk to you, I want some real names." We both showed him our identification and he said, "Well, I'll be dammed, you got me good."

Being in the Homicide Unit brings back some great memories for me and also some that are not so good. I intend to share some of them with you in this book. I can honestly say that while in the unit, I worked with the finest bunch of homicide detectives that could have ever been assembled in one unit. I know that sounds like bragging, but it can be backed up by the number of solved homicides the unit had in the years that I was there.

Now that I am retired, people still ask where I worked while in the police department. Although I worked in several units in my twenty-five years, I like to tell them I worked in the Homicide Unit. I always get the same reaction, "Wow, I bet that was exciting." Even when I talk about the other units that I worked in, it always gets back to the Homicide Unit and they love to hear stories about murders. I tell stories and I am always amazed at the different responses that I get. Some people say things like, "You must have seen a lot of terrible stuff." I usually don't respond, but I think to myself, in a city that averages three hundred murders a year, you bet your sweet ass I saw some real terrible shit. I can remember one of my relatives, one that never lived anywhere near the city, asked me why there are so many murders in the city. Actually this was not the first time I had been asked this question and my answer was always the same, "I don't know." The reason that I give the short answer, is because if I go on with what I believe is the correct answer, it will generate debate that I would rather not have. I could say that in certain parts of the city, the people have no regard for life. I could say that certain sections of Baltimore are drug infested and have been since the 60s and guess what, nobody gives a shit. I could say that in most homes in the bad neighborhoods of the city, there is usually only one parent and that is the mother. I could say that the preachers, educators, activists, and politicians really don't want to change anything. The preachers just get up in the pulpit and talk about how bad things are and then pass the collection box. The educators don't want to make any waves, so they just pass the bad kids, to get them out of their class and on to the next teacher who don't give a shit either. The activists are interesting people; they come out of the woodwork once in awhile and hold candlelight vigils on the corners where the murder happened. I save the politicians for last and that is where they usually are, last to do anything. In cities like Baltimore, hell you could be the worst piece of shit on the earth and you can get elected.

You ask what the solution is and I would say, how about mandatory sentences without the possibility of parole. Oh yeah, how about the death penalty and a quick death penalty, not one that allows you to wait about fifteen years to run through every appeal possible. My final suggestion is to give the streets back to the cops and let them smack the bad guys around a little.

After all these years retired from the department, I still get frustrated when I read about the crime in the city. I have noticed lately that murders in the city don't even get the front page anymore; they are stuck on page three in a small paragraph.

I am going to move on with some stories about my years in the Homicide Unit. I am not really a bitter person; I just love Baltimore and want to see it become a safe city.

The Teacher and the Prankster

I had some great trainers in the Homicide Unit, but the best was Detective Sergeant Rod Brandner. I was assigned to Rod's squad when I went to homicide. Rod was the sergeant, but you never really thought of him as the supervisor, just as one of the guys. He always worked very close with all his detectives. He never went home until the work was done and his detectives were done. Rod was one of the most interesting people I have ever met in my life. If you talk to anyone that was in the Homicide Unit when he was there, they will tell you the same thing. I could go on and on with stories about Rod and all the pranks that he pulled on guys in the unit, especially the guys in his squad. Rod was the most knowledgeable homicide investigator and supervisor in the unit. Being around Rod and watching him was like on the job training. As I am writing this story, I am thinking back on all the jokes and tricks he pulled on the guys.

Rod also played on the Homicide Unit softball team and I was the manager. He was our pitcher and a real good one at that and just loved to play softball. We did not play in any organized softball leagues; we just played other units in the police department. We also played the states attorney's office team and a few teams that were with other police departments around Maryland. I do have to admit that we were not that young of a team. We really just played for the enjoyment of being together and drinking beer after the games. At some of the games we actually had beer in the coolers on the side lines. I have had players ask me to take them out of the game early, just so they could drink some beer. Rod was the man; he loved to pitch and took it very serious and absolutely hated to lose.

I think that Rod and I bonded right off the bat, because we were both Marines. As everyone knows, the closeness that Marines have is something that really can't be explained. I guess it speaks for itself when you say honor, courage, and commitment.

I will tell you a story about Rod that I will never forget. I had been promoted while assigned to Rod's squad. I had been in the unit for five years prior to getting promoted. The unwritten rule back than when you got promoted while working in detectives, was that you spent one year in patrol as a uniform sergeant. I left homicide and worked my one year in patrol and then was asked to come back to homicide. I worked in Rod's squad as a detective and now I was a homicide sergeant and again working on the same shift with Rod. I was thrilled not only to be back in the Homicide Unit, but also working alongside my mentor, Rod Brandner.

My squad was working the midnight shift and it was summer time and very hot in the homicide office. We had no windows that would open in the office and the air conditioner was not the greatest when it worked. I wrote a report to the captain saying that it was very hot in the office at night. I asked if we could get some big fans to be placed in the office, to help cool it down a little. Well, about one week later, they placed about four large commercial type fans in the office and it seemed to work. Well, Rod wrote a report to the captain forging my signature saying that now it was too cold in the office at night. He asked in the report, if the fans could be taken out. He also included in the report that we might now need some space heaters in the office.

The next morning, the captain, who was Joe Di'Carlo at the time, called me in and started by saying "What the hell is wrong with you Sergeant.?" I did not know what he was talking about, because I didn't do anything recently that would provoke him. He went on to say, "One day your cold and then you are hot, make up your damn mind, what you are." I just sat there trying to figure out what the hell he was talking about. Finally he said, "If you want to control the temperature, I'll send you back to patrol, where you can ride around and roll the window up and down as many times as you want." I finally had to say something, so I said, "Captain I have no idea what you are talking about." That set him off and he threw a report at me. After I picked it up off the floor, I saw that it had my signature on it. I read the report and it was addressed to the captain from me. The report went on to say that since the fans have been put in the office, that I was cold at night and could we take them out and get some space heaters put in the office. I looked at the signature again and at first I was thinking, this is my signature. I was thinking that I must have written it, but then it hit me like a ton of bricks; it was Rod. I started to laugh and that pissed off the captain even more. I said, "Captain, I have the answer to this report, it was Sergeant Brandner that wrote this report, not me." He looked at me and I don't think he believed me at first, but then I told him, "No way would I write a report asking for space heaters after I had asked earlier for fans." I told him to look close at the signature and although it looked like mine, it was not. At this point I was getting a little more relieved and the captain broke out in a roaring laugh. He said, "I will get that bastard, if it is the last thing I do." The captain then came up with a pretty good plan. He told me to go back out in the homicide office main room where all the detectives had their desks. He said he was going to come out into the room and start to bust my ass in front of everyone about the report that I had written. He said that he would really get loud and wanted to see Rod's reaction.

Well, it went great. The captain came out in the main office and it was crowded with detectives and he started on me; he said, "Sergeant Ellwood, you stupid son of a bitch, what the hell is wrong with you" and he commenced to read the report. He went on to bust me real good and as I looked around the office, no one was laughing. I noticed that Rod had a smirk on his face that was both a smile and a real concern that the captain was busting me in front of all the detectives over something that he had done. The captain turned to Rod and said, "I am glad I have sergeants like you Rod, the kind that never bitch like Sergeant Ellwood does." Rod could not take it any longer and said, "Captain I wrote that report." Well, the office got real quiet, because no one knew what was going on. The captain wanted to continue to be serious; he could only burst out laughing and said to Rod, "Get your ass back in my office right now." Well, now it was my turn to laugh and laugh I did and so did the entire office, who by now had pretty much figured out that Rod was up to his tricks again. When Rod came out of the captain's office, he at first looked real serious. When he got to his office, he and I went in and we almost pissed in our pants laughing. It was so bad, that we had to lock the door.

There are so many stories about Rod, but sadly, later in life after retiring from the department he became very ill, suffered a lot, and passed away. He developed a condition that took his eyesight. He had heart bypass surgery and then for some serious medical condition, his leg was amputated. He was in the hospital recovering after being in a coma for eight days when the most tragic thing you can imagine happened. His wife Rose, the love of his life, was on her way to the hospital to visit Rod and had a heart attack on the hospital parking lot and died. At his wife's funeral, Rod was brought to the church in an ambulance and was wheeled down the church isle on a stretcher and placed next to his wife's coffin for the service. It is something that all who attended will never forget. The tears were flowing that day in the church from all of us tough guys who worked in the Homicide Unit. We dealt with death on a daily basis, but nothing like this.

I must tell you this final story about Rod that I will cherish for the rest of my life. Rod was still in the hospital after the death of his wife and on an early Sunday morning, I decided to go and visit with him. I walked into his room in Union Memorial Hospital and he appeared to be sleeping. I sat in a chair outside the room and the nurse told me to just go and stand by his bed. Well, I stood by his bed and when I turned away from looking at him, he scared the hell out of me. He sprung forward in the bed and hollered, "Holy shit I must have really died this time and I know I am in hell, because Dick Ellwood is here." Well, we laughed as hard as we did when we were working in the Homicide Unit and that brought back some great memories. He was glad to see me, but not as glad as I was that I made the decision to come and see him.

I could tell he was a little uneasy by being confined to the bed. You need to remember, this guy went blind, had major heart surgery, was in a coma, his wife died, he lost a leg, and was still making jokes. I can honestly say that Rod was the toughest Marine I have ever known. I knew Rod's military history and even though he had performed brave and honorable service to his country in the Korean War, these were the roughest times of his life. I stood by the bed and before I gave him a gift that I got for him, I asked him how it felt to be in a coma for eight days. Well, that was just another opening for him to get me and he did, he said, "How the fuck would I know how it felt you dumb shit, I was in a coma" and we laughed again. I was now feeling really good about coming to see him. As I stood there, I wished like hell I could do something for him. I then did something that even to this day, I can't believe I did it, but I did. I gave him a gift and because he was also in the Marine Corps, I gave him a book about the history of the Marines. At first you would say, well that was nice, but do you remember the part where I told you that he was blind. I handed him the book. He looked in my direction and in a manner that only Rod could do, he said, "You are not the brightest son of a bitch in the world; is the book in Braille." This time the laugh was so loud that the nurse came in and asked if everything was alright and it was, it really was.

I will always look back at that hospital visit and have that wonderful memory. I have lots of stories and memories of Rod from the Homicide Unit and the softball games. I stayed at the hospital for a couple of hours that day. We laughed a whole lot and it was great to see that big smile back on his face. When I left the hospital, I could not drive out of the parking lot. I just sat there with no one around and cried. I guess you are thinking that Marines don't cry, but if you didn't cry that day, you were not human.

Very sadly, shortly after that visit Rod died. When I heard that he died, I was mad at myself for not going to visit him more often. I guess now that I am getting older, I want to be around all my cop friends, especially the ones that are going through some tough times.

At the funeral for Rod, they asked if anyone wanted to get up and say something about him and many did and I am glad. I sat there with tears in my eyes. I knew that I could not get up in front of people and talk about Rod, I just couldn't do it. Rod touched so many lives and will always be remembered by everyone that worked in the Homicide Unit back then. I have promised myself that if I ever finish this book, I plan on dedicating it to him and a few others that have touched my life over the years…God bless Rod Brandner.

Fired and Hired - All in One Week

I could go on and on with homicide stories, but one that I want to tell was both a good time in my life and also one of the worst. In 1977 a Baltimore police officer who was only on the job for eleven months was shot and killed in northwest Baltimore. The shooting occurred about noontime in a residential neighborhood. The officer was a young police officer and was gunned down by a mental patient who had wrestled the officer's gun from him. The mentally deranged assailant actually stood over the young officer and shot him five times in the head. I assisted with the investigation which was not that involved, because justice was served on the streets of Baltimore that day. The gunman was shot to death by responding police officers and that's the only part of the story I like. What happened to this cop killer is what you call street justice and I wish there was more of it.

What followed after assisting with the investigation, is what turned out to be a nightmare and a real life changer for me. We worked the investigation until about 6 PM. We all went to our favorite watering hole, the Calvert House; to do what we did best, drink. The Calvert House was the hangout for most of the Homicide Unit when they got off the day shift. It could be as many as ten to fifteen detectives there for happy hour each day. It was an interesting place, as the owner loved police officers. She would let us all run a bar tab and pay her at the end of the month. This was a good setup, but it turned out to be a disaster for some. As you can imagine, if you are allowed to run a bar tab, you will drink more than you usually would.

Well, we were drinking and I can remember that I had not eaten anything the entire day and drinking on an empty stomach is a roadmap for disaster. We were all talking about the officer who was murdered. When cops get killed, it seems like a tradition that other cops get together and mourn his loss over a few drinks or in this case, lots of drinks. Well, I had more booze than I should have and by about 10 PM, I was totally wasted. One of the other detectives who was just as drunk as I was, started heating me up. He said to me, "If you were any kind of a cop, you would go out to the house of that no good bastard who shot the cop and shoot his brother or someone in his family." I know this sounds crazy, but you have to remember we were really belting down some booze and it was not beer, it was hard liquor. After being needled for awhile by this fellow drunken cop, I finally told everyone I was leaving and going home. I left the bar and got in my car. As I sat in the car, I was thinking about what the detective was telling me in the bar, about going out to the cop killer's house and killing someone in his family.

I started to go home, but it kept bothering me and I was thinking of this young police officer who went to work that day and was now dead. I thought of his young wife and his two year old daughter that we met when we went to the house to tell his wife that he had been killed. I thought of all the senseless murders that happen every year in Baltimore by thugs that have no respect for human life. I thought about when I was a young cop and my kids were young and what would life have been like for them, if I had been killed in the line of duty. I pulled the car over and sat there for awhile. I knew that what I was about to do was wrong. I was about to make the biggest mistake of my police career.

I knew the address where the cop killer lived, because we had sent some detectives out there earlier in the day to talk to his family. I don't really remember a whole lot, but I did drive to the address. In the condition I was in at the time, I don't know how I made it. I pulled up to the house; I guess it was about 11 PM. I went to the door and rapped on the door. Some elderly lady answered the door and I asked if the guy who killed a cop earlier in the day lived at this address. I am calling this guy the cop killer in this story for two reasons: one is that it is not important what the hell this dirt bags name is and the other reason is that I really can't remember what his name was. I also don't think he was worthy of any research on my part. After I told this lady what I wanted, she slammed the door and then some man came to the door. The man was elderly and identified himself as the father of the cop killer. I asked him if he had any other sons in the house. I am sure he could see I was drunk and closed the door and called 911.

Uniformed patrol officers came to the house and they knew who I was and put me in the patrol car. I am not sure what they told the people in the cop killer's house, but apparently whatever they said, it worked. The uniform officers told me they were going to take me down to the homicide office. They told me that it would be better if I could get some sleep, sober up, and go home in the morning. I am not sure of all the particulars, but I found out later that one of the officers drove my personal car down to the police building. The officers took me up to the Homicide Unit office. The shift sergeant, Donald Estep asked me if I wanted a ride home and I said that I did not need a ride. Well, Donald, who was a good friend of mine, up to this point, suggested that I go in the room where they usually keep the prisoners and get some sleep. He said that in a few hours, he would have someone drive me home. I argued with him and started to leave and he said, "You are in no condition to go anywhere and if we have to, we will forcibly keep you here." He had a couple of detectives escort me to the interview room. I sat in the chair; they put handcuffs on me, and hooked me to the chair. I guess I was there in the room for about an hour, when I convinced them that I had to go to the bathroom. They took off the cuffs and let me go to the bathroom by myself. I actually did go to the bathroom, but after that, I got on the elevator. I went down to the garage, found my car, and drove out of the police building.

I really don't remember much of how I got there, but I later found out that the police got a call that a man was lying on a bench at the Greyhound Bus Terminal. The call to the police dispatcher was that the man in the terminal had a gun hanging from his pants. Police officers came in the terminal and woke me up and took my gun. This time, they again took me back down to the Homicide Unit. The sergeant, who was really pissed off and some detectives put me in the interview room. They put handcuffs on me and tied me up with rope; yes they actually tied me up with rope. I do remember being tied up and I thought they were kidding, until they left the room. I tried to sleep, but could not, it's not easy to sleep when you are handcuffed to a chair and tied up with rope, even if you are drunk.

About 5 AM, the dayshift lieutenant, Charlie Kearney came to work in the Homicide Unit. He was briefed and was told I was in the prisoner room. He came in the room, looked at me and said, "You are disgusting, I am getting you a ride home. I'm putting you down today as taking a vacation day." Well, here is where I really screwed up, I told the lieutenant, "I don't want a damn vacation day." I can remember exactly what he said, which was, "Your ass is fired." I told him, "I don't give a shit if I'm fired or not." The lieutenant told two detectives to take me home and also to drive my car to my house.

I have to now give you a little scenario of what was happening in my life at that time. I was married with two kids. I lived in a real nice house in the suburbs. I had thirteen years on the police department. The most disgusting thing, now that I look back on it; I was on the promotion list for sergeant. I was number nine out of a hundred police officers on the promotion list for sergeant and I get fired. Let's all say it together, "How fuckin dumb can you be."

I got to my house and as any drunk would do, I went straight to bed. I did not even take time to tell my wife what had happened. I just wanted to sleep and pull the covers over my head; maybe this was all a bad dream. I guess when two detectives bring you home and you are drunk, there ain't many believable stories you can come up with for your wife. I am sure she was probably worrying about me all night and hoping that nothing had happened. I also had two kids at that time. I don't know if they ever heard this story, but they are hearing it now. I am sure they understand what I did was wrong. It was something that happened and no way in hell, am I playing it down. It comes under the category of shit happens, especially when you drink.

Later that day I woke up and that's the hard part, to wake up and start to realize just what the hell happened. I didn't really have a grasp on the entire picture, so I called Sergeant Brandner. He filled me in and the more he told me on the phone, the sicker I got. I hung up the phone and I just sat there thinking this is the end of the world for me. My thoughts were that everything that I had worked hard for in the police department would be down the drain, because of some stupid act on my part. I did not know where to start to apologize. There were so many, including my wife and kids and all the cops that had to deal with me the night before. Later that day, Sergeant Brandner and another homicide detective, Ron Mikles came to my house. Rod told me that the captain had sent them to get my badge and gun. I gave them the badge and gun and when they left, I tried to pull myself together. I was trying to come up with some rationale on how it happened and how could I explain it to anyone who would listen. As I lived in the house where my wife and kids also resided, I figured this might be the best place to start. I told my wife the whole story and as you can imagine, she just shook her head and couldn't believe it. She kept saying things like, "How could you do that now that you are on the sergeant's list? How could you disgrace yourself and your family, especially your father?" Well, I had no answers and like a good Marine, I just took my lumps. I knew that the worst was yet to come and that thought alone, kept me sick for several days afterwards. I can tell you that about a year or so later, I got a divorce, but it was not just because of this incident, it was many other things that played a part in my divorce.

A couple of days went by and I had heard nothing from anyone in the police department. I was starting to come to the very sad conclusion that my career was over in law enforcement. I was thinking how I would explain this to my father, who was so proud that he had two sons on the police department and now, one was fired. I had explained it to some close cop friends, but I can tell you they did not fully understand how something so stupid like this could happen. I can't blame them, because the more I thought about it, it made no sense. If I had only continued home that night, instead of letting the booze convince my brain to take justice into my own hands. The only thing I am really grateful for to this day is that nothing happened at that house, or I would be writing this book from a cell.

This is one of those moments in life, when you talk to God and say things like, "God if you get me out of this, I will be good the rest of my life. I will go to church every day and twice on Sunday." Well, maybe God was listening and wanted to give me another chance. I got a call from the homicide Captain, Jim Cadden. I can't repeat what he said on the phone to me, but you can bet that I just listened. I just kept saying, "Yes sir, yes sir, yes sir." I was hoping that some part of the conversation would be the part where he says, come back to work. He did not quite say come back to work, but he did say he wanted me to be in his office the next day. He said that he would decide how to proceed with some type of punishment. I can remember that there were no goodbyes said on the phone, he just slammed the phone and that was the end of the conversation. It was one of the best conversations I had with anyone in a few days.

The next day, I put on a nice suit and tried to look real good for the meeting with the captain. I knew that this could possibly be the most important day of my life. I got there early and I was surprised that all the detectives in the unit had some nice things to say and wished me well. These guys had all worked with me on murders and we all got along great. I could sense that they were pulling for me and that under similar circumstances, they were probably thinking, it could be me. I sat outside the captain's office and at precisely the time he told me to be there, I knocked on the door. He opened the door and said, "What the hell do you want?" That scared me because he is the one who set up the meeting. I started to answer and he said, "Just sit your ass over there. When I am done with real police business, I will deal with you and your foolishness." Now I was really, really scared, but there was nothing I could do but sit in the chair and hope that he was having a better day then it appeared.

I looked around the homicide office and watched all the detectives moving about and talking about what they were going to be doing that day. I knew this is what I wanted again in the worst way. The more I sat in the chair, the more stares I got from people in the office. In the morning, the homicide office was one of the busiest places in the headquarters building. All the news reporters were roaming about trying to get a story. There was also some brass from the department who were there talking about murders that occurred in their districts. While I sat there, I know that my five day deodorant pad was failing me big-time. I could feel beads of sweat running down my back, but I didn't dare take off my suit coat. I felt like I was interviewing for a job and in some ways, that's exactly what was I was doing. I was interviewing to get back the greatest job anyone would want and the job that I was so proud of getting just a few years earlier.

I had a lot of thoughts going through my head, like being number nine on the sergeant's promotion list. I was also thinking about getting promoted and being a detective sergeant in the Homicide Unit. All of this depended on the captain and every time the captain's door opened, I looked in that direction. The captain would just look in my direction and say nothing. He knew exactly what he was doing, making me sweat it out. After all, this guy was a pro at interrogating people. He knew that the longer I sat and watched the other detectives go about their job, it would tear at me. He knew it would eat me up inside and he was absolutely correct.

Well finally it happened, the door to the captain's office opened. He pointed his finger at me and said, "Get your sorry ass in here." I went in and now you can imagine that I am sweating like a marathon runner. I stood in front of his desk and he did not say anything; he was reading from a report. He looked at me and said, "Shut the door stupid and sit your ass down." If your thinking to yourself as you read this, why would this professional police captain talk to someone like that? Well, I don't care what you think. He could have called me every fuckin name in the book, smacked me around the room, and I would not have said a word. I knew I was in for the reaming of my life and this was the guy who could do it better than anyone in the police department. Captain Cadden was as tough as they come; he had been in the Eighty Second Airborne in World War II. He had made several parachute jumps in Germany behind enemy lines. He didn't talk about the war much. There were times when we were at a bar or a retirement party and after a few drinks, he would get tired of me and others talking about the Marines. He would jump in and tell us how it was in the old days when he was in the Army Airborne.

I sat in the chair in front of his desk and his first statement was, "If those fuckin windows could open, I would throw you out." I was glad for the first time while in the Homicide Unit that the windows did not open. He stood up and started walking around my chair. He just went off on me about how I should be ashamed of myself and how I have let him and everyone else down, especially my father. I won't repeat all of the language, but I am sure you get the idea on what happened. The professional reaming went on for what seemed like hours, but it was probably only twenty minutes and then he let up a little, just a little.

He left the office and slammed the door and I just sat there too damn scared to move. He came back in and said, "Get your ass out of here; you have just received the biggest break of your life." He told me to report to Sergeant Brandner and get back to solving homicides. He said, "If anything like this incident ever happens again, I will personally make sure you get fired." I stood up and tried to shake his hand. He said, "Richard, I will shake your hand at a later time when I see how sincere you are about this opportunity I am giving you." I thanked him a few times and assured him that nothing like this would ever happen again and I left the office.

I stood outside his office for a few minutes to gain my composure and to start the normal breathing process again. I know I needed to do one thing and that was to go home and change my clothes. I felt like I had sweated off several pounds just being in that office. I also wanted to do one more thing before I went home. I went and talked to Sergeant Brandner and he was sincerely elated that I was back in the squad. Rod shut the door to his office and he gave me a little talking to. It was nothing like I had just gone through with the captain. I told Rod that he would never have any trouble out of me in the future and we shook hands. I started to leave his office and he said, "I think I have something you will need." He reached in his desk and pulled out my gun and badge. I walked out of the homicide office and strapped on the gun and badge. What a great feeling, as I walked through the building to the elevator. I got on the crowded elevator, took off my suit coat and proudly displayed my equipment; I am back in business.

On the drive home, I had so many thoughts going through my head. I was thinking what a great opportunity I had just received. Also, how so many people had been pulling for me and how stupid you can be when you drink too much booze. I now had my hopes up that if things went okay for awhile; I might get promoted to sergeant. I can tell you that for the rest of my career in the police department, I often thought of that time in the captain's office and it kept me straight. I had the chance years later to talk to Captain Cadden about this incident. Like the gentlemen he was, he just brushed it off and said, "It was no big deal." I told him that it was the biggest deal of my life and I will remember it as long as I live. He just smiled and this time he did shake my hand.

STEAM CRABS WILL GET YOU PROMOTED

In June of 1978, I got promoted to sergeant and from the previous story, you are probably wondering, how in the hell did this guy get promoted. In October of 1977, while in the Homicide Unit, I wanted to get promoted so bad, that I studied promotion material every waking minute that I could. I knew at that time that I had about twelve years on the job and it was a now or never moment for me. Contrary to some of the stories I have told, I was actually a hard working detective with a lot of pride, most of which I carried over from my four years in the Marines. I am not proud of some of the stupid shit I did in the police department. I can tell you that when I retired, I was very proud of my twenty-five years with the police department. I can also attest that from the huge number of people that attended my retirement party and the many accolades and certificates I got, it validated my overall opinion that I had really made a difference. I feel that I was well respected by my peers during the twenty-five years on the job.

In 1977, I took the sergeant's promotion test along with about thirteen hundred police officers. Only one hundred would eventually be placed on the civil service promotion list. Out of the one hundred on the promotion list, it was customary within the police department that about fifty or sixty would probably get promoted. It was important to score high on the written test, oral interview, and the proficiency score. The total points were forty for the test, forty for the oral interview, and twenty for the proficiency score.

After the written test scores were published, I was elated to find out that

I had a high score that put me in the top twenty. The next step would be the oral interview which would be conducted by three senior police officers from police departments outside of Baltimore. I knew that for the proficiency part, I needed the twenty points from my commanding officer.

I decided that I would talk to the captain; yes this is the same captain that took me back on the job after being fired, Jim Cadden. I knew that the captain was a fair guy, but he had five detectives in the Homicide Unit that had also passed the sergeant's test. He would have to provide proficiency marks for all five detectives. I wanted to pick the best time to approach the captain. My first thought was that I would wait until he stopped with the guys to have a drink after work. I decided that might not be the way to go; I wanted to make it more professional. I decided to wait for an afternoon that I thought he might be in a good mood and then approach him. Finding the captain in a good mood would be hard to determine, as he had the same look most of the time. I guess you could call it a poker face or his homicide game face. One way of deciding if he was in a good mood would be to see how many murders the unit had in a week and how many were solved. The captain lived and died with the Homicide Unit results. He would want a one hundred percent clearance rate if that was possible. In Baltimore, a city that averaged three hundred murders a year that was not possible. I was tight with the captain's secretary, Kim. I was sure she would help me out if I approached her and laid out my plan. After talking to Kim and promising to buy her a drink the next time we were at the Calvert House, she agreed to help. She told me that the best time to talk to the captain was about 4 PM. He was preparing to leave the building and probably stopping for a couple of drinks before he went home. She told me to hang around the office and when she knew he was alone and seemed to be in a good mood, she would give me the sign that it was okay to try to talk to him.

I got the nod from Kim one day at about 4 PM and walked by the captain's open door. I wanted to see if he would acknowledge me and he did not. It took three trips walking by his door, before he shouted, "Okay Ellwood, what the hell do you want? I am a busy man and I'm getting ready to go home." I walked in and asked how he was doing. He gave me that look, the one that was saying what I already knew: it was four o'clock and he had been through a long day. He wanted to get the hell out of the office. He motioned for me to sit down and said, "Quit beating around the bush with pleasantries and get it off your chest." I asked if it was okay to shut the door and he said, "Oh shit, what the hell have you done this time?" I shut the door and assured him that I was not in any trouble. I told him that I just wanted to talk to him about something very important. He pushed back in his leather chair and put his feet on the desk and said, "Tell me what it is and talk quick, you are almost into my drinking time." I don't know where I got the courage, but I knew that this was a once in a lifetime chance of getting promoted. I mustered up some strength, sat up straight, and said, "Captain, I want to get promoted more than anything in this world." I was surprised that he did not come back with some off the wall comment. He put his feet on the floor, leaned forward, and said, "How can I help?" After being surprised at his attention to what I had said, I told him that I really need the twenty points for the proficiency mark. I said, "If I don't get it, I don't think I will get promoted." I was surprised again, when he said, "Richard, I have been around a long time. I have been fortunate to get promoted several times and the first and most important promotion is to sergeant." He went on to say, "I can remember years ago when I was in the same position that you are in now. I can appreciate your frankness in what you are asking me." He went on to say, "I am sure you know that five detectives in the Homicide Unit have passed the written test. They will also want the twenty points for proficiency." I tried to interrupt and tell him why I deserved the points. He stopped me and said, "I intend to do the right thing with each detective that passed the test." He said that he wanted to be fair. He said he has already given it a lot of thought. He said that out of the five detectives, he feels there are only two that deserve the full twenty points. He said, "Rather than you and I sitting here on my drinking time, I will just tell you that I will carefully consider each detective's work in the Homicide Unit." I could see that he wanted to end it there, as he was moving toward his overcoat and looking at his watch at the same time. I thanked him and asked where he was stopping for a drink. He said, "I am not telling you, because you guys drink too much and you are not getting me in any trouble." He laughed and walked out of the office.

The oral interview was scheduled and each police officer interviewed would have forty-five minutes in front of a three member panel. The interviewers would only know your civil service eligibility number and would not have your name. The day I was scheduled, I was as nervous as you can imagine. While you are waiting to go into the interview room, you are trying to think about what they will ask you. From prior interviews, most of us knew some of the routine promotion questions; for example, what would you do if someone in your unit showed up for work and you smelled alcohol on their breath or if you had a female in your unit and the guys were harassing her, what would you do? We all knew that going into the interview and having a bad interview would just about eliminate you from any chance of getting promoted. I can remember that I was scheduled for 1 PM, which would mean they had just returned from lunch and I would have to talk loud and make my answers interesting or they would probably fall asleep.

I got to the police building and the interviews were being held on the sixth floor next to the Police Commissioner's Office. I had not spent much time on that floor, because it was where most of the bosses had their offices. It was decorated with expensive paintings, nice furniture, and plush carpets. I waited in a small room that connected with the actual interview room and the nervousness continued and the beads of sweat started. I kept looking at my watch and now it was 1:10 PM and it seemed pretty quiet in the interview room. Than it happened, a female who I had never seen before came in the room and I can remember that she was very attractive and for a few seconds I took my mind off the interview. She said, in a very pleasant voice, "I assume you are Richard Ellwood" and I said, "You assume correctly and who might you be." She told me she was with the civil service commission and her job was to assist the people doing the interviews. She told me that I would be in the interview room for approximately forty-five minutes and the interview would be recorded. She started to leave and I asked how long I had to wait and she said, "They should be back soon. They are still at lunch, just relax."

Well, about fifteen minutes went by and then the interview door opened and a man called my number and said, "Come on in and have a seat." I went in and waited for him to take his seat with the other two men and then I sat down and faced all three who were on the opposite side of the very long table. I tried to look around the room and I can remember there was absolutely nothing on the walls and very little paperwork on the table. They introduced themselves to me, only saying what police department there were with, but did not give their names. I remember that all three held the rank of captain and one was from Detroit, one from Chicago, and one from Washington, DC. The guy from Chicago seemed like he was in charge and sat in the middle. He started by saying they would ask questions in turn and either of them could then have follow up questions on my answers. He said that the interview might take forty-five minutes, but that depended on my answers. When he said that, I remembered reading about interviews and it said that when asked a question that you know something about, that you should stretch it out as long as possible. The first question came from the Detroit captain and he asked me why I was not in uniform. I found that to be a strange first question, but I felt good that I knew the answer to the first question. I guess it was an ice breaker because he had to assume that I was a detective or I would be in uniform. I told him that I was a homicide detective and was told to report for the interview in a suit as opposed to a uniform. He said I was the first person to show up with a suit and he was just wondering.

The interview moved along pretty smoothly. I stretched out my answers as much as possible. I would not dare look at my watch, but it seemed like I was in there for at least an hour. I must say that as the interview moved forward, I started to feel more comfortable with these guys, because during some of my answers, they would interrupt and say how long they had been in law enforcement. The guy from Chicago told me he worked homicides early in his career. I felt like they were actually getting casual with me, but I did not want to let my guard down. I laughed when they laughed, I nodded my head when they said something, I sat upright in the very uncomfortable chair, I looked directly at the person when responding to their question, and controlled my sweating as much as possible.

It appeared they were running out of questions and they were actually looking at their watches and then the most unusual situation occurred. The captain from Detroit asked me if I knew where they could get some good steamed crabs in Baltimore. I smiled and waited for him to say he was just kidding me, but that did not happen. When I knew he was serious, I figured this is my chance to make a move that would either make or break this interview. I told them that I was the manager of the Homicide Unit softball team and that our uniform sponsor was the best crab house in Baltimore. All of sudden, it was as if we were buddies having a drink at a bar and the Detroit captain said, "That sounds great. Can you let us know where it is and maybe give us some directions?" At that point, I almost forgot where I was and was about to say, hell, not only will I tell you about the crab house, I will take you there, pick up the check for the crabs, and we can drink beer all night. Thank God, I did not do that, but I did tell them the name of the place, which was Bo Brooks Crab House and it was the absolute best place for crabs in Baltimore. I then may have gone out on the limb a little and told them when they got to the crab house to ask for the owner, Leon Rutherberg. I told them, he would make sure that as police officers, they would get the best crabs he had. I started to think, was this a trap and they were pulling my leg and I had just trashed the entire interview. The three of them all stood up at the same time and the Chicago captain said, "Well, that's the interview and you did very good and thanks for the tip about where to get the crabs."

I can remember leaving the police building and thinking what a dumb shit I was to talk about crabs at the most important interview I would ever have. I had a drink later with some guys and I was telling them the story about the interview and the crabs and they laughed and said, "You blew it man, you ain't getting promoted." I left the bar and on the way home, I was thinking what if they do go to Bo Brooks tonight and get crabs. I decided to call Leon, the owner of Bo Brooks and a guy who loved cops. I know that is why he spent a lot of money for uniforms for our softball team. I called Leon and told him the story and he said, "No problem, I will look for them and take care of them." I asked Leon to call me the next day and let me know what happened. I also told him that if he talked to them, not to mention my name.

The next day, I got a call from Leon and he said that they were there and he took care of them. He gave them the biggest crabs he had that night. He told me that they stayed about two hours and did some serious drinking along with eating the crabs. I asked if everything went okay and he said, "Yeah, it went fine, I picked up their tab and they stayed and actually had some more drinks at the bar." After talking to Leon, I did not know what to think about the interview, but one thing was for certain, no matter what happens, it was too late to change anything and I would just have to wait and see what the score was for the interview.

About two weeks after the interview, I received a letter in the mail from the Baltimore Civil Service Commission. They would compile the three scores and place you on the list of the one hundred eligible for promotion to sergeant. When I got the letter, I went off to a quiet place and opened it very carefully and was almost shaking as I held the letter that could change my life. The letter stated the results of the written exam, the proficiency mark, and the oral interview marks for the position of sergeant. The letter went on to state that the marks have been compiled and attached you will see your standing on the promotion list. I could feel the old familiar sweat beads forming on my neck and back as I looked at the attachment to the letter. The attachment listed the one hundred people who had made the cutoff. I started by looking in the middle of the list and did not see my name, but as I scrolled up toward the top, I almost fell on the floor; there I was at number nine. I started screaming and shouting that I did it, but no one was home, so I guess my neighbors were wondering what the hell I did. I calmed down a little and started to look for the individual marks. I was again shocked when I saw thirty-six for the written, twenty for the proficiency and thirty-eight for the oral interview. My thoughts were of Captain Cadden giving me the twenty points for the proficiency mark and those three captains giving me a thirty-eight for the interview.

I will always remember that interview and have told others over the years that when you go into a interview: just relax, stretch out your answers, make a good appearance, act like you are having a conversation with some friends, and if you know where a good crab house is, let them know.

Promoted and Assigned to Tactical SWAT

I was promoted on June 28, 1978, and my assignment orders were to report to the Tactical Unit. When promotions in the Baltimore Police Department were to be made, there would be a meeting of the command staff and the list of people being promoted would be presented to the group. I have been told that it is like a professional football draft. Each member of the command staff would try to get the sergeant they wanted assigned to their unit. I had a good reputation in the police department and was told later, that several members of the command staff tried to get me in their unit. I was also told later that the captain of the Tactical Unit, John Schmidt, who was also a Marine, made a strong case for me. He said that he had plans to reorganize the Tactical Unit and he felt that a former Marine would fit in good with his plans. He had made in known that he wanted the Tactical Unit to be more efficient and better trained.

I reported to the Tactical Unit and was told to go see Captain Schmidt, that he was expecting me. I knew Captain Schmidt when he was a uniform patrol sergeant in the Central District. I worked in his squad and considered him a very good cop. As we were both Marines, we hit it off good and we had teamed up many times in the area we worked and made some good arrests. He got promoted to lieutenant and then to captain and we did not really see much of each other, except for a few times when I would see him in the headquarters building.

I walked into his office and it was as if we were long lost brothers; he grabbed me and shook my hand, as only he could. Captain Schmidt was a huge man and very strong. When he shook your hand, you could almost cringe, except for the fact that it was one Marine shaking the hand of another Marine and we don't cringe. He shut the door and told me how excited he was to get me in the Tactical Unit. I told him that I was also very excited to be there, which was a real stretch of the truth on my part. It was not that I wasn't excited; it was that for the past six years, I was a detective and was used to detective work. We talked about old times when he was the sergeant and I worked for him. He had a hell of a memory and brought up situations that I had totally forgotten about. He said he had to go to a command staff meeting and would introduce me to my new shift lieutenant, John Wagner. We walked down the hallway and went into a small office and the first thing I saw on the lieutenant's desk was the Marine Corps flag. I knew things would be okay. The captain introduced me to the lieutenant and said, "John this is your new tactical sergeant and he is a Marine, just like us." Well, anytime you meet someone and they say they are a Marine, the first question is, when were you in the corps and that was his first question to me. We talked briefly about the Marines and the captain went to his meeting. He said that when he got back he wanted the three of us to go to lunch.

Lieutenant Wagner was a real spit and polish guy and you could see from his uniform, his office and the way he carried himself, that his Marine days were being carried over into the police department. I am very proud of being in the Marines, but I must honestly tell you that I was not a spit and polish guy after I got out of the Marines. I could tell from his appearance that I would have to step it up a little. I would have to resort back to my Marine days when I worked on my shoes for two hours; to the point you could see your face in them. I was thinking that this might be just what I need to get back to some form of military life and have more structure in my everyday activities.

I talked to the lieutenant for at least two hours and he gave me a tour of the Tactical Unit which took up the whole second floor of the headquarters building. He talked solely about the Tactical Unit and how he and the captain wanted to make it the best unit in the state. As we walked around, I could see that this guy had the respect of the personnel in the unit. As we passed people, all I heard was: good morning lieutenant, how are you lieutenant, yes sir lieutenant, and thank you lieutenant. I don't think anyone even saw that I was with him. He talked about a lot of things and on some topics, he lost me. I knew that I needed to shape up on my military and tactical language real quick, to fit in with this unit. You have to remember that I had just came from the Homicide Unit, where things were laid back. In this unit it would be different and more like the military. I was excited to get promoted and determined to make a good impression in my first supervisory assignment.

Later when we went to lunch, I tried to keep up with the conversation, but I knew some of what they were talking about was going right over my head. They talked about many things; for example, the budget for the unit, new purchases of equipment, and training. This was stuff that I had not been involved in as a detective. I did what anyone would do that is not in tune with the conversation, I just nodded once in awhile and agreed with whatever the hell they were talking about. I guess it worked, because after lunch we had another meeting in the captain's office and this time they went into much more detail about how they were going to reorganize the unit. They told me that I would be a big part of the changes, along with the other three sergeants in the unit. The captain said that he wanted to change the name of the SWAT team, which stood for Small Weapons Assault Team. He said that others in the command staff thought that it was too offensive and with that I started to laugh. I stopped laughing when I saw that no one else was laughing. I said, "Excuse me Captain, can I speak freely?" He said, "Please feel free to speak freely anytime you want; that is why I got you in this unit." I told the captain and lieutenant that, "When you have the occasion to use the SWAT team, you want to put the fear of God into the people or person you are using the SWAT against. I am not sure what you would change it to, but if I were a bad guy and knew that the SWAT was coming after me, I would be real concerned and probably surrender." I guess I did not make my point, because the captain said it was already decided by the police commissioner that the name would be changed. The captain said it was not a contest to come up with a new name for the SWAT, but he had already received many suggestions. He started to throw out some acronyms for the changing of the name. Some of them were good and some of them we all laughed at. The captain read from a paper that had all the suggestions for the new name. The one name that made the lieutenant and I roar with laughter was, Fast Assault Response Team. I am not sure how much time the captain put into the list of names he had, but the lieutenant and I figured out this one right off the bat. The acronym for that unit would be the FART. As we were all having a good laugh, I told the captain, "I will feel a little embarrassed to tell all my friends that I got promoted and I am now in charge of the FART". We got serious after that good laugh and the captain decided that the new name for the SWAT would be the QRT, which stood for; Quick Response Team. We all agreed that it sounded like something we could live with and thus the QRT was formed and is still in existence today. I still have my QRT pin and the distinction of being among the first sergeants to be certified in the QRT.

The lieutenant told me that the squad of patrolman that I would supervise consisted of thirteen men. He informed me that the structure of the Tactical Unit consisted of two lieutenants, four sergeants and each sergeant had thirteen patrolman assigned to their squad. The unit I would be supervising was currently working the 5 PM till 1 AM shift. The lieutenant said that my squad would be in for roll call at 4:30 PM. He asked that I stay around and meet them. He said that they were working at this time without a sergeant. The lieutenant told me that the average age of the men in the squad was twenty-three years old and that they all had prior military service. At that time in my career, I was thirty-four years old. I thought that was young, but twenty-three was real young. The lieutenant told me that they were good police officers, but a few of them had some wild tendencies. I asked what he meant and he said, "It is better that you make that determination after you work with them for awhile." He also suggested that as this was my first supervisory position in the police department, that I be firm with the squad. He said that it would be important to get control right from the start and make sure there was no doubt in their minds that you are in charge.

Well, around 4 PM, the squad that I was taking over started to mingle in the roll call room. I decided that I would not wait for the lieutenant to introduce me to the squad. I walked in the room and went around to each officer and introduced myself. I was surprised that some of the guys told me that they had already heard about me and they knew I was coming from the Homicide Unit. A couple of the more outgoing guys said that they heard that

I like to party. I squashed that real quick and said, "Whoever told you that is wrong; I am hardly a partier by any means." I was thinking that the last thing I need in my first supervisory position, is to get the tag of partier. Even though I was only thirty-four years old, some of these guys looked like kids to me. Don't get me wrong, they were all strong looking guys and I am sure they could handle themselves; boy was I about to find out.

We were all told by the captain that for the next two weeks, the entire Tactical QRT would train like they have never trained before. The goal was to become a top notch and respected unit within the department. He said that the training would take place at Fort Meade Army Base and other locations around the state. The captain gave the entire unit a Marine Corps gung-ho type speech in which he told them that there would be no nonsense. He told the unit that if anyone did not take the training serious, they would be dismissed from the unit immediately and sent back to a patrol district. The captain said that the training would be rough and that those that cannot meet the new standards would also be sent back to a district. At that point he asked if anyone wanted to opt out of the training before it started. He said that there would be no hard feelings, and as expected, he got no responses.

The two weeks of training was very rough and brought back some memories of my days at Parris Island in Marine Corps boot camp. During the training, I could see in my unit who would be the "go to guys" and who would be the guys that might want to test me. No matter where you work, there is always a small element that will see how far they can go with a new boss. It is something about vigorous training that brings the best or the worst out in people. I can say that during this training, I saw a tremendous amount of effort. I also saw a real determination to make the grade and have the bragging rights that we were the first unit trained under the new title of QRT.

While we were at the Fort Meade Army Base, we fired several weapons that would later be purchased by the department and used by the QRT. We did extensive training on hostage situations, crowd control, and other areas that a quick response team would be needed for.

In the second week, we did some training at the Baltimore Fire Academy. We trained on entering burning buildings and how we could use the fire department on hostage situations. While at the Fire Academy, the lieutenant decided to have training on repelling from buildings. The Fire Academy had a building that was over a hundred feet high, which is equivalent to a ten story building. I can tell you that I was not too excited about this training, as I am not fond of heights. The thought of repelling off a ten story building, put the absolute fear of God in me. I tried to be casual about it and told the lieutenant that I would pass on this training because I did not like heights. He seemed okay with it at first and I just stood around while the repelling instructor started his class. He instructed the unit on how to hook up to the ropes and how to go off the top of the building. He also instructed on how to scale down the side of the building without ending upside down. After the initial training which lasted all of about thirty minutes, the instructor said that he would take five men at a time to the top of the building. He said he would take groups of five at a time until everyone had repelled. At this point I was trying to slide away from the group and hope that no one saw me. I was acting like you do when you are in school and the teacher asks a question that you do not know; you slide down in your desk hoping that she will not see you. Well, this worked for awhile, until the lieutenant came over to me and said, "If you don't want to repel off that building, that's okay, but I am going to do it." He said in a Marine DI's voice, "I think that your unit would expect their sergeant to do what they do." He also told me that after the first group goes off the building, he would break the training and I could think about it over lunch. Well, at this point my stomach was turning and the last thing I wanted was lunch. I could just imagine that if I did go up and repel, someone below would be wearing my lunch.

At lunch, the lieutenant was cool and talked about a lot of other things, but did not mention repelling off the building; that is, until we were heading back to the training area. He said, "Look, I will leave this up to you, but I am going to do it. I know that the other three sergeants are probably going to do it, but it is up to you." I could tell by his voice and demeanor that he really wanted me to repel off this building with the rest of the unit. If for nothing else, just to say all the supervisors did it. I started to think that he was probably right and if I did not do it, I would probably not have the respect of some men in the unit.

We got back to the training site and after a brief talk by the repelling instructor, who was also a Marine and in great shape, I decided to say the hell with it and just do it. What was the worst that could happen; I could fall on my head and die, or be crippled for life, not a problem. I did not want to wait to be the last one off the building, so I slipped in with the third wave. I have to admit that I was as scared as I was back when I was in Marine Corps boot camp. The only difference was that I was not being slapped around by a drill instructor. I pretended that nothing was wrong, but I am sure it was obvious to the others that I was scared shitless. I guess the out of control shaking was the big clue.

The time came for me and the third group to go to the top of the building. The only way up was the stairs and with the equipment I had on, it seemed like climbing Mount Everest. This was a ten story building and each story is ten feet, so that makes the top of the building one hundred feet off the ground. I got to the top and it started to sink in that I could die going off this building. I know that is a stretch, but when you are as scared of heights as I am, it's reality. I also knew that this instructor was real good and he would not let anything happen to me or the others. I had actually watched a few repel off the building prior to climbing the steps and they appeared to have no problems. I knew that this was the first time repelling for most of these guys also. When it came time for me to approach the point at which you actually step off the top of the building, I was stepping very gingerly. The instructor picked up on it and told me that no way in hell would he allow anything to go wrong. He also said that he would go off at the same time and be alongside me on the way down. We were checked out with our harness gear and all the ropes and I don't know if I stepped off the building or crawled off of it, but either way, I made it off. I repelled down the building and the key was not looking down until you were almost at the bottom. I slipped up one time and the instructor who was going down with me told me what to do with the guide rope and everything turned out okay. I got to the bottom and I know my legs were shaking, but I made it and all the guys were clapping, as if I had just done something amazing and I had. I was standing around trying to settle down. The lieutenant came over to me and shook my hand. He said, "You know what, let's go up and do it together to show this group that Marines don't fear a damn thing." The lieutenant grabbed my arm and said, "Let's go

Marine." Well, this time I was actually pumped from all the shouting from the guys and said, "Semper Fi, do or die, let's go Marine." The lieutenant and I went up and repelled off the building and it was great.

As time went on in the Tactical Unit, I started to like it. The guys in my squad were all top notch guys and a great bunch to be on the street with. We had a lot of situations where we used our training, like hostage situations and other situations where people were barricaded in homes and buildings with weapons. When we encountered these situations, our procedures were that four officers and the sergeant would enter the building with an additional four man unit and a sergeant as backup. All of the situations that we encountered during my time in the Tactical Unit were very serious and all were handled with the utmost professionalism. I am proud to say that the best part was that no one got hurt. The guys took pride in the equipment they used and were always coming up with better techniques.

I can remember one situation where we had a black man on the west side of Baltimore holding a small child hostage. The story was that he had broken up with his girlfriend and when they had argued, he tried to stab her. She reported that she ran from the apartment and left the baby there. She called the police and the first responding patrol units called for the QRT after they had made several attempts to have the man release the baby. We responded to the scene and after setting up the perimeter and making other assignments, I went to the second floor of the apartment building. I was with a four man unit and we made our normal entry. This was a shaky situation and the logistics were not good, as there was only one entrance to the apartment where the man was with the child. The first thing I did was to call the apartment and try to talk the guy out. While I talked on the phone, the man said that if anyone tried to enter the apartment he would cut the child's throat. The information was relayed to the command post, which was about a block away from the scene. I was instructed to use all caution and not to enter the apartment unless I received instructions from someone in command of the situation. The person in command would be the major from the Western District who was on the scene and outside the building.

We positioned ourselves in the hallway and I tried to talk to the guy through the door. He would only respond back by saying that if anyone came in, he would cut the child's throat. We could hear the child crying and it was disturbing to think that if we were not successful, this child could die.

We waited in the hallway for over an hour and nothing was changing, so one of the guys came up with what I thought was a great idea. The idea was for me to talk to the man and position myself close to the door. I would tell him that I could not hear him, in the hopes that he would move closer to the door. When the man would move closer to the door to talk to me, one of the guys would run and knock the door down. I chose Pete Bullock, who was six feet, four inches tall and weighed in at about two hundred and fifty pounds. I told Pete to get a running start from down the hallway and just knock the door down. I was thinking about checking with the major who was outside in the command post truck. I knew what he would say, because usually the high ranking bosses did not want to make any waves, at least nothing that would come back to bite them. I also thought that by the time the major thinks it over; we could have the situation resolved.

I figured if we were lucky, we would knock the bad guy to the ground with the door and Pete on top of him. The game would be over and we would all go home. I decided to make the decision on my own and not ask for permission. I also knew that if anything went wrong and the baby was harmed, it would be my ass. We discussed it and could not rehearse it; with the exception of Pete measuring the length of the hallway and practicing his run and leap for the door.

Well, it could not have gone any better if we would have had time to practice. Pete got down like a linebacker and when I was talking to the guy, I gave Pete the signal. Pete ran at full speed and took the door off the hinges with the first try. The door fell on top of the bad guy and the knife went flying across the room. The baby was sitting on the bed and was not hurt; not even crying. I have to admit that I had my doubts if it would work and even when Pete was heading for the door, I thought of stopping him. But as big as he was, he would have probably taken me through the door with him. As we were removing the door from the guy, he started to fight us and that was a mistake, a big mistake. We handcuffed the guy and took his bloody body out of the building. I was approached by the major who wanted to know what happened. I was going to make up some story, but I was proud of what we did and I told him the truth. He called me to the side and told me that I had violated his orders to not enter the apartment unless he gave the okay. I told him the plan was well thought out, which was a lie. I also told him that it was my decision and it was based on the conditions at the time. I also told him that I did not feel that I had time to seek anyone's approval. The major pulled me to the side away from other bosses and said, "Dick, I know you did the right thing and everything turned out great. But we have procedures in place in the department and you did not follow them." At this point, I was prepared for the worst, but to be truthful, I really didn't give a shit. The situation was over and the baby was fine and that was all that I cared about. The major asked me if I understood the importance of following procedures and I assured him that I did. I was about to put up an argument, when he stopped me and said, "If anyone asks you who gave the order to enter that apartment, tell them I did" and he walked away.

The bad guy was arrested and charged with the stabbing of his girlfriend, abduction of the child, and resisting arrest. Before the trial of this creep, he actually made a formal complaint through his attorney to the FBI Civil Rights Unit. His complaint was that we violated his civil rights. I have no idea why they accepted his complaint and I laughed about it when I first heard of it. I was later contacted by the FBI who wanted me to give them a statement about the incident. I met two agents in the police building and through the advice of the police department legal section; I told them that I had no statement to make. I informed them that whatever was written on the official police report was all that would be provided. I don't think they liked it, but they accepted it and a few months later the department got a formal letter from the FBI stating that the complaint was unfounded. Can you imagine this asshole making a complaint that his civil rights were violated? I have heard of some silly shit in my day, but this was one of the weirdest.

I had many situations in my first supervisory role in the Tactical Unit. I really enjoyed my time working in the QRT. In 1980, I got a call from the new captain of the Homicide Unit, Captain Joe De Carlo, who asked me if I wanted to come back to Homicide. I told him yes and I left the Tactical Unit with mixed emotions. I felt that we had started something special with the QRT. The unit was finally getting the professional recognition that we were looking for when we conducted all the training. I also feel that the year that I put in Tactical QRT made me a better supervisor and I would not change that experience for anything.

The young men that were in my squad were tough on the street and really cared about each other. Their professionalism showed each time we would go on a hostage or barricade situation. Each member of the unit made sure that they did their job and made no mistakes that could possibly get their buddies hurt. When I left the Tactical QRT, I really missed those guys. It was a real pleasure for me to watch their careers. Some of them got promoted and a few actually moved up the ranks to join the command staff.

When I left the unit, they gave me a party and boy was it a party. We held it at a local bar and I think it went on until about four in the morning. I told you earlier that these guys were a tough bunch. They worked hard and played just as hard. That night, QRT could have stood for "Quite a Rowdy Team."

Button Button - Who's got the Button

It was great to be back in the Homicide Unit as a detective sergeant and having my own squad. It was as if I had never left; people were still being murdered on the streets of Baltimore at alarming rates. One of the most intense murder investigations I supervised as a homicide sergeant and also worked on was as bizarre as you would ever imagine. I had just returned to the Homicide Unit and was learning how to be a homicide sergeant after spending about one year in patrol. One of the first murders my squad got when I returned was a senseless murder of a young girl. The crime was so horrific that after we solved it, the investigation was written up in a magazine called True Detective. It qualified with the magazine as the murder investigation of the year. It was selected because of the manner of death and the quality of the investigation by the Baltimore Police Department and the Maryland State Police.

In April 1980, a young girl name Dena Marie Polis was reported missing by her parents. She had left home in Essex, Maryland, to visit her boyfriend in Glen Bernie, Maryland and that was the last time her parents saw her. She was eighteen years old and a very attractive young lady, who according to her parents and friends loved life. About three days after she was reported missing, her body was found in a sewer in the Fells Point section of the city. Her partially clad body was discovered by a passerby who saw her legs sticking out from the sewer. The body had been dumped in the sewer and from examination seemed to have been deceased for at least several days.

I responded to the crime scene location with Detective Jimmy Ozezewski, one of the more senior investigators in my squad. After a careful and thorough crime scene investigation, the body was recovered and taken to the Medical Examiner's Office. At the scene of the recovery of the body, there was no physical evidence, other than the clothing on the body. All indications early in the investigation revealed that the victim was most likely murdered at another location and dumped in the sewer in Fells Point.

At the Medical Examiner's Office, fingerprints were obtained which positively identified the young lady as Dena Polis. During the preparation for the autopsy, a small brown button was recovered from the bra of the deceased female. It would have been very easy to miss this button, but for the good work of the doctors at the Medical Examiner's Office and their expertise. The button could have fallen out at several locations: the crime scene, the sewer or the vehicle that transported her body to the morgue. The button was recovered and marked as evidence. It would later be a very important part of both the investigation and the criminal trials of the suspects. The autopsy revealed that the cause of death was strangulation. There were also multiple bruises and abrasions on the body, some of which may have occurred when the body was forced into the sewer. The autopsy also revealed that the young lady had been vaginally and rectally raped.

After the identification of the body, the family of Dena Polis was notified. Several members of the family came to the homicide office and gave statements. We were looking for any information they might have on Dena's friends and others that she associated with. The only information obtained was that on the last day that Dena was seen, she had received a ride from her uncle and aunt. She was allegedly dropped off at the intersection of Pratt and Light Streets in downtown Baltimore. The uncle and aunt were identified by the family as Bernard Stebbings and his wife, Annette Stebbings. The family members indicated that Bernard and Annette offered Dena a ride to the city, where she was going to catch a bus to go visit her boyfriend. No family members interviewed thought anything suspicious about the uncle and aunt. The family members thought that after Dena was dropped off in the city, something went wrong from there. The only negative information early in the investigation about the uncle and aunt, was that Bernard was a heavy drinker. We also learned that Bernard was about twenty years older than Annette and did not treat her well. One family member told us that Annette was mentally challenged or a little slow as he put it.

At the morgue, that's what we called it, but the official name is the Medical Examiner's Office or ME's office, it was determined by the forensic autopsy that the body of Dena Polis was most likely moved several times before being dumped in the sewer. It was also determined by forensic examination that the body was deceased for at least twenty-four to forty-eight hours prior to being discovered in the sewer. During the early stages of the investigation by Detective Jimmy Ozezewski, Detective John Hess, and myself, we canvassed the area of Pratt and Light Streets in downtown Baltimore. This was the area that the uncle and aunt said they had dropped off Dena. We also talked to Dena's boyfriend, looked through Dena's personal items at her house and distributed photos of Dena to the media. All of these efforts proved fruitless.

The big lead that kept coming back to us throughout this investigation was the uncle and aunt dropping Dena off in the city. We decided to have the uncle and aunt come down to the Homicide Unit where we could take a detailed statement from both of them. Detective Oz (we all called him Jimmy Oz) called them up and set a date for them to come to the Homicide Unit. At this point they were not suspects, only witnesses. On the date they were supposed to appear in the Homicide Unit, Bernard called and cancelled the appointment and really did not have a good reason. Detective Oz made another appointment and on that date, Bernard called again and said he was having car trouble. Bernard asked for another date, but Oz was not buying his story this time. Oz told him that we would come and get them and bring them to the office and take them home after the statements. Oz informed Bernard that it was very important that this get done immediately. Bernard tried to get out of coming, but Oz insisted and Bernard said, "Maybe I can get my van to work. I will be in the homicide office later this afternoon."

Bernard and Annette Stebbings came to the police building and signed in at the front desk. Detective Oz went down to the desk and escorted them up to the Homicide Unit. On the way up, they told Oz that they received a ride down to the police building from a friend. When they walked into the Homicide Unit, I advised them that we needed to take their statements, as they may have been the last people to have seen Dena alive. I told them that our procedures were to take their statements separately and directed each to an interview room. Detective Oz interviewed Bernard Stebbings and Detective Hess interviewed Annette Stebbings.

As the interviews were proceeding, information was filtered back to me by each detective and I tried to coordinate the information that seemed important with both investigators. Detective Hess at one point asked Annette how she got to the police building and she said she drove down with Bernard in the van. She said they parked across the street from our building in a parking lot. I would point out that Annette seemed to be mentally challenged and that was the information we had received from family members. I slipped a note to Oz about what Annette had said about coming down to the building in the van and parking across the street. Oz confronted Bernard with what Annette had said and he reluctantly admitted that the van was across the street from the police building. I sat in the interview room with Oz and Bernard for a few minutes. I told Bernard that we need the truth from him and lying about how they got to the building, was not a good start. I informed him that if he did not fully cooperate and tell everything he knew about the day he allegedly dropped off Dena downtown, that we could hold him in city jail as a material witness to a murder. I don't really think we could have done that, but it seemed to get his attention, so what the hell, you do whatever you have to do, to solve murders.

Detective Oz asked Bernard if we could look through the van and at first he said no. Oz told him we could do it the easy way or the hard way, which meant we would obtain a search warrant for the van. Bernard reluctantly signed a form giving us permission to search his vehicle. We obtained the keys and the van was driven into the police building. Bernard then made a real interesting and important statement. He told Detective Oz, "If you see blood in the van, Dena was drinking a beer in the van on the day we dropped her off downtown and cut her hand on the can." Detective Oz already knew this was probably not true, as he had attended the autopsy and also reviewed the final autopsy report over and over and there was no mention of a cut on either of Dena's hands, other than the scrapes from being put in the sewer.

While the van was being examined by the crime lab personnel, the interviews continued. I think we all knew that we were on to something big with these two. While I was sitting in my office, coordinating the information being received, Detective Oz came running in very excited and shut the door. His face was lit up like a Christmas tree and he could hardly contain himself. He then blurted out the most unbelievable statement I have ever heard in my homicide career, "Bernard is missing a button on his shirt." At first it didn't hit me, then it did, I knew it had to be the shirt he wore on the day he probably murdered Dena. The button recovered at the autopsy, probably came from the shirt he had on. We were so excited that we had to regroup to control ourselves so that Annette, who was in the next room, did not hear what was happening.

I called Detective Hess out of the room and told him about the button missing from Bernard's shirt. He flipped out just like Jimmy and I had done. An occurrence like this is rare in homicide investigations, so when it happens, you thank the homicide Gods and celebrate. We stood in the hallway and planned our strategy, now that we had something to work with. We were sure that either Bernard or Annette or both of them had murdered Dena Polis. As luck would have it, while we were doing our planning, the crime lab technician examining the van called the office. He said they had recovered blood from the van, some wood chips, and some hair fibers. As it was now all coming together, it was really important how we proceeded. There was no doubt in our minds that we now had the killers of Dena Polis. We knew that every move we made from this point forward would one day be scrutinized in a court room, as it is in any murder trial.

We decided to do what we did in a lot of investigations when you have two people involved: we would zero in on the most vulnerable suspect. In this case, we decided our best move would be approaching Annette and laying our cards on the table. We now had the shirt with a missing button, some blood in the van, and the early lies about driving to the building. I went back in the interview room with John Hess and believe it or not, she asked us what all the excitement and hollering was about.

We knew that this was a crunch time moment, a make it or break it situation. John told Annette that we had found out certain things about her and Bernard. He told her that we feel that she knows something about the death of Dena. Well, we were shocked with her response. As it rarely happens, we in the Homicide Unit are not quite used to suspects confessing outright to murder. She stood up and said to our shock and surprise, "I killed her, but it was all Bernard's idea." I think we stood there with our mouths open and for a short period of time, no one could say anything. I knew we had what we wanted, but now we needed details. I told Annette that she has now done the right thing and we need a detailed statement from her about the murder. I was surprised that she did not cry or seem upset. Her frankness may have had something to do with her mental condition. I don't want you to think that we took advantage of a mentally challenged person. Annette was very capable of knowing what was happening and as we later found out from the statement, she probably wanted to confess to something that she felt Bernard had caused.

John proceeded with taking the statement from a very cooperative Annette. After the statement was obtained, I was convinced that she knew exactly what she had done. We felt that she was only telling us because there was no way out and she did not know what Bernard was saying in the other room. She possibly believed that he was blaming the murder on her.

We wanted to approach Bernard and tell him that Annette had confessed, which actually was the truth. We knew that he would think we were bullshitting him and just trying to trick him into a statement. Jimmy Oz went back in with Bernard and laid it all out for him. We were hoping that he would make it real easy and would also give in and confess. Bernard was much older than Annette by twenty years and more savvy about police tactics than Annette, as he had several prior arrests. Bernard leaned back in his chair and then with a cockiness, he leaned forward and said that he did not care what Annette had said, he did not kill Dena. He refused to give a statement, but went on to say that Annette has some mental problems and is easily led astray. He also said that he felt that we probably pushed her to make the statement. He was then advised by Jimmy Oz of his rights and he refused to sign the form. He stated that he could not read and write. He sat back in his chair and said, "I guess I probably need a lawyer."

Annette on the other hand seemed like she wanted to talk forever and that's what we let her do. She went into graphic detail about the rape and murder of Dena. In some points it was so graphic that even a hardened homicide investigator, like John Hess would cringe. She basically stated that she and Bernard gave Dena a ride downtown, but on the way, Bernard offered Dena a beer and asked if she wanted to take a ride and have some fun. Annette stated that Dena agreed to go for a ride, but told Bernard that she had to be back at a certain time, because she was meeting her boyfriend. Annette stated that they drove out of the city and into Harford County. Annette stated that Bernard had often talked about how pretty Dena was and he actually told Annette that if he had the opportunity, he would love to have sex with her. Annette stated that while they were driving, Dena was in the rear of the van and Bernard whispered to Annette that he was going to pull the van over and have sex with Dena. Annette said that at first she thought Dena would go along with it, but when he stopped the van and went in the back of the van, Dena asked what was happening and started to cry. Bernard started to get on top of Dena and was having a hard time. He told Annette to help hold Dena down. Annette said she got in the back of the van and tried to hold Dena down, but she was fighting them. Annette said she decided to straddle Dena's chest while Bernard was having sex with her. Annette said that she had her hands around Dena's throat and it seemed like Bernard was taking a real long time and she asked him to stop. Annette said, "Bernard was laughing and would not stop." Annette said, "I was mad and started to choke Dena." She said she was real mad that Bernard would not stop and when he would not stop, she started to choke Dena more. She said that at one point, Dena was not struggling anymore. Annette said that Bernard got off of Dena and was still laughing. Annette said that Bernard wanted to have sex with her now and she punched him. She said she told him that he enjoyed sex with Dena too much and she would not have sex with him. Annette said that Bernard got out of the van and drank a beer and Dena was just lying there and was not moving. Annette said that she tried to wake Dena up, as she thought that she had passed out, but Dena would not wake up and had no movement at all. Annette said that she panicked and started to scream and told Bernard that she thought Dena was dead. Bernard just laughed and drank another beer and told Annette to just let her sleep for awhile and then he would drive her back to the city and drop her off.

Annette said they stood outside the van for about thirty minutes and then Bernard got back in the van. She said she could feel the van moving and when she looked in the back of the van, Bernard was having sex with Dena and she was still not moving. Annette said that she thinks Bernard was drunk and he was talking crazy. Annette said that after awhile, he said, "I think you're right, she is dead." Annette said that she started to cry and Bernard told her to keep quiet and that he would take care of everything and no one would find out what happened. Annette said that Bernard covered Dena with some cardboard and started to drive back to the city and was still drinking beer.

She said that they pulled over for awhile and talked about what they would say to Dena's parents about giving her a ride to the city. Annette said that when it got dark, they started to drive around the city and by now, Bernard was drunk and still talking crazy. He told Annette that she needed to stick to the story and to leave the rest up to him and that everything would be fine. Annette said that she was crying and telling Bernard how bad she felt about what happened to Dena. She said that Bernard punched her in the chest and called her a fat fuckin whore. Bernard told her that if she didn't stop crying, he would kick her ass. She said that they were in the city, but she did not know the area. They finally pulled over in a vacant lot and Bernard said he wanted to get some sleep and they would get rid of the body later. Annette said that Bernard slept and she was still crying, but she was trying to be quiet, because she was afraid of Bernard. Annette said that Bernard slept as if nothing had happened and she just sat in the van and once in awhile she would look back and see Dena's body under the cardboard.

Annette said that about three or four in the morning, Bernard woke up and drank another beer and wanted to have sex and she refused. She said that Bernard told her that they were going to drive around and look for a spot to dump Dena's body. She said that they drove for about an hour and then Bernard said, "This looks like a good spot" and pulled the van over to the curb. Bernard told her to wait in the van and he opened the back doors and moved the body close to the door. She said he then used a pry bar to open a manhole cover and she said she could not believe what he was doing. She said that he took Dena's body and forced it into the open manhole and put the cover back on. Annette said that he got back in the van and told her again what the story would be if anyone asked about riding Dena to downtown Baltimore. Annette said that they went home and Bernard went to bed and she stayed up and cried.

The information received from Annette was that the actual murder of Dena Polis took place in Bernard's van and the location where they parked was outside the Baltimore City limits. We determined that the actual location would most likely be Abingdon, Maryland, so I made contact with the Maryland State Police for their assistance.

I received a call from Detective Sergeant Bill Jacobs of the Maryland State Police and after giving him the reader's digest version of what we had determined, he immediately responded to our Homicide Unit. I did not know it at the time, but this would be the start of a long friendship with Bill Jacobs, who we all called "Jake." I don't want to get off the topic, but Jake and I had a lot in common. We were about the same age, Marines, played tennis, and we were Detective Sergeants in police departments.

When Jake got to the office and after we briefed him, it was decided that we would ask Annette to drive with us and show us exactly where the murder took place and she agreed. We drove to an area of Abingdon, Maryland, and with very little trouble, she pointed out an area in the woods where the murder took place. The State Police Crime Lab Unit responded and they recovered some evidence that would be very crucial in the trial of Bernard and Annette. Later, Bernard and Annette were transported to the Harford County Sherriff's Department where they were both charged with the murder of Dena Polis. The charges were placed in that county, because the actual murder took place there and then the body was dumped in the city.

At a preliminary hearing both Bernard and Annette Stebbings requested that their trials be moved out of the Harford County court system and the request was granted for Bernard Stebbings, but Annette's trial was to be held in Harford County.

The trial of Annette Stebbings was held first and after about one week of testimony, she was found guilty by a jury and later sentenced to the death penalty by Harford County Judge Albert Klose. The sentence of Annette would make her the first woman to get the death penalty in Maryland. During the trial, it was brought up by her defense attorney that she was mentally challenged and probably went along with the murder, because she was terrified of Bernard. The testimony and evidence was overwhelming and when her statement was read to the jury, there was no doubt in the jurors' minds that she knew exactly what she was doing and was a willing participant.

During the trial for Annette, I never really felt sorry for her, even knowing that she was manipulated by Bernard. I am sure that Bernard took advantage of her mental capacity and the fact that he was twenty years older than her. I actually did not see much remorse from Annette during the trial and we did find out after the trial that she and Bernard were writing letters to each other from their jail cells. Her statement was so riveting that most of the jurors cringed when certain parts were read in the courtroom and I think that sunk her.

Bernard Stebbings' murder trial was moved to Salisbury, Maryland, which is on the eastern shore of Maryland, near the resort town of Ocean City. Everyone in law enforcement who would testify was put up in hotels in Ocean City, which is only about twenty miles from Salisbury. We had about ten law enforcement personnel that would testify. Then there were the prosecutors, the crime lab technicians, the forensic pathologist, and a few other witnesses that stayed in various hotels at the beach. Salisbury was not a sleepy little town, but having such a high profile murder trial in town, drew a lot of attention and the courtroom was packed each day of the trial.

Bernard was convicted and also given the death sentence, which was well deserved. The murder trial got a lot of publicity, in both Salisbury and back in Baltimore. The trial lasted longer than anticipated and the evidence and testimony were overwhelming.

The jurors from Salisbury were decent hard working people and most of them had a background in farming. I could tell during the trial that what they were hearing probably seemed like something out of a Hollywood movie. I know that when the doctor from the Medical Examiner's Office testified about the autopsy and went into graphic detail about what Bernard did to Dena both before and after her death, was very compelling. The judge had instructed the jurors prior to the doctor testifying, that what they were about to hear could be very upsetting and he was right. During the trial, Bernard just sat there showing no emotion. Bernard was skinny, with long black hair and to me, he had that Charles Manson look. He never took the stand in his defense and the only rebuttal that his attorney provided, was that he did not kill Dena, that he only had sex with her. His attorney contended that Bernard had no intentions of killing Dena when he got in the back of the van. The entire defense in the trial was that Annette was the person responsible for Dena's death.

The investigation and outcome of the trials were written up in True Detective. I still get a lot of kidding from Jake and others involved in the investigation, because throughout the story in the magazine, it talks about, Sergeant Ellwood did this, Sergeant Ellwood did that, Sergeant Ellwood said this, and so on and so on…not too much said about Jake and the others. I figure, what the hell, I was the one being interviewed for the story and I told it the way I saw it. I am only kidding, when I say that I did it all, because I did not, but I love to kid those guys.

I have been carrying a large button with me ever since that article came out in the magazine. It has been a standard procedure with guys at our reunions and retirement parties, to ask me to tell the "Button Story." I pull out the big button and tell the story. In no way do I carry the button out of any disrespect toward Dena Polis or her family. I carry it to show the dedication of all the people that worked on that murder. I took investigating murders very serious. Remember the plaque on the wall in the Homicide Unit that states "No greater honor could be bestowed upon a human being than to investigate the death of another human being."

I investigated many homicides during my time in the Baltimore Homicide Unit, but this was probably the one that I will never forget and most proud that "We" solved. Dena Polis was a young, beautiful person with her whole life ahead of her and it was cut short by of all people, her relatives. Both Annette and Bernard originally received the death penalty, but after a few years, they appealed the sentence and it was reduced to life in prison without the possibility of parole.

It has been thirty years since the murder of Dena Polis. I think she would be about forty-eight years old if this horrendous cruel act did not take place. She probably would have been married with children, possibly a grandmother, but two deranged people changed all that. I have never really wished the death penalty on anyone, but on these two bastards, especially Bernard, I would have personally pulled the switch.

I only hope that they have lived a miserable life behind bars. I can imagine that one day, some do-good outfit will want to take their case in front of the courts and ask that these two old people are shown mercy and released from prison. I hope some cops come to the nursing home and get Jake and I and wheel us into the courtroom, so we can make sure these two killers don't ever see the outside world.

The Sheraton Hotel - Dukes of Hazard Almost Career Ending Story

I told you in the previous story that all the law enforcement personnel on the Bernard Stebbings' murder trial stayed at hotels in Ocean City. The hotels were close to Salisbury, Maryland, where the trial was conducted. I stayed with John Hess and Jimmy Oz in a high rise hotel on the ocean side. From what I remember, it was a beautiful place and had a nice pool: story about the pool to follow. We were in Ocean City for a week and needless to say that when we were not in court testifying, we did what cops do best when they are bored, we drank.

One night we all went to the Sheraton Hotel and we were drinking and having a good time. John Hess decided he needed to take a piss. He also decided that the bathroom was apparently too far away, so he pissed in a large flower pot near the bar. As you might expect, this drew some attention from the bartender and the manager. Some guy pissing in a flower pot in a crowded nightclub just might draw a few stares. I don't quite remember how it all got started, but the bartender grabbed John and then some guy that we did not know got involved. In no time at all, it seemed like the whole place was fighting. Well, someone hollered "the cops are coming" and if you can imagine this, we all started to run out of the place...yes, the cops were now running from the cops...don't have any sensible reasoning for this, but it happened. We ran out to the parking lot and we all jumped in my unmarked police car and yes, we were making our getaway from the police, in a police car. I drove up Ocean Highway at a pretty high speed and I could see the emergency lights of the Ocean City Police car in the rear view mirror.

I decided to do a Dukes of Hazards maneuver; I am sure you have seen this on TV. I made a real quick right turn and headed straight for the beach. I had the headlights out and apparently going too fast and the next thing I knew we were airborne. The car landed in the sand on the beach. It was a miracle that no one was injured. The Ocean City police car continued up the highway and apparently did not see the Dukes of Hazard move. We just sat in the car for awhile and I assume everyone was stunned by such a stunt. I was a little surprised also. Good thing we were drinking. I think I shocked the state troopers. They didn't know whether to get out of the car and run or not. Everyone just stood around sort of dazed. Jake said, "What the fuck did you just do, you crazy bastard?" The city cops, John and Oz just sat in the sand and were laughing their asses off. I am not sure what I was doing, but I do remember thinking that this was crazy and how in the hell would I get out of this one.

We now had to figure out how we would get the car out of the sand. The only thing we could think of was to call a tow truck. Well, we did get out of the sand and miraculously there was no damage to the car. That would be the only good thing that happened that night. We drove back to the hotel and like a bunch of gangsters we tried to hide the car in the rear of the building. I later found out that the Ocean City cop got my tag number and when he called in for a listing, he was told it was listed to the Baltimore City Police Department. I can only imagine his reaction to find out that he had been duped by a Baltimore City cop, but I am sure he also knew that he would have the last laugh.

Well, it got interesting from here on, as the night duty officer on the Ocean City Police Department called the duty officer in Baltimore and told him about the incident at the Sheraton and the chase. The Baltimore duty officer, Captain Gil Karner checked with the police motor pool and found that the vehicle was checked out to me and he called my home. He asked my wife, if she knew where I was and naturally she said, "He's in Ocean City for a homicide trial."

Back at the hotel in Ocean City, we were celebrating and more drinking of course. Not sure what the hell we were celebrating. I mentioned earlier that

I would get to the part about a swimming pool. This was a very scary thing and I cringe even today when I think about it. Everyone in the hotel room was drinking and settling down for the night. I was drinking and standing out on the balcony. I decided I might be able to jump into the swimming pool from the balcony ledge. Naturally, as good drinking buddies usually do, they egged me on and I started to climb over the rail. I am not sure who stopped me, but someone did and that was a good thing, because we were on the 13th floor of the hotel. Just as a side note, there was no water in the pool. It had been drained after the summer vacation period, thank you Jesus.

As if you have not already heard enough craziness in this short story, there are actually a few other episodes that occurred while down the ocean for the Stebbings' trial. Most of them I have heard from Jake, because quite frankly, I don't remember. I do know that the word got back to the police department in Baltimore and we knew we were in a world of trouble. I was called into the colonel's office when we got back to Baltimore. I explained the incident at the Sheraton as a misunderstanding; sure, someone pissing in a flower pot in a crowded nightclub is a misunderstanding. I know the colonel did not buy the story, I wonder why. The saving point for us was that the Ocean City Police did not want to pursue the matter. Later, it was also dropped by the Baltimore Police Department. I took the blame for the incident and rightfully so, because looking back on it, someone could have been seriously injured or killed over my stupidity. This story actually falls under the all too familiar category of "Dumb Shit" on my part and yes, again booze played a major part in all of our foolishness in Ocean City.

The only good thing that came out of the trip was that Bernard Stebbings got the death penalty and that was our mission to start with. I thank God that no one was seriously injured. I think mentally, I scared the shit out of all the guys on the ride up Ocean Highway and the night I tried to jump in the empty pool. I do have to say that the Dukes of Hazard stunt was pretty neat.

The morning after all this happened, I was sleeping or I should say, recovering. John and Oz came to get me and said that the captain of the Homicide Unit was on the phone and wanted to talk to me. I remember both John and Oz physically holding me up to the phone. The captain was pissed and wanted to know what the hell happened at the Sheraton Hotel. I told him that I would have to call him back and he did not want to hear that and said, "You better have a good story or your ass is in deep trouble." I was told that when I hung up from the captain, I looked at my wrist and said "Damn, someone stole my watch" and John said, "It's on your other wrist, stupid."

I waited about an hour and several cups of coffee later before I called the captain. I was making better sense this time and I told the captain that there was an incident at the Sheraton Hotel. I told him that I would go to the Sheraton and also talk to the Ocean City Police before I left to return to Baltimore. I was hoping that it could be straightened out, but my only shot, was to give it a try. I assured him that everything would be fine and I would explain it all when I got back to Baltimore. The captain at that time was Joe Cooke and he was a good guy. I knew that I had to come up with a half believable story. If the Ocean City Police were satisfied, everything would be okay, or at least I'd hope that would be the case.

I did talk to a Ocean City Police major who seemed to be amused by the whole story. He was laughing when I was telling him what happened. He told me that the officer who chased me on Ocean Highway was unhappy about not catching me. The major said he would talk to the officer and calm him down. He also said that as long as the manager of the Sheraton Hotel did not want to press charges against anyone, he would dismiss the whole incident. I was really appreciative of this major's attitude. I told him that not only did I appreciate what he was doing, but all the other guys appreciate it also. He pulled me to the side and said "Look, I have been a cop for twenty-eight years; I have done some stupid ass things also and as long as no one got hurt, it ain't no big deal."

I can honestly say that when all this went down, I sure as hell thought that we were all getting fired. Maybe not everyone, but I thought I was getting fired, demoted, transferred, or something.

When we got back to Baltimore and went back to work on solving murders, we all felt better. I know that the captain hung this over my head for a long time. He never pursued any departmental charges against me or anyone and that was a good thing. I did have the occasion to be out with him one night and I told him the real story. I thought he would be mad, but he laughed his ass off and like me, he loved the part about the Dukes of Hazard stunt.

Doctor Russo – Unsolved Murder

In 1981, a very prominent doctor who had an office on Harford Road in northeast Baltimore was brutally murdered while he was seeing patients in his office. When I say he was brutally murdered, I mean he was shot several times at point blank range. People talk about murders; in terms like, brutal, horrific, and senseless. If you think about it, they are all that way. A murder is a murder; nobody is more deader than the other dead person.

Dr. Sebastian Russo was extremely well liked in the community where he lived, which is also where he had his medical practice. The doctor would charge whatever a person or family could pay for their visit or treatment. He was known to charge nothing if you could not pay. This was an absolute shocking murder to the neighborhood and his many patients. He was an old time doctor who would actually go to houses if people could not get to his office. At various times during the day and early evening, there would be lines outside his office with people waiting to see the doctor. He lived across the street from his practice, which made it very convenient for him to stay open for most of the day and early evening to see patients. He dealt mostly in cash and did not have a very good bookkeeping process. He would record in a book what he charged and what he received from his patients. He did not have any help in the office. People would just come in and put their name in a book and wait their turn to see him. The layout of the house he practiced in was a typical Baltimore rowhouse on Harford Road in northeast Baltimore. The doctor would see the patients in the back of the first floor of the house.

On a March night in 1981, the normal crowd of Doctor Russo's patients was forming a line on Harford Road to see him. They would fill the office waiting room which was on the first floor and some would extend out the door onto the street. On this particular night, at about 8:10 PM, there were still about sixteen people in the waiting room. A black man came into the office area and walked directly to where the doctor saw patients. The people in the waiting room later told us that they did not think anything of it; as the man seemed confident and did not appear that strange. Most people in the waiting room told us that they thought he was either delivering something to the doctor or had been there earlier and was paying the doctor. The doctor always kept the door to the actual treating room closed and when someone came out, the next on the list would go in to see him.

Well, this black man was in with the doctor for only about five minutes. He casually walked out, closing the door to the office behind him and walked by the people in the waiting area. Some witnesses told us that they think the man had pulled his green windbreaker jacket up over his face as he exited the front door. Most witnesses told us that they did not really hear anything unusual while the man was back with the doctor. When the man walked out of the building, the next person on the waiting list went back to see the doctor. When she opened the door, she screamed and saw the doctor lying on the floor. He had a large pool of blood near his body. She told us that at first she thought the doctor had passed out. She said that when she bent down to try to talk to him, she knew something bad had happened. She observed a large amount of blood in the chest area and the doctor was not moving. She went screaming from the office as others came in and tried to assist the doctor, but he was dead on the scene from gunshot wounds to his chest.

The police were called and when the uniform officers arrived, several of the people that were in the waiting room had already left. Doctor Russo was pronounced dead in his office with three gunshot wounds to his upper torso. The uniform police officer first on the scene was Officer Bob Groncki from the Northeast District. Groncki did an excellent job in preserving the crime scene, keeping witnesses on the scene, and calling for the Homicide Unit and the Crime Laboratory.

I am sorry to say that what I am about to tell you, was an absolute disgrace to the Homicide Unit and the Baltimore Police Department. I was a detective sergeant in the Homicide Unit at that time, but I was detailed to the Sex Offense Unit. When I came into work the day after the shooting of Doctor Russo, the office was abuzz with several reporters and a few members of the command staff. Doctor Russo was not only a well liked and prominent doctor, he was also a member of the Sons of Italy, which was a very large and well known organization in Baltimore comprised mostly of Italian Americans. The police commissioner at that time was Frank Battaglia. The commissioner was a long time member of the Sons of Italy and a personal friend of Doctor Russo. The Sons of Italy was a very influential group in the city and many high ranking members of the police department were members. Needless to say, the murder of Doctor Russo got lots of attention from the police commissioner and others in the command staff.

I was not even in the office long enough to get a coffee, when the captain of the Homicide Unit, Joe Cook, called me into his office and shut the door. He told me that there were no arrests and no suspects in the murder of Doctor Russo. He told me that he was taking me off the detail in the Sex Offense Unit and putting me in charge of the Doctor Russo investigation. He told me to pick three detectives from the Homicide Unit to work on this special task force, which he said would start immediately. I asked why the two detectives that were on the scene last night when the doctor was murdered were not continuing with the investigation, as this was usually the procedure. He pushed on the door that was already shut and this time he locked it. He asked that I not repeat what he was going to tell me. The captain said that he did not want the two detectives to work the investigation, because he felt that some unprofessional things were done on the crime scene at the doctor's office. He said that he did not want to elaborate too much at this time, but felt more comfortable with assigning different detectives to the case. I told the captain that I would get with the three detectives and review the reports. I told him that I would review the recovered evidence immediately and update him on how we were going to proceed. The captain said that he had already been called to the police commissioner's office and was told that he should do whatever it took to make an arrest in the doctor's murder. He told me that the commissioner suggested that he use as many detectives as needed. The captain was told that if he needed anything he was to come directly to the commissioner for help. The captain said that he would allow me to work whatever hours that I needed, but he wanted to stay in constant contact with me as the investigation proceeded. He thanked me for taking the assignment and I went and notified the detectives that they would be on this task force to investigate the doctor's murder.

We met in a vacant office next to the homicide office that would now be our home for several weeks to come. All of the reports on the murder and recovered evidence were brought into the office. I asked each detective to take some of the reports and read them and make notes. I also asked that they review all the crime scene photos and recovered personal property of the doctor. I informed the detectives about what the captain had told me and that the police commissioner was watching this investigation very closely. I did not go into why we were picked to conduct the investigation. These guys knew the procedures and asked why we were getting the case and not the two detectives who were originally on the scene. I told them that it was the captain's decision and maybe down the road, we would get that answer. I asked that all the reports and evidence be looked at very carefully. I knew these three detectives very well. It was Norm "Lefty" Lesnick, Steve Danko, and Donald Kincaid; they were top notch homicide investigators. I told them that all eyes in the command staff of the department would be on us and that we could not leave any stone unturned in this murder investigation.

Well, it did not take long to see that something was not right with what we were seeing and hearing about the original crime scene at the doctor's office. I was looking at the crime scene photos along with Lefty and Steve. We could not believe what we were seeing. The body of Doctor Russo was photographed in different locations in his office. He was lying up against his desk, he was lying in front of the desk, and he was lying close to the office door. One of the detectives came to me and said that he was a little confused. He said that a report said that some evidence was recovered, but there were no receipts from the evidence room that the articles were ever turned in. I closed the door and figured this was a good time to tell the guys some of what the captain had told me. I told them that the captain had emphasized how important this investigation was and that he had to report daily to the commissioner on the progress. I also told them that he was not happy with the original crime scene investigation. I told them that if mistakes were made on the crime scene, we would not cover up anything and deal with each situation as it surfaced. I asked if anyone had any problem with working on this investigation. It was very possible that their fellow detectives may have screwed up the initial investigation. They said that they did not have any problems and were anxious to move forward.

While we were discussing individual assignments and the overall game plan, I was approached by Sergeant Paul Lioi who worked in the Arson Unit. I had known Paul for several years and he was a great guy. His office was on the same floor as the Homicide Unit and we had talked on several occasions. Paul told me that he was related to Doctor Russo by marriage. He said that he had met earlier in the morning with the doctor's wife. Paul told me that the doctor's wife had viewed the body of her husband and noticed that his wrist watch was missing. She told Paul that it had been in the family for many years. She was wondering if it had been taken by the assailant or did the police take it off the body. Paul also asked if some Italian money had been recovered from the office. He asked if a large amount of cash had been taken by the assailant or was it recovered by the police and turned in as evidence. I told Paul that I would have to check these things out, as I had just been assigned to the case. I told him that I would get back to him when I found out something. I asked the detectives to review the reports and check and see what evidence was recovered on the murder scene and what was turned in. I was later told that no articles were turned in to our Evidence Control Unit as being recovered on the murder scene. I found this to be very unusual that on a murder scene of a very prominent doctor, that no physical evidence, other than photos and diagrams would have been turned in.

I decided to call the detectives that were on the scene of the murder that night. I started with a detective that I knew pretty well, Ron Carey. When I talked to him on the phone, what he said surprised me. He said, "Sarge, I am not sure what happened last night. There were so many cops on the scene, anything could have happened." I asked him what he meant by that and he said, "Things were out of control on that scene. It did not seem like anyone was in charge." I asked why he allowed that to happen and he said, "There were people on the scene that out ranked me" and he told me who they were. I told him that was no excuse for what happened. I asked him if a watch, Italian money, and other money were recovered on the murder scene. He at first said he did not know and then said, "Maybe you should check the other detective's desk." I asked why anything recovered would be in someone's desk and he said, "Like I told you, things were a little out of control last night." I told him that I would want to discuss this further when he got to work.

I went to the desk of the other detective, Dave James, and opened the top drawer. Sitting right there was a watch and what appeared to be foreign money. I was actually shocked and before I took it out, I called Lefty over to witness what I found. I asked Lefty to submit the articles to the Evidence Unit. I called Detective James at his home and his attitude on the phone was very negative, but par for this guy. I never really liked his attitude. I asked him about evidence recovered on the Doctor Russo murder scene. He hesitated at first and asked me why I wanted to know. I told him that I was assigned by the captain, to the investigation of the murder of Doctor Russo. He said, "Why would they take the investigation away from me and my partner?" I told him that I did not want to discuss it with him on the phone. I asked him to come to the Homicide Unit and he said, "I will talk to you when I get in tonight for work." Well, about that time, I had enough of this guy. I told him as calm as I could that he was to come to the Homicide Unit within the next hour or I would be out to his house. I did not wait for a response and hung up the phone. I went back in the office and I am sure the other detectives could see that I was upset. Steve asked what the problem was and I told him that I did not have a good feeling about what went on last night on the crime scene. The detectives agreed with me and said that after reviewing the reports, looking at the crime scene photos, and checking what little evidence was collected on the scene, we certainly had our work cut out for us. I told the guys, because of what little was done on the initial investigation, we were now operating from a disadvantage in our effort to catch the murderer of Doctor Russo.

Later that afternoon, I was in the office. The shift lieutenant, who was also on the scene the night of the murder, came into my office. He shut the door and flopped down in my chair. I never really got along with this lieutenant and he had only been in the Homicide Unit for about eight months. He acted like he had been there for years. He had the attitude that because he was a lieutenant, what he said was the gospel and was not to be questioned. He was not a very friendly guy. As he entered the office on this occasion, he was smiling and acting like we were the best of friends. He relaxed in my chair and said, "I heard that the captain gave you the Doctor Russo case." I just nodded my head and could see that something strange was about to take place. He leaned over the desk and in a very low voice he said, "Don't make any waves." He sat back in my chair and smiled. I asked him what he meant by that statement. He gave me that shitty smile he had and said, "I am only going to say this one time and I hope you do not repeat it." He leaned over the desk again and said, "I know some things were not done right last night on that murder scene, but you now have the opportunity to make things right." At this point, I did not care if this guy was a lieutenant or a general. He was asking me to cover up some things that as far as I was concerned bordered on extremely unprofessional conduct. He got up and started to leave. I said, "I would like to tell you something before you go." He turned to face me with his hand on the doorknob and in his very snippy way, he said, "I think we are done and I hope you get the message." Well, that infuriated me more and I stood up and said, "Lieutenant, let's make one thing very clear. I have been assigned this investigation by the captain and he has placed his faith in me that I will conduct a thorough and professional investigation." I went on to say, "I know that a lot of things went wrong on the murder scene last night and nothing will be covered up or overlooked." I told him, "If I determine that there was any wrongdoing on that scene, I will make recommendations to the captain that those involved be transferred out of the Homicide Unit." He started pulling on the door and I said, "If the acts go beyond simple investigative mistakes and appear to be criminal, I will present them to the captain and recommend that criminal charges be considered." Well, I certainly got his attention this time and he sat back down in the chair and the arrogant attitude seemed to dissipate. I could see that he had the feeling of losing control and that kind of made me feel good in a perverse way. I started toward the door and said, "Lieutenant, if you have no further need for me, I have a homicide investigation to work on" and I walked out of the room.

I went for a walk on the floor to collect my thoughts and to think through what had just happened. In all my years on the job, I had never had that kind of conversation with a boss. I did not want to go to the captain at this time, because it was still early in the investigation. I was not really sure what went wrong on that murder scene.

I worked my way back to the office and the detectives were busy making notes. We had a short discussion and decided that we needed to go back out to the crime scene, before any further discoveries were made. The guys that were assigned to me for the investigation were detectives with a lot of years in the Homicide Unit. I had all the faith in the world that they would work hard and do the right thing to solve this murder. The detectives went out to the murder scene. I told them to call me if they had any good news; we sure as hell could use some good news. I stayed in the office and tried to make some sense of the whole thing. I reviewed the official homicide crime report that was written by the uniform officer and finally something looked good. The report was very well written and went into much detail. I was very impressed with the way the officer went into everything that happened from the time he arrived until the time he left the scene. The Officer was Bob Groncki and he worked patrol in the Northeast District. I think at that time he had about eight years on the job. I thought that because the officer was on the scene the entire time, it would be important for me to talk to him. Maybe he could shed some light on the activities of our homicide investigators. I called the district and got his home phone number from the desk sergeant and called him. I was surprised to get him on the phone. I figured he would probably be sleeping, because he worked on the murder most of his shift. The officer was very informative and pleasant to talk to. He went into much detail, some of which was not in other reports. I asked him if he could come to the Homicide Unit when he came to work for the 4 PM to midnight shift and he said that he would.

Officer Groncki arrived at the Homicide Unit at least two hours before I expected him and was very eager to participate in the investigation. When I first met him, he impressed me, not only with his neatness in uniform and his attention to detail, but it was something else. I think it was an inner feeling that you get about someone and I got that good feeling about Groncki. I told him that I appreciated him coming down to the office and I was also impressed with his report that he wrote on the murder. I also told him that I had information that some things might not have been handled properly by the homicide investigators that were on the scene. When I told him that, he smiled and said, "Sarge, I am only a patrol officer, but I have to be honest. I was not impressed with the way things went last night on that crime scene." I talked to Groncki for quite awhile and some of what I thought happened on the scene was coming to light and now made better sense. I was so impressed with Officer Groncki, that I asked him if he would he like to be detailed to the Homicide Unit to work on this murder. Well, you would have thought I just told him he hit the Lotto; he sprang forward in his chair and said, "Sarge that would be great, if you can make it happen." I told him that I could not promise anything, but I would approach my captain. The police commissioner had told my captain that he could have whatever he needed to solve this murder. I think Groncki must have thanked me a dozen times before he left the homicide office. I told him I would call him as soon as I knew anything.

Later that same day, the two detectives that worked the initial homicide scene came into work for the 4 PM to midnight shift. I told both of them that I wanted to talk to them and they both started to walk into my office. I stopped them and said I wanted to talk to them separately. I knew who I wanted to talk to first. I also knew that I had to be very careful with this conversation. If it came to the point that one of them admitted something that could be conceived as improper or unprofessional, I would have to ask for a written report. I called in Ron Carey first, because he seemed to want to cooperate with me. I wanted to let the other guy sit and wonder what was happening. Detective Carey was actually a good guy. He apparently just went along with the other detective on the murder scene that night or possibly he did not know what happened. I asked him about the photos showing that the body had been moved around the doctor's office. At first he said he was not sure what happened. He then said that he was probably busy interviewing witnesses. He said that the other detective was the one who handled the actual crime scene in the doctor's office. I asked about the money and the watch that were not turned in. He said he knew they were recovered, but assumed the other detective would turn them in. I told him that the scene investigation was not very good and that I would be making a report on all the discrepancies that we were finding. I told him that I expected much more from him or any investigator on a crime scene. He hung his head and said, "You might be right. I don't know what the hell I was thinking about last night." He asked if he was in any trouble and I told him that I would hope that no one is in trouble. I told him that I needed to get to the bottom of all this and quickly move forward with the most important job at hand and that was to catch the person who murdered Doctor Russo.

I called the other detective, Dave James, into the office. He did not have a very good reputation as a homicide detective and just seemed like he was biding his time in the unit. He would be what we called a "hanger on"; somebody who talks a good game, but really don't know what the hell they are doing. I told him about what we had found; the weird scene photos, the failure to turn in the doctor's watch, and the money that was recovered from his desk. He said that he intended to turn in the articles when he got back to work the next day. I told him that was a clear violation of procedures. I asked him what else went on that night that I should know. He looked surprised and asked what I meant. I said, "I don't think there was a very good job done on the murder scene." I told him, "If my investigation shows any more violations of procedures, I will recommend to the captain that you be transferred back to patrol." I think I now had his full attention, so I said, "If I find anything that would be considered criminal, I will report that with recommendations also." He got up to leave and I asked him if he understood. He was almost out the door, when he said, "I think you are blowing things out of proportion." I made sure that before he left the office, I repeated what I had said and told him that I would get back to him real soon.

Later in the day, I met with Lefty, Donald, and Steve and we went over what we had found out so far. One of the detectives told me that he read a statement from one of the witnesses that was sitting in the doctor's office when the black man came in. The statement from the witness was that she saw the black man run from the doctor's office after the shooting. Another witness reported that the suspect took off a green windbreaker jacket and threw it down the sewer about a half block from the doctor's office. I asked the guys if any of the police reports indicated anything about checking the sewer for the jacket and they said no. Steve stated that several people that were in the doctor's office at the time of the shooting had reported that the black man who went into the doctor's office had a green thin windbreaker jacket on. I told Lefty and Steve that they needed to go back out to the crime scene and check that sewer. They went back out and when they went down in the sewer, they recovered a very dirty and wet green windbreaker jacket. The jacket was photographed in the sewer, recovered, and turned into the Evidence Control Unit. When I was told about the green jacket being found, I was again furious. I called the two investigators that handled the initial scene investigation back into my office. I told them we recovered a green windbreaker jacket from the sewer about one block from the doctor's office. At first they said that they were not sure they had that information while on the scene. They then changed their mind and said they intended to go back out and check the sewers in the area for the jacket. At this point I knew that I had enough of their negligence or stupidity and just told both of them to get the hell out of the office.

I was called into Captain Cook's office and he asked for an update on what we had done and where we going with the investigation. I guess the captain picked up that something was wrong by the way I looked. I started by saying, "OK, I need to be straight with you captain." I told him that I would normally not report to him with simple mistakes made by detectives on a murder scene. I told him I had something that needed to be addressed and it is becoming a real hindrance to the investigation. I told him what had happened and he got up and shut the door and said, "Tell me again and this time, give me more detail." I told him what had happened and he asked me for my opinion on what I thought should happen to the two detectives. I told him that one of the detectives should be transferred immediately. I told him that the possibility was there that he could eventually be charged departmentally with violating police procedures. The captain said, "What about the other detective?" I told him that the other guy knows he did wrong, but seems to be cooperating. I suggested that with a reprimand he probably should stay in the unit. The captain at first told me that he was surprised and a little shocked. He then told me he agreed with my recommendations and would have to run this by the colonel for approval. He told me to continue with the investigation and if I needed any help to let him know. He then gave me some much needed good news and told me that the request to have Officer Groncki detailed to homicide was approved.

This investigation of the murder of Doctor Russo went on for about three months and there were many twists and turns. I think at several times during the investigation, we thought we had our killer, but it did not pan out. We worked this investigation nonstop, until we had a file cabinet filled with reports.

As of the writing of this short story, the murder of Doctor Sebastian Russo is still an unsolved murder and resides in the "Cold Case Files" in the Homicide Unit. After all these years and no arrest, it really does not sit well with me even to this day. I know that others in the Homicide Unit over the years have picked up this investigation and added to the reports. I would imagine there are several file cabinets. Now that I am retired and have lots of time, I often think about this murder. I rehash what happened over and over and have actually had dreams about continuing to work this murder. Maybe one day, a tip will come into the Homicide Unit and some young aggressive detective will jump on it and break this case. I know the current captain of the Homicide Unit; he used to work in my squad. Maybe, if I call him and ask if I could review the files, I might see something that was missed.

I must say that in all my years in the Homicide Unit, I observed nothing but dedicated work from the detectives. I only tell this story to show you that if investigators involved in a homicide investigation are not working on the same page, we only help people get away with murder. Working in the Homicide Unit is the toughest assignment in the police department. It takes a toll on you mentally and physically, not to mention your family life. I think that the detectives originally involved in the investigation of Doctor Russo have retired from the job. I hope that they also think about this murder, but I doubt it. Did they ever take time to read the plaque on the wall in the Homicide Unit?

CHASING CHINESE FOOD

In June of 1982, I worked a very strange murder investigation with Detective Lenny Willis. Lenny was an excellent cop, very smart, and a meticulous dresser. I remember working some murder scenes with Lenny where he was sorry he came to work looking like a banker, instead of a "gumshoe". Lenny was the intellectual in the unit or at least we let him believe that. Many nights when murder took a little break in "Charm City", we would sit around the homicide office and have some really involved discussions. If Lenny did not get his point across, he got real angry. Some nights, even if we agreed with him, we would get him all worked up by just disagreeing with anything he said. He knew we were getting on his case most of the time and no harm was done. We always ended most of our in-depth discussions with a little laughter. Then the phone would ring and we were out in the streets of Baltimore where all Lenny's liberal ideas went right down the drain.

We got a call one night to respond to a homicide at the home of a very prominent black doctor, Norman Thompson. Doctor Thompson was a surgeon at Sinai Hospital in northwest Baltimore. He lived about two miles from the hospital in a fairly new development where several other doctors lived. When we got to the house, the doctor's body was still on the scene. He was lying about four feet from the front entrance to his townhouse. The doctor was fully clothed and had several stab wounds to his chest.

We learned from the uniform officers that responded to the house, that they received a call from a next door neighbor. The neighbor said that she heard screaming and some loud noises coming from the doctor's home. The uniform officer who was first on the scene said that the front door was slightly open. The officer said that when he pushed it fully open, he saw the doctor on the floor. He said that he checked for a pulse, but knew from the amount of blood in the chest area that the doctor was dead. The officer said that the neighbor also told him that the doctor lived alone and was not married as far as anyone knew. The neighbor stated that the doctor was very quiet and most of the time, they didn't even know if he was home.

As we waited for the morgue wagon, we looked around the house. We were being very careful not to touch anything before the crime lab could get there and do their thing. The uniform officer told us that he and others had checked the house also, mainly to see if anyone was in the house. They said they wanted to see if any of the other entrances were tampered with and they were not. He said that they found nothing out of the ordinary throughout the house. When we examined the doctor, we found three stab wounds to the mid to upper chest area and a large cut on his right hand. We estimated the doctor to be at least six feet, four inches tall and weighed about two hundred and fifty pounds and he appeared to be fit for his size.

As we looked around the house, we noticed that there was very little furniture in any of the rooms, except the master bedroom. We later found out that the doctor spent most of his time either at the hospital or at a female friend's home in northeast Baltimore. We also found out later that the doctor had purchased the townhouse to be near the hospital. I assumed that because he was a bachelor, he did not need much furniture.

The body of the doctor was removed from the house and taken to the Medical Examiner's Office for an autopsy, which would be done the next morning. Lenny and I finished up with the crime scene and after taking photos, dusting for prints, talking to neighbors, and sketching the crime scene, we left. We knew that this would be a tough investigation, not that they all weren't.

None of the neighbors, other than the person who had called the police had heard or seen anything that would help us in the investigation. We decided to go to Sinai Hospital and talk to some of his colleagues. We wanted to learn something about the doctor's friends and habits or pretty much anything we could learn. It was frustrating; all we had now was a dead doctor.

The staff at Sinai Hospital was stunned at the news of the doctor's death. Everyone we talked to, spoke very well of the doctor. The only information we received, was that he had recently purchased the townhouse so that he could be closer to the hospital. We were told that he frequently worked out to control a weight problem. In addition, we found out that he had no known relatives in the Baltimore area. We were told that he dated a lady that lived in northeast Baltimore. Along with this information, the only activity that the doctor seemed to enjoy was going to the racetrack. The staff at the hospital was very helpful and also had information on his family. They told us that they would want to make the notification to the family and we agreed. The doctor had family in North Carolina and the hospital staff also wanted to assist the family with funeral arrangements. Anytime someone else says they will make the notification to the family, is fine with me. The worst part of being in the Homicide Unit was going to someone's home and telling the family their loved one has been killed. It takes a special approach and tact to go to someone's home and deliver that message. I knew from experience, when you drive up to someone's home, usually in the early morning hours, they probably already know something is wrong. On some notifications, the only thing we got to say was, "We are from the Homicide Unit" and no more had to be said. It never really got easier; I have seen some veteran homicide investigators get emotional when they deliver that horrible news. I always compared it to a military notification of a soldier's death, when several uniform military men walk up the path to a home. As a parent or spouse, you already know that they are there for one reason.

The next morning, Lenny and I went to the morgue, another part of working in the Homicide Unit that I never liked. I will never forget the very potent smell in the basement of the Medical Examiner's Office. It hits you, as soon as you get off the elevator in the basement. If you think about it, even now, it comes back to you. The morgue was a fairly new building and had the latest equipment available in forensic pathology. The building was supposed to have chemicals running through the ventilation system to offset the smell that came from the actual autopsy room, but it didn't work real well for me.

If you have never been to a morgue, it is hard to explain, especially one that averaged about thirty or forty bodies a day for autopsies. The morgue was a state facility and all deaths in Maryland that did not have a doctor's certificate that listed the cause of death, were taken to the morgue for an autopsy to determine the cause of death. As the morgue was located in Baltimore City, it was very convenient for our Homicide Unit, because it was downtown next to the University of Maryland Hospital.

Lenny and I walked into the autopsy room and even though it was a Saturday, the room had about thirty bodies on the tables ready for autopsies. Just to see all those bodies on tables waiting for the doctor to do his thing was about as eerie as it gets. The procedure in the autopsy room in the morning consisted of a real degenerate looking employee that was called a diener, who would open the skulls of the bodies on the tables. This guy looked like something out of a Frankenstein movie. He had the biggest head you ever wanted to see and by coincidence, he was the guy who opened all the dead heads. The diener uses an electric saw and just goes around the top of the head, until it is open and the brain is exposed. It makes a buzzing sound that if you close your eyes and think about it, you can hear it and recall the smell. Apparently he is good at it, because all my years in the Homicide Unit, he was always the man with the saw. He had another job and that was to open the chest of the deceased, so the doctor would not have to perform that nasty job. He was pretty good and he knew that on certain autopsies, he would not open the chest. His untrained cutting open of the chest might disturb the examination of gunshot or stab wounds. In certain cases, the doctor would open the chest, but the diener would be right there watching because he loved his job. So for the most part, when you walked into the autopsy room in the morning, you saw naked dead bodies on the tables with the top of the heads sawed open and the chest opened. It actually looked like a meat market.

Lenny and I found Deputy Medical Examiner, Doctor Martin, who had already completed the autopsy on our victim. Doctor Martin was a guy who seemed to enjoy what he did and that always amazed me. I wondered if he had failed a lot of subjects in medical school and decided to be a pathologist. Hell, you can't make mistakes when you're working on a dead person and they sure as hell ain't going to complain. Doctor Martin was a good guy and really enjoyed working with the homicide detectives. He would always call the office to follow up and see if we solved the murders when he performed the autopsy. This morning, he was in a good mood, don't know why, but he was and he told us that our victim, Doctor Thompson died from three deep stab wounds to the chest. He told us that one of the stab wounds pierced his aorta and was probably the fatal wound.

We were getting ready to leave when Doctor Martin called us over to the table he was working on and said, "Your victim had stab wounds that were inflicted in a downward motion." At first it really did not mean anything to me, but the doctor went on to say, "Because your victim is six feet, four inches tall, the person who stabbed him is most likely taller than your victim" and now this made a lot of sense. He went on to say that he had removed substance from the victim's stomach and he thinks that it is Chinese food. He feels that the victim had a meal approximately two or three hours prior to being stabbed. Doctor Martin stated that he would hold the substance removed from the victim's stomach and suggested that we visit Chinese restaurants in the area where the doctor lived. Visiting the restaurants could possibly tell us more about the approximate time of death. It was not much, but maybe we would find a Chinese restaurant that could tell us the doctor was eating there and had company.

Well, we left the morgue with a little bit more then we had, which wasn't much. We started to check the Chinese restaurants in the entire area around where the victim lived. I did not realize how many there were until we started to check. At each restaurant, we showed a photo of Doctor Thompson. I know that we must have visited at least ten or more Chinese restaurants and no one could remember the victim being in their place recently.

We did get a lead that the doctor frequented Pimlico Race Course. Pimlico is located in the area of Sinai Hospital and the information was that he was there the day of the murder. The information was called into the homicide office by a guy named, Curt Motton who had played baseball for the Baltimore Orioles. Mr. Motton reported that he was with the victim at the racetrack. He also said that Roy Hilton, a former football player with the Baltimore Colts was there with him and the doctor. Motton said the other guy was retired from playing professional football and hung around the racetrack all the time. When he said the name, Roy Hilton, I sure recognized that name. I had watched this guy play football for many years. Motton reported that the three of them were at the Pimlico Race Course all day and that Doctor Thompson had won a lot of money betting on the horses. Motton reported that when they left the track, they had a few drinks and Doctor Thompson and Hilton decided to drive to Charlestown Race Course. Charlestown was open in the evening hours and was located in West Virginia, just over the Maryland line. Motton stated that he went home and did not see either of them the rest of the day.

When Lenny and I talked about this new information, it hit us like a light bulb going off in your head. The ME Doctor had said that the stab wounds were in a downward motion on the victim. The victim was six feet, four inches tall and having been a Colts fan, I knew that Hilton was real tall. We got an old media guide from the Colts football team. Roy Hilton, who was a defensive end was listed as six feet, eight inches tall. Lenny and I just looked at each other and then that homicide smile came over both of us: the one that says, I think we got something here.

We decided to go back out to the victim's house and look it over a little better before the family sold it. We went in and it appeared that it had not been disturbed. The black fingerprint powder was everywhere and blood was still on the floor near the door. We decided to check every room to make sure we did not miss anything. After checking the bedroom and living room, we looked around in the kitchen. The cabinets were pretty much empty, with only some cereal, coffee, sugar, cookies, and a few other items; a total bachelor's pad. I opened the refrigerator and there wasn't much in it. There was some stale milk, some cheese, and a couple of diet sodas. On the bottom shelf, there were about ten small containers of diet fruit cocktail. I checked the dates on the fruit cocktail and they were fairly current. I am not sure why, but it hit me that after being told by the hospital staff that he watched his weight, he probably ate a lot of diet fruit cocktail. We decided to take the fruit cocktail with us on a crazy hunch. We took it down to the ME's office and asked Doctor Martin to check the fruit cocktail and see if that is what was in the victim's stomach and removed during the autopsy. We told Doctor Martin that we had checked every Chinese restaurant in the area and that nobody had seen the victim in their place. Doctor Martin took the fruit cocktail that we gave him and went downstairs and got the substance he had removed from the victim. He examined both of them and looked at us and said, "Gentlemen, I am sorry I sent you on a wild goose chase." He went on to say that he now felt that both of these substances appeared to be the same texture and it was in fact fruit cocktail and not Chinese food. We were not upset with the doctor, since he was only trying to help; if nothing else, we now knew where every Chinese restaurant was in the city. The only thing finding the fruit cocktail proved was that after being at the Pimlico Race Course, the victim may have come home and eaten the fruit cocktail before he left for Charlestown. But we really did not have any more information than we had before this discovery. He lived alone and no one could say if he came home first or not. Doctor Martin did confirm that with the substance in his stomach being in the condition is was, he most likely did not eat again after eating the fruit cocktail. The time table would fit in with the trip to Charlestown and the return trip to his home.

We decided our next best course of action was to take statements from Motton and Hilton. We called Mr. Motton and he was very cooperative. We went to his home and took a statement in which he outlined his time with the victim on the day of the murder. Motton also told us that Roy Hilton was not employed. He said that after playing football for the Colts and later playing for a couple of other teams, he appeared to be in financial trouble. Motton stated that when Hilton came to the track, he would cash winning tickets for others that were winners on the races. Motton stated that he would do that because of taxes. If you would cash a winning ticket at the track and it was substantial, they would record your social security number. Mr. Hilton, because he was not employed, would take ten percent of the winnings when he cashed the winning tickets. This process would allow the real winner to not have to pay taxes on their winnings.

Lenny and I had canvassed the entire neighborhood where the doctor lived and talked to his colleagues at the hospital. The only information we got, was that the doctor was well liked by everyone at the hospital. The strange thing was that no one really knew much about his activities away from the hospital. A couple of his friends did say that he talked about loving to go to the racetrack. We assumed that because it was so close to the hospital, he could do that frequently. The neighbors told us that they rarely saw the doctor and hardly ever saw anyone going in his home. We checked his financial status and he had no problems with his finances.

The hospital posted a reward on the local TV stations and with the Crime Stoppers program. A few leads came in, but they did not amount to anything. Lenny and I decided that our next course of action was to ask Mr. Hilton to come into the homicide office and give a statement. We actually did not know how to reach him and we asked Mr. Motton if he could contact Hilton and have him call our office. The next day, I received a call from Hilton and we discussed his acquaintance with Doctor Thompson and he was very frank and upfront. He seemed genuinely disturbed and upset about the murder of Doctor Thompson. I asked him to come to the homicide office and he agreed. That afternoon, I got a call from the front desk that a Mr. Hilton was in the building. I asked Lenny to go down and meet him and bring him back up to the office. Well, when he walked into our office, everyone just stopped what they were doing and just stared at Mr. Hilton. I don't know if they were staring because they actually knew he was a former player with the Baltimore Colts or just the mere size of this man. He was humongous and literally had to bend down a little to come in through the office doorway. He took a seat in our little waiting area in the Homicide Unit and the stares continued. I was thinking that we might have an autograph signing right here in the office.

Lenny and I went in the sergeant's room and talked to Sergeant Brander on how exactly should we handle the questioning of Mr. Hilton. Rod, in his ever sheepishly grin that he had, said, "Maybe Dick should take him in the room and smack him around a little." Well, we laughed at that, because even if we were to smack him around, we would probably need the entire Homicide Unit to get the job done. This guy had been throwing offensive lineman around in the NFL for at least ten years.

We had a little information on him and we knew that he had played for ten years in the NFL; most of the time with the Baltimore Colts. We knew that toward the end of his career, he was with a couple of other teams. We decided that I would take the statement from him, with Lenny sitting in the room for support. We went in the interview room and again, he literally had to bend down a little to get in the room. He sat across from us and now staring directly at him, I could really appreciate how big this guy was. I could only imagine how much it probably hurt when he hit those smaller offensive linemen during his playing days. I wanted to jump right into the statement, but I could not help but tell him that I was a huge Colts fan. I also told him it was a pleasure to meet him in person. Lenny looked at me like, what the hell are you doing; we have a murder of a prominent doctor to work on and you are sitting here star gazed at our possible suspect. I picked up on the look that Lenny gave me and started in with the interview and put my homicide game face on.

After getting all the upfront questions answered; like, personal information, where are you living, who do you live with and are you employed. I started to get into what I always referred to as the meat of the statement. I asked him to tell me about his relationship with Doctor Thompson. He sort of hesitated and said, "Before we start, do you think I had anything to do with his murder?" I looked him directly in the eyes and told him, "I will tell you what I tell everyone that comes to the homicide office. I appreciate you coming in to talk to us and until you give this statement, I have no inclinations either way if in fact you were involved in the murder of Doctor Thompson." I went on to say, "The mere fact that you have volunteered to come to our office to talk to us makes me feel like you do want us to find out who murdered a friend of yours."

I told him that, "Until we find who killed the doctor, everyone in Baltimore is a suspect." He seemed to be a little more at ease and said, "Before I came down here, I did call a lawyer, to get some advice." I told him that it was certainly up to him to have a lawyer present during the interview. I told him if that were the case, we could postpone this statement until such time that he could obtain an attorney. He took a big breath in that big body and said, "So far you guys seem to be treating me pretty good, so let's continue with the statement."

I started back with my line of questioning which was; tell me about your relationship with Doctor Thompson. He stated that he had met the doctor through some mutual friends and he mainly saw the doctor at the racetrack. He said that he had not been to the doctor's home, but has been to dinner with him. He said, he really enjoyed being around the doctor. He said that he last saw the doctor on the day he was murdered and they were at Pimlico with several friends. He said that the doctor was having a great day with betting the horses and he did cash a few winning tickets for the doctor. He said he would cash the winning tickets and get about ten percent of the payout for the ticket. Hilton said that they stayed at Pimlico until the last race. He said that the doctor decided that because he was having such a great day, he wanted to go to the Charlestown Race Course. He said that the doctor wanted to see if his winning ways would continue. Hilton said that he drove with him to Charlestown and they stayed at that track for about four races. They drove back to Baltimore and the doctor dropped him off at his car, which he left on the parking lot of the Pimlico Racecourse. Hilton said that he went home and that the doctor did give him about a hundred dollars. He said he did not want to take the money, but the doctor insisted. When they were at Pimlico, the doctor ran into a few people he knew, but Hilton said that he did not know them. He said that Doctor Thompson had a few drinks at Pimlico and a couple more at Charlestown, but he felt that the doctor was fine when he left him. He said that he went home and believes that the doctor did the same, because he talked about having to be at the hospital early the next day.

When I knew I was getting down toward the end of the statement, I asked Hilton if he knew who killed the doctor and he said that he did not. I asked him how much money, did he think Doctor Thompson had on him after winning at two racetracks. He said, "I am not real sure, but I would guess his winnings were about twelve hundred dollars." He went on to say, "I only say twelve hundred dollars, because on the way back home he was talking about how much he started with at Pimlico." Hilton paused for a minute, then said, "I think he mentioned he had about twelve hundred dollars, I could be wrong about that amount." I asked him if he knew of any enemies that the doctor had and he said, "To be truthful, I don't really know much about Doctor Thompson." Hilton said, "From what I have seen and heard, he is a good doctor and people like him." I asked him if he knew how the doctor was murdered and he said, "All I know is what I have read in the paper and heard on the news, I assume he was stabbed."

Usually when we get to the end of a statement, we really try to push some buttons to see if we can get them to say something that would lead us to continue with the questions, but with him I really got the impression that he was sincere with his answers. I have been wrong in the past, but for as big as Hilton was, he did not give the impression that he would murder someone. I told him we were almost finished, but I wanted to talk to Lenny outside the room and would be right back.

Lenny and I went back in the room with Rod and we kicked it around about the statement. I told Rod that even if he was involved with the murder, we had nothing else to go on. I told Rod that in my opinion, we should just thank him for coming in and if anything came up in the future, we could get him back in. Rod, who never did like anybody who came to the homicide office to leave, unless they were in handcuffs and charged with murder, looked at me and said, "I really do think you should go back in there and smack his ass around and get a confession." I told Rod, "If anyone is going in there and smack this guy around, I want to make some wagers and my money is on the big guy."

Rod agreed with me and I went back in the room and had a little chat with Hilton. He seemed a lot calmer now that he was not giving a formal statement, maybe now was the time to ask for his autograph. He talked about having some money problems, but was now getting things back in order. He said that if he heard anything in his circle of friends about the murder, he would give me a call. I thanked him and when he got up, he kept getting up and again it was amazing how big this guy was. His handshake was putting a hurtin on this hundred and fifty pound little white boy tennis player.

Well, Lenny and I worked this case diligently for about one month straight, as much as we could, because in Baltimore City the murders just keep coming. We worked every tip we received and the reward that was posted by the hospital got up to about twenty thousand dollars. Usually when rewards are out there in a murder investigation, you get some good leads, but in this case, there was nothing good.

I am not sure who murdered Doctor Thompson, but maybe the ME's office was wrong about the angle of the stab wounds, since he was wrong about what was in the doctor's stomach. Maybe it was a random robbery where the doctor answered the door and was overwhelmed by his attacker. Maybe it was a female acquaintance and something went wrong or she felt jilted by the doctor. Maybe he was drinking and slipped and fell on the knife...three times...who the hell knows.

I do know that if you are a doctor in Baltimore and you get murdered, you probably don't want me to investigate it. As you have read in these short stories, my record with investigating doctor murders is not that good. I did have some other murder cases involving doctors and they were solved, so why in the hell am I writing about the unsolved ones. I guess, as the old homicide mentality comes out in us retired guys, we want to share the unsolved murders, with the thought that someone reading these stories will come forward with information to break these murders.

BABIES ARE NOT EXEMPT FROM MURDER

I have come to realize that working homicides for a period of time makes you a little jaded in your thinking about society. It's almost inevitable that over the years working murders, you become hard. This would be especially true in a city that averages about three hundred murders a year. The murders that I could not stomach doing my years in the Homicide Unit, were the senseless murders of little children and especially babies. I have handled murders of babies that would make you sick, especially if you had to sit in the same room with the person responsible and take their statements.

I had an investigation involving a lady, I don't even like to call her a lady, who lived in the Cherry Hill section of the city. This no good bitch placed a three month old baby in her microwave and turned it on. Without going into details, you can imagine what happened and if you can't, I will tell you that the baby cooked and literally exploded in the microwave. I don't want to go on much more with this story. The lady gave me a statement, in which she said that the baby was the devil. She said that she was told by evil spirits, which were always in her head to kill the baby. The saddest part is that when this sick bastard went to court, her attorney pled her guilty by reason of insanity and he was backed up by several doctors. She was sent to a mental institution and she might be out on the street today. Usually, they only keep you until they feel you can go back into society. Let's think about this for a minute, who makes that decision and what the fuck are they thinking about, if they let a son of a bitch like her back in society. If I had my way, she would put in the biggest microwave I could find and her fat ass thrown out on the highway for the buzzards to feast on.

I really don't enjoy talking about them, but let me tell you about another murder of a baby that I investigated. I worked this baby killing with one of the best homicide detectives in the unit, Furrie Cousins. Furrie had worked homicides for over twenty years. He was a master at interviewing and talking to people. It seemed like he knew everyone on the west side of town. The original story on this baby's death, as reported to the uniform police officer, was that the baby had died in an apartment in west Baltimore. When the mother was finally found, she said she did not know anything about the baby's death. The baby was a boy about ten months old and was found in a clothes closet by a neighbor of the mother, who was visiting and called the police.

The patrol officers arrived at the apartment before the mother had returned home and called for an ambulance. The ambulance was called as a formality and they pronounced the baby dead on the scene. The ambulance crew told the officer that the baby was extremely emaciated. The child was covered with feces. The ambulance crew told the police officer that in their opinion the baby may have been dead for a period of time.

Furrie and I were called to the apartment, which was in a real bad neighborhood in west Baltimore. I can't begin to describe this apartment, but if you can imagine the worst conditions possible, then this is what the apartment looked like. There were liquor bottles, beer bottles, and drug paraphernalia all around the apartment. There was food caked on the stove and "Red men" running all over the walls in the kitchen. If you have never heard about "Red men", they were medium size roaches. These roaches were apparently a rare species of roaches, because I had only seen them in west Baltimore. I had seen roaches when I grew up in the city, but our roaches were black. The inside of the closet where the baby was found was something I will never forget. Along with the fecal matter, roaches, and the smell; there were pieces of moldy bread, chicken bones, empty milk cartons, and just a bunch of junk. The baby's body was photographed and removed from the closet and taken to the Medical Examiner's Office for an autopsy. If you have never seen an autopsy of a small baby, it is something that will stay with you your entire life.

The conditions in that apartment were the worst that Furrie said he had seen in his twenty years on the job. When you were standing in this apartment, you felt as if you were in the poorest country in the world. But we were not; we were in probably the richest. I don't think that the people living in those conditions could be human. After seeing the body of that baby, I knew that we were dealing with people that were worse than animals.

We left the apartment and threw our plastic jumpsuits in the first trashcan we saw. In that neighborhood, a trash can is hard to find. We were driving back to the Homicide Unit, when I almost made the mistake of asking Furrie if wanted to stop and get something to eat, but I caught myself. Shortly after we left the apartment, the patrol officers spotted the mother walking in the neighborhood. They transported her down to the homicide office. She was placed in the interview room. I was surprised that she was fairly well dressed and appeared to be clean. We decided that we would both go in the interview room and Furrie would be the lead guy. I would be there for support or just to smack the shit out of this bitch, when she got to the part where she said she loved her baby.

Furrie was a real professional, he had done this for twenty years and always kept his cool. I was thinking that this would be the one that would put him over the top. Before we went in the room, Furrie put his arm around me and said, "I know how you feel, but no matter how we feel about this baby's death, we need to get a statement from this bitch." He also said, "We need to get her to tell us what led to this baby's death and then we will charge her with murder." I can tell you that this was probably the nastiest bitch I have ever talked to in my police days. She just sat there and every question Furrie asked, even the simple ones like, what is your name, she would say, "I ain't did nothing and I want to get the fuck out of this place." Well, even mild mannered Furrie was having enough of this bitch and he got a little loud with her. She started to answer some questions. Her story was that she had this baby with an old boyfriend. Basically, the new boyfriend did not want anything to do with the baby. She said that when she was with her new boyfriend, she would put the baby in the closet and take him out after the boyfriend left the apartment. She said that she noticed lately that the baby was getting sick. She said he was throwing up and messing himself. She said she didn't know what to do. I didn't jump in the conversation, but I knew that was a lie. When the baby was found, he did not have a diaper on and we did not see any in the apartment. She went on to say that she periodically would put some food in the closet with the baby; such as, bread, some chicken, and milk. Furrie went on with the interview and I could see it was getting to him and I sure as hell knew it had already gotten to me.

Well, just when we had thought we heard it all, she had the balls to say, "I'm hungry, do you think you can get me something to eat?" I can still to this day visualize the expression on Furrie's face. He reached over the interview table and grabbed her by her shirt. He said, "You sorry fuckin piece of shit, you starved your baby to death and you want me to get you some food." He released his grasp and she fell back in the chair. She started calling us every name in the book. Furrie got up and said, "I have had it with this bitch." Furrie was the senior man, so he asked me to finish the statement. I had never seen him like that before and as he left the room; I could see that he was visibly upset.

I finished the statement and she was charged with the murder of the baby. I think it may have been one of the hardest statements to take in my career. I did everything I could to stay calm, because there was no one left to take the statement; Furrie was not talking to this piece of trash anymore. When I was done, I told her that she would be charged with the murder of the baby and she didn't seem to be fazed. She just looked at me and said, "I didn't kill the fuckin baby." I think that statement alone if read in the proper context in a court room, would be the nail in this bitch's coffin. We usually did get some food for suspects that were going to be in the homicide office for a long period of time. I can guarantee you, she did not get any food from us, she may have gotten it at the jail.

The next morning, the ME Doctor determined that the baby did in fact die from starvation. How they ever performed an autopsy on that tiny baby, I will never know.

I remember at the trial, Furrie was testifying and he was damn good at it. He laid it on heavy for the jury. He made sure he told them the part about asking for food during the interview. At that point in his testimony, the defense attorney jumped up and said, "Detective Cousins, isn't it a fact that when she asked for some food, you grabbed her by the throat?" I was thinking, damn is the jury going to take this as some sort of brutality or a threat to get the confession. Furrie was good on the stand, he looked directly at the jury and said, "Yes, that is true, sir. I was only thinking of that poor baby when she said that and for a moment, I lost my cool." The silence in the courtroom seemed like it lasted for minutes, but it was probably seconds. The judge spoke up and said, "Detective, I can understand how you must have felt. I would have done the same thing." Well, the defense attorney was furious and told the jury that the only reason she gave us a statement, was because she was threatened. The jury was made up mostly of black females. As the testimony went on from Furrie and then the ME Doctor, you could see the jurors cringing on every word.

I am glad to say that she was found guilty and sentenced to thirty years in jail. But as I write this, I bet she is just as plump as can be, because she is now getting three square meals a day and a roof over her head; she could give a shit about the death of that baby.

CONTRACT MURDER ON ONE OF OUR OWN

I handled a contract murder on a Baltimore City Police Officer that was really interesting. When it is one of your own, you get more attached to the investigation. The cop worked in the Northern District and had about five years on the job. He walked a foot patrol post in a high crime neighborhood around Greenmount Avenue and Twenty-Fifth Street.

The short story is that when the police officer left his home at night to go to work on the midnight shift, he no sooner would shut the door that his wife would be heading out to the bars. I don't know how long this was going on, but one night his wife was in a bar in Fells Point. Fells Point is close to the Baltimore Inner Harbor and has many watering holes. After some drinks, she told a guy she was with, her husband was a cop. She told him she would really benefit financially if her husband would be killed in the line of duty. She asked the guy if knew anyone that would kill her husband. The guy she was talking to was working as an undercover informant for the Drug Unit in the police department. This informant later called the supervisor of the Drug Unit and told him the story.

We got involved in the investigation, because we handled contract murders. This was more than just a contract murder, it was one of us. We decided to have one of our homicide detectives go with the drug informant to the bar. We wanted to see if the officer's wife would solicit him to kill her husband. We decided that Detective Lenny Willis would be perfect to play the part of a hit man. Lenny was street smart; we were confident that he could dress and play the part perfect. We hooked Lenny up with the drug informant. We also placed a recording device on Lenny, so that we could get the conversation at the bar on tape. With the conversation recorded, it would make the eventual arrest very simple.

We had detectives watch her house. They saw her husband leave for work around 10:30 PM. He was heading for his district for 11:30 PM roll call. While we were planning this investigation, we decided that we would not tell the police officer what his wife was planning. We decided it was best to wait until we got a recording and knew that she was serious. Shortly after the officer left his house, the detectives watching the house saw the wife leave. The detectives in an unmarked car followed her to Fells Point. We were notified she was on the move and Lenny and the informant headed for the bar. We wanted the informant to engage in conversation with her. The informant did not know that Lenny was wearing a wire; we wanted the conversation to be genuine. The informant introduced Lenny to her as being from Philadelphia. Lenny asked her what she wanted done and how much was she willing to pay. Well, she did not pull any punches; she stated loud and clear on the recording, "I want my husband killed." She said, "If he is killed, I will get a hundred thousand dollars from the federal government and his full police salary for the rest of my life." Lenny did not have to do much talking. She told him that she would give him five thousand dollars up front money and ten thousand dollars when the job was done. She talked about how her husband was always talking about how bad the neighborhood was that he patrolled. She talked about how she could not stand him anymore and she would be set for life with him out of the picture. We were outside the bar in a van and we could hear the conversation and it was sickening to hear her talk about her husband who was one of us. Lenny was doing a great job, but I am sure he was feeling the pain for this bitch's husband. Lenny did not have to talk much, but when he did, he sounded like a real hit man.

We decided that we would make the arrest when we knew that we had the conversation clearly on the tape. Lenny was instructed to leave the bar and ask her to meet him later to get the upfront money. We decided that we would take down all three of them, to give the appearance that the informant and Lenny were not on our side. We wanted her to think that we would be talking to the drug informant and the hit man about the soliciting to commit murder. The tape recording was very clear and legible, which was a surprise. We have had occasions where sometimes in structures like bars, the recording did not come through very good. Everything went perfect on this case and we had all we needed to move forward with the arrest.

About one hour later, she left the bar with some guy. When they got into a car, we approached the car and identified ourselves and arrested her. We took her down to the Homicide Unit. The shift lieutenant decided that we needed to get her husband off the street, just in case she had made arrangements with someone else to do the job. The officer was called into his station by his supervisor and before they told him what was happening, they took his gun from him. The officer was transported to the Homicide Unit and without letting him see his wife; we took a statement from him. The officer, throughout the statement, denied that he had any idea that his wife was leaving the house late at night after he went to work. As a matter of fact, this officer told us that he did not believe what we were telling him and it must be a misunderstanding. He went on to say, "Maybe someone is lying about my wife." I told the officer that I could understand how he felt, but we knew what we were talking about and that we have a tape recording of his wife hiring someone to kill him. As weird as it might sound, this officer still insisted that we were wrong and that his wife would not do anything like that. I decided that it was time to play the recording for him. The officer asked if he could see his wife. I told him that this was now a criminal investigation and although he was one of us, we had to do things by the book. I told him that he could not see his wife at this time. He seemed pissed that we were going by the book. I knew that one day down the road, this would be in criminal court and I wanted to make sure we did it right.

I asked two homicide detectives to come in the room and be there when I played the tape. I did not know if this guy would go off or not, he certainly had every reason to. I played the tape and even though it was recorded in a bar, it was remarkably clear. The officer slid his chair up close to the table so he could hear. When it got to the part where she said she wanted him killed and she would pay money to have it done, he made a statement that shocked me and the detectives in the room. He said, "It can't be true, she don't have that kind of money." I was expecting him to break the table and chairs, punch the walls, and scream about how he could not believe she would do this to him, but he did not.

When the tape was finished, he asked if this was all a joke and that really surprised me. Did he think we were going to take our valuable time in the Homicide Unit and play a nasty fuckin joke on a fellow police officer? I asked him why he did not believe us. He just sat there with his head in his hands and the tears started to come. I don't know why it took so long, but he finally got it. I knew there was nothing I could say at this point to make him feel better. I felt bad for him, but I felt good that we intercepted that conversation and acted quickly. Who knows, if we did not get the information from the informant, we might be investigating his murder.

I asked the two detectives to leave the room. I told him that I can only imagine what he was going through. He stood up and punched the wall. He composed himself a little and asked if he could hear the tape again. I told him it would probably not do him any good to hear it again, but he insisted. I played the tape and he just put his head in his hands again and said, "Why would she do this to me? I love that woman." He asked again if he could see her and I told him that she had been drinking and was arrested in a car with another man. I did not think that it would be wise for us to allow him to see his wife. Hell, we could have a murder right in the homicide office. We made arrangements for him to be driven home and his wife was charged with soliciting to commit murder.

During the trial, she took the stand on her own behalf and had a rosary around her neck. She looked a whole lot better than she did that night in Fells Point. She looked like a mother with two kids, as she sat in court holding a Bible. She told the judge that she had been going through a rough time during that period. She said she was using drugs and hanging with some bad people. She told the judge that she really did not want her husband killed. She also told the judge that since this had happened, she made bail, and they are living together. She said she feels that they can work it out and stay married. Well, needless to say, the judge and the jury were astounded at what she said. They had already heard the tape that was recorded in the bar. Her husband actually took the stand in her defense and talked about what a wonderful wife and mother she was. He testified that he feels she just made a terrible mistake and asked that she not be sent to prison.

The judge instructed the jury to consider all the facts and especially the recorded conversation. The judge informed the jury that they should not let the fact that her husband is a police officer, influence their decision. The judge stated that a crime had been committed and even if her husband wanted to forgive her, it did not diminish the seriousness of the case.

The jury was deliberating for about two hours and when they returned, they informed the judge that they had reached a unanimous verdict. The judge asked her to stand and he told her that the jury had found her guilty as charged. The defense attorney, apparently feeling that he would get a light sentence for this client from the judge, stated that they were prepared for sentencing. The judge went on talking for about ten minutes. He actually looked at the police officer and asked him to come to the front of the courtroom. He told him that had it not been for these detectives, you might not be here in this courtroom today. He said that he is obligated because of the abundance of evidence to send his wife to prison for a long time. He looked directly at the officer's wife and sentenced her to twenty years in prison.

I don't know this as a fact, but we have been told that her husband often visited her in prison. We also found out that he paid the defense attorney for the trial and to file an appeal. We learned later, that after a few years in prison, her sentence was reduced to ten years. I am only guessing, but they may very well be back together today, as one happy little family. I don't know about you, but my thinking with this situation is that there ain't any second chances. She took her shot and fucked it up. I know that if I heard a tape recording with my wife's voice and she said, "I want my husband killed," that would probably be enough for me to pack my shit and hit the road.

Happy Homicide Holidays

Let me tell you how we spent some holidays in the Homicide Unit. A couple of times during the year that come to mind when I worked homicides were Christmas and New Years. On Christmas, we worked the night shift with just a few detectives. I can remember the Jewish community coming to the Homicide Unit. They would come to the office, bringing corned beef sandwiches and other Jewish delicacies. They would usually get to the office around 9 PM on Christmas Eve and they would answer our phones. This kind gesture would allow some detectives to go home and be with their families.

Murder did not take a rest during the Christmas holidays; people continued to be murdered in Baltimore. We were called out on a murder one Christmas Eve about 10:30 PM to the Cherry Hill section of south Baltimore. We went to a house which was in a very low income and high crime area. The first thing we saw was a black guy lying under the Christmas tree with a big knife in his chest. I can remember that the house was extremely hot, as lots of people that lived in the projects would leave their oven running with the door open and the regular house heat blasting away.

I was out on this murder with veteran Detective John Hess. I can remember when we walked in the house, John looked at me and we could hardly control our laughter. I know that you are thinking what a disrespectful bunch of assholes these guys are, but you had to be there to appreciate it. The dead guy was literally under the Christmas tree with the knife in his chest. The Christmas gifts were wrapped and under the tree with the dead guy. People were sitting around drinking beer as if nothing had happened. It was a small house and with all that was going on, it got to be real crowded in the living room. I told the uniform officer to call again and see when the morgue wagon would get there. I wanted to get that dead body out of the house and away from the children. There were several kids in the house and I kid you not, when I tell you they were running around playing, as if nothing had happened. There were several adults in the house. Although this was a crime ridden neighborhood, this dead body was in their house; not on the street where they could just walk by and ignore it. Because no one else had the common decency to do it, I took an afghan off the couch and put it over the dead guy. I left the knife in his chest, so that the Medical Examiner could remove it at the morgue, which was normal procedure. I was wondering why no one in the house took the knife out of his chest. When it happened, did they try to take it out or just say, "Fuck it, he's history, keep wrapping the presents?"

I told the oldest female who apparently was a grandmother to take the kids upstairs. It was late on Christmas Eve, they should probably go to sleep or Santa might not stop at their house; maybe they thought we were Santa. What a fuckin crime that I have to tell adults to remove kids from the living room where a man is under a tree with a knife in his chest. He was about as dead as you can get; were they waiting for him to pop up and say, "Merry fuckin Christmas."

Here I am on Christmas Eve, in this roach infested, overheated, piece of shit house in Cherry Hill; my two kids are at home in bed and all excited about Santa coming. I am standing in a room where the temperature is about one hundred and fifty degrees, trying to talk about Christmas to kids that probably watched a murder.

It was one of the weirdest feelings I have ever had on a homicide scene. I did not even know these people. I was pissed that they would allow small children to stay in a room with a dead man with a big knife still in his chest. I was thinking, would every Christmas in the future for these kids, bring back this memory? Would they wake up in the morning, wondering where the nice man that was sleeping under the tree got to? Did anyone in that house, really give a shit how it affected those kids? Would Santa come down the chimney, see the dead man and get the fuck out of the neighborhood as fast as Rudolph can move the sled? As you can tell, I had a lot of questions. My main question was who put the knife in sleepy man's chest?

When the kids were finally out of the room, we moved forward with our investigation. I really did hope the kids were dreaming about what they were getting for Christmas. I went in the kitchen and asked what had happened and the weirdness continued. I waited for a reasonable answer, but no one spoke up. Nobody said anything and now I am really pissed. I said, "Listen folks and listen good, in case you can't see it or just want to ignore it, there is a dead man under your Christmas tree. He is in your living room and as I see he is not gift wrapped, I am assuming that he was not put there by a cruel fuckin Santa." I said, "I will ask one more time about what happened; then everyone will be spending the rest of Christmas Eve and most of Christmas down at the Homicide Unit." I could tell from the looks on the faces around the room that they knew what happened. It was a matter of who was going to say something first. After a few minutes, an elderly man who was apparently a grandfather said, "We was all sittin around. The door opened and this guy came stumbling in. He fell under our tree and that's all I knows." I looked at John and probably at the same time, we said, "Get your fuckin coats on, we are going to the Homicide Unit." I think this hit home with the kids' mother, who magically realized that we were not buying that bullshit story. She said, "I ain't spending no fuckin Christmas in the poo-lice department, I'll tell you what happened."

I took her to the side in a small bedroom. She told me that the guy under the tree was in their house earlier in the evening. She said he had been drinking pretty good. She said, "He left out and came back and was arguing and trying to fight with my friend." She went on to say, "They got into a big fight and my friend got a knife from the kitchen and stabbed the guy in the chest and ran out of the house." She told me she knew the name of the guy and where he lived. She said she would go down to the Homicide Unit and the rest of the family did not need to go. Well, we overruled her on that and took most of the family to our office. We left the grandmother with the children. We got statements and identified the guy who did the stabbing. He was later arrested that morning and charged with murder.

When I got home from work that Christmas morning, my wife and kids were still sleeping. I sat in the living room looking at the tree and it was more beautiful than ever. The best part was that there was no one under the tree with a knife in his chest. I sat there real quiet, enjoying my tree, until I heard the kids moving around upstairs. I went and got them and told them that Santa sure was good to them this Christmas.

I watched as they came down and the sight of all the presents just overwhelmed them. They did what all kids do; they commenced to just rip into the packages and it was great. I totally concentrated on my kids that Christmas morning. I could not help but think of those kids in Cherry Hill and what they had gone through. I hoped that somehow they would get through it and have a good Christmas. I was wondering, did they come down in the morning and ask where that man with the knife in his chest got to. Maybe they thought he got caught trying to steal the presents; after all, they did live in Cherry Hill.

DECK THE HALLS IN THE HOMICIDE UNIT

On Christmas in the Homicide Unit, we always had a decorated tree with the lights, the bulbs, the tinsel, and we usually added a little something that most Christmas trees did not have. We hung photos of murder victims on the tree. One Christmas someone actually put a small knife in the chest of one of the wise men. I think that even upset a few of the more decent Christian members of the unit. The captain did not appreciate it either. At the bottom of the tree, next to the manger scene, we would put some bullets, handcuffs, a blackjack, and a nightstick. On that wise man with the knife in his chest, we actually had some red nail polish to make it look real. I almost forgot about Saint Joseph who would normally be kneeling around the manger. On our scene, he was hanging on a limb with a rope around his neck. I know you are thinking we were some sick bastards and you could very well be correct. It was all in fun, maybe a morbid kind of fun, but nevertheless it was our fun.

It was hilarious to watch the visitors to the office; they would walk by the tree and then perform the biggest double take you ever saw. The first year that I watched the tree being decorated, I thought at first they were kidding. The guys that did it were serious, later I was one of them. I mean we actually were picky on what photos would go on the tree. We were precise with the position of the knives and the rope around Saint Joseph had to be the right knot. I don't think the captain liked all the attention that the tree got. He never told us to take it down. I think one year, word got up to the police commissioner about the tree in the Homicide Unit and we had to clean it up a little.

I know that we did not mean any disrespect with decorating the tree that way. I attribute it to just some idle time before the phone rang.

214

New Year's Eve Murder Lottery

New Year's Eve was another night that was interesting in the Homicide Unit. We always started a pool or lottery to see who could pick the exact time of the New Year when the first murder would occur in Charm City. The money was collected and I think it was five dollars from each person who participated in the pool. I can remember, some years the winnings got up to over two hundred dollars. The money got even bigger over the years, because we included some outsiders; like the crime laboratory and detectives in other units on the floor.

In the pool, you had to be very precise on your guess. I mean it had to be damn near the exact time of death. If someone got shot and did not die until later at the hospital, we had to check with the doctor and see what the exact time of death was. I can tell you that it usually did not take long into the New Year before someone was a winner at the expense of someone being a loser. I remember one year, the winner was Augie Buchheit. I think he won about two hundred and twenty dollars. The first confirmed murder that year was eleven minutes after midnight, not sure why it took so long.

We were real serious about this pool and guys that did not win, would check with the hospitals the next day. They wanted to make sure no cheating was going on. The detective who was on the crime scene of the first murder of the year, did what he had to do at the crime scene, the next thing he did was to call the winning detective. We would call guys at home to let them know they won and how much was in the pool. Again, I guess you think this is nasty shit, but no one was hurt by us having a pool on the first murder. It was not like we were going out and killing someone just to win the money, or at least I don't think that ever happened.

Arson Unit – Burn Baby Burn – 1983

After almost ten years in the Homicide Unit as a detective and a detective sergeant, I felt it was time to move on. The opportunity came in 1983 when the sergeant in charge of the Arson Unit made it known that he was retiring. I never thought I would want to leave the Homicide Unit. I knew that I had given it everything I had. The time at work was starting to get to me. When you get thoughts about leaving a unit, it must be time to go. It was not that I was tired of investigating homicides, because I was not. I just wanted to get involved with some other type of investigation that would suit me better in a second career when I retired. I knew from friends that had already retired, that when you retire from police work, not too many insurance companies want to hire someone that investigated murders. They would prefer someone who worked in auto theft, white collar fraud, or fire investigation.

I got word that the sergeant in charge of the Arson Unit, Paul Liou, was thinking about retiring. I knew that there would be a lot of interest from other sergeants in the department to get that job. The Arson Unit was one of the few units in the Detective Division where the supervisor was issued an unmarked police vehicle to take home. I also knew that the arson supervisor received extensive training in fires and bombings. The Arson Unit assignment very much interested me and hopefully could lead to a job in the insurance industry when I retired.

In 1983, I had about eighteen years on the job. I knew that I could retire in another seven years or sooner if they lowered the retirement age and years of service. If I could get the Arson Unit position, it would not only provide me with a great opportunity to have in retirement, it would rekindle the sparks: pardon the pun. I was feeling a little burned out in the Homicide Unit, pardon the pun again. By feeling burned out, I mean that the longer you are in the Homicide Unit and all you see day in and day out is murder; you get a morbid and nasty slant on life. I knew that a change of scenery would do me good. The change would be good, not only in my professional life, but also in my personal life.

I knew the arson sergeant pretty well, as I had worked a few arson homicides with his unit over the years. Paul Liou was a good sergeant and he loved the Arson Unit. He was divorced and had recently met someone who lived in Florida. The word was out that he would be retiring soon and moving to Florida. I knew that just talking to Paul would not land me the Arson Unit job. I decided that out of respect for him, I would talk to him before I approached anyone in the command staff.

I met Paul for a drink after work one day. After some small talk about his divorce and his new girlfriend, I got right to the point. I told him that I was interested in taking his place in the Arson Unit. Paul was a good guy and told me that several other sergeants in the department had already approached him about the job. He said he would tell me exactly what he told them. He at first told me that he thought I would do very well in the Arson Unit, because of my background in the Homicide Unit. He also told me that he had heard nothing but good things about me. He said that he might have some say in who gets the job, but if I knew any bosses in the command staff, I should start asking them to talk to the police commissioner on my behalf.

We had some more drinks and I thanked Paul for the information and he wished me well. I started to think about who I would approach to try and get the Arson Unit. I made a list of who I would go to and discuss the position. I had a few people on the list, but as important as this was, I needed to get to the boss who could get it done. I knew the Chief of the Fire Department at the time, Pete O'Connor and that seemed like a good place to start. I knew that the supervisor of the Arson Unit had to deal directly with the Chief of the Fire Department on various issues. I knew Pete from being at happy hours and some affairs that he attended over the years. I knew that he was a good Irishman and we had talked about the Irish neighborhood that I grew up in. We had shared a few stories about people he knew from that great Irish neighborhood, the "Tenth Ward." I also knew that Pete frequented a bar in the Fells Point section of the city after he got off of work. I decided the best place to discuss this with Pete would be his favorite hangout, the bar with a great name, "The Horse You Road In On."

I decided to go to the bar and hopefully Pete would be there. I figured that over a few beers, I could pitch myself to him for the arson job. Well, it did not take long to run into Pete. It was my first try and it appeared that he had been in the bar for quite awhile. I knew this was good, because sometimes things get done when one of the participants is feeling pretty good after a few drinks. I approached Pete and he was alone. He seemed pleased to meet me and asked me to join him for a drink. We talked about the old neighborhood. We also talked about the fire department and the police department. I can tell you without any doubt, Pete O'Connor was the most well liked fire chief the city ever had. Pete was a real gentlemen: he loved his men and they could go to him with any problems they had. That was evident as the bar started to get crowded and most of the patrons were firemen. I knew that if I did not take my shot, I would lose him to his firemen buddies. The guys were all trying to buy him drinks, so I had to move fast. I asked him if I could discuss something with him and he said, "Sure, but let's get some drinks first. If you are going to ask me something that will require me to do some thinking, I think best with a few beers in me." I figured this was good and I was actually prepared to buy him all the beers he needed. I knew that I might have to stay with him as long as it took to get his help in getting the Arson Unit job.

I did not pull any punches and came right out with it. I said, "Pete I have known you a long time. I respect you as a man and also as the chief of the fire department." Pete looked at me with those big green Irish eyes and said, "If you know me that well, then you should also know that you don't have to beat around the bush. What do you need?" Well, we got another beer and I told him that the sergeant in the Arson Unit was retiring and I wanted to get that job. After he guzzled his beer and had a good Irish belch, he looked at me, grabbed my hand, and said, "Dick, you got the job."

Well, at first I thought it was the beer talking, but he pulled out a pen and some paper and asked for my home phone number. I asked how he was going to make it happen. He seemed a little annoyed with me and said, "Hey Irishman, you asked me to do it and I said I would. Leave the rest to me and drink your beer, the night is young."

I made sure that night that I did not get drunk and I slipped out of the bar after I thanked Pete. I could see that it was going to be one of those nights for Pete and his firemen. I was excited that I met with him. I knew that although he was a heavy drinker, he was a very sincere man and he would do it if he could. My dilemma after talking to Pete, was do I now try to talk to someone high up in the police department or just leave it to Pete?

At that time in my career, I knew a lot of the bosses in the police department. It would be no problem approaching them, but sometimes when you approach too many people, it can backfire on you. I decided that I would approach one person in the command staff that I had the utmost respect for, Leon Tomlin. Leon was a colonel in the department and one of the finest men I had ever known. He was also one of the most honest people you would ever want to know. I felt comfortable about approaching Leon. I would tell him about talking with Pete O'Connor, because Leon also knew Pete very well. I met with Leon and told him the same thing that I had told Pete; I want the arson unit job. Leon said that I need not worry and he would talk to the police commissioner. So between Pete and Leon speaking up for me, I felt real good about getting the position.

I got called into the chief of detectives' office about two weeks later and I was told that I would get the Arson Unit position. When I knew for sure I was getting the job in the Arson Unit, I knew I had to go in and tell the Homicide Unit captain so there would not be any hard feelings. I told him and he was fine with it and wished me well. He thanked me for my years in the Homicide Unit. About two weeks later, I moved over from the Homicide Unit into the Arson Unit. I did not have to physically move that far. The Arson Unit office was located down the hall on the same floor with the Homicide Unit.

When I started in the Arson Unit, I wanted to learn all I could about fire investigation. The detectives assigned to that unit were very experienced and I wanted to be on par with them as soon as possible. I also decided that I would need to spend some time at the fire department as I would be working real close with them. My first visit to the fire department was to thank Chief

O'Connor. Without his help, I probably would not have gotten the job. I then decided to visit the Fire Investigation Bureau which consisted of fire investigators who held the rank of captain. Most of them had over twenty years experience in the fire department. I would be working very close with them and I needed to learn as much as I could, as fast as I could.

After a few months in the Arson Unit, I applied to go to the National Fire Academy which is located in Emittsburg, Maryland. The National Fire Academy was the top training facility for fire investigation in the country. I was in a hurry to learn, so I also applied to go to the Federal Law Enforcement Training Center in Georgia. I was somewhat surprised that the department approved both schools for me. I was now a little apprehensive about going, because I was brand new at this. I knew that fire investigation involved some in-depth training in fire science, along with the actual fire scene investigation.

After I completed these schools, I felt a little better about fire investigation. I was more comfortable when I was out on the fire scenes with the much experienced fire captains. I became very good friends with one particular fire investigator, Captain Gene Thomen or as everyone called him, "Pops" Thomen. Pops was a great guy and we hit it off right from the start. I knew that if I hung around him, I would learn the street smarts about investigating fires. I can remember being out on fires with Pops and he showed me things about fire scenes that were never really covered in the formal schools. We would also meet after work and have a drink and we would talk about fires. I owed a lot to him, as I gradually became a fairly decent fire investigator.

I was the supervisor in the unit, but I enjoyed working on fires so much, that I would take turns in the rotation when we got called out to a fire scene. The only downside to getting called out on fires was that most of the time the call came either very late at night or in the early morning hours. I can remember on some cold winter nights, the phone would ring and I knew what it meant. It was the fire department dispatcher and the message was, "Sergeant Ellwood, this is Lieutenant Casmire, fire department dispatcher, they need you on a fatal fire." I would get the address and put on warm clothes, which I kept close by in the bedroom. I would get in my police vehicle and I just loved to wake up the neighbors, as I hit the siren when I pulled out from my development. My wife hated when I would do that, but I loved it. The vehicle

I had was neat. It had a police radio, a fire department radio, a public address system, and my favorite part, the siren.

I loved going on fire scenes with my mentor, Pops. He would do some things on fire scenes that absolutely amazed me and some of them were pretty dangerous. It seemed like he had been doing it so long that the danger part did not even faze him. I saw him one time on a church fire that had destroyed the church and just being inside was dangerous. Pops was just walking along and I was following him, when all of sudden Pops was gone. He had fallen through the floor all the way to the basement. As you can imagine, I was scared to death and was calling for help. Just then, I heard Pops holler up to me that he was all right. I went down the basement with a few firemen and we helped him out of the building. When he got outside, the other guys were kidding him that this was a great fall and that he could now retire on a medical disability. Pops just laughed and brushed himself off. He did have a small gash in his leg. He refused any treatment, which I knew he would and we continued with the investigation.

I learned so much from Pops on the fire scene, but I also learned a lot from him when we would meet at the bar to have a few drinks. He was a few years older than me and had that weathered face from all the cold nights on the fire scene. He was very smart and by that I mean he was loaded with common sense, which I admired in people. I respected his opinion on lots of things that were going on in my life at that time.

Pops retired from the fire department and we had a great party. I think that is when I realized how many friends he had and how he must have touched their lives also. Sadly to say, a short time after Pops retired, he was diagnosed with cancer and although he fought the good fight, he passed away. After his death, I missed him a lot and being out on the fire scenes was never the same without his guidance and especially his laughter. I will never forget him and I am sure he is looking out for his buddies up in that big firehouse in the sky.

A FAMILY WIPED OUT IN ONE FIRE

Working in the Arson Unit, you see some fire scenes that are etched in your memory forever, especially the fire fatalities. I have been on many fire fatalities, but the one I will remember the most was a fire in the 2700 block of Tivoly Avenue. Nine people died in the fire. I arrived on the fire scene after responding from my home, siren blasting. The fire was almost under control when I got there. I talked to Battalion Chief Chuck Schultz, who was in charge. He informed me that he had multiple deaths in the house and none of the bodies had been removed yet. I don't know why, but when he said that, I assumed he meant maybe three or four victims at most. He never really told me a number. I would soon find out that it was much higher than three or four. Our procedures in the Arson Unit were that we would not go onto the fire scene until the fire was totally out and the battalion chief gave us the okay.

On this fire, I was with Detective Bill Cysyk who had received the call and also responded from home, siren blasting I hope. Bill was the on-call detective in the Arson Unit that night. As the supervisor of the Arson Unit, I responded to all multi-alarm fires, all fire fatalities, and bombings. I was glad that Bill was on this fire with me that night, because he was probably the best arson detective in the unit.

We finally got the okay to go in the house and we were directed to the second floor front bedroom. While we were walking up the heavily damaged stairs, the lieutenant in charge told us that we should be prepared for what we were about to see. Well, nothing could have prepared us for what we did see. It was a scene that you just stared at and wondered at first, what the hell am I looking at. I can only describe it today as the most horrific sight I have ever seen. It was also probably the worst that any of the firemen on the fire ground that night had ever seen. There were no lights in the house, which had received massive damage. We had powerful flashlights to get around on the very dark fire scene. When I directed my light towards the front windows of the bedroom, I had to stare to make sure I was seeing what my eyes were telling me was there. I will try to describe it as best I can, but I will not do it justice. In total there were nine bodies, literally stacked against the wall of the bedroom directly under the windows. The fire had been extremely intense in that room and on the entire second floor. The fire personnel, who were fighting the fire, did not know the bodies were there until they knocked down the flames. The bodies were near the windows because as in many fires, people don't realize how fast the smoke takes over your body. As you breathe it in and in the excitement of a fire, your breathing enhances and thus you are taking in more smoke. No one will ever know the last thoughts and moves of these people. The mere fact that they were near the window, would lead you to believe that the adults in the group thought they could either get out the window or would be rescued near the window. The scene was so bad, that some of the fireman fighting the fire had mistakenly struck a couple of the bodies with axes, as they were chopping into the floor to ventilate the fire.

I stood there with Bill and we had no idea what our next move would be to investigate this fire. Would we have the bodies moved, would we first have photos taken, or would we leave them there until it got light outside? We were getting looks from the firemen standing around, so something had to be done. I told Bill to call for the police crime lab to process whatever scene there was. Just then, I saw the Fire Department Chaplain come up the steps. I knew the chaplain from being on other fire fatalities with him. He was an ordained Catholic priest who gave his time to be a volunteer chaplain with the fire department. He walked over to me and then looked at the carnage near the window. He put his hand on my shoulder and said, "God have mercy on us." He asked me how many bodies were there and before I could answer, the lieutenant said, "I think there are nine Father, but I can't be certain." The chaplain then asked everyone in the room to please kneel and pray over the bodies with him. You could have heard a pin drop, except for the sound of all the fire engines that were still outside. I don't know what faith all those firemen in that room were, but they took off their helmets, put down the hoses, and axes to pray over bodies of people they did not know. Bill and I did the same: we knelt and prayed. The chaplain seemed a little shaken up. I am sure he had never presided over anything in his life that would come close to what was in this room. The chaplain had a rosary around his neck and held a small Bible. If it wasn't for those two things, he looked like a firemen, because he had all the fire gear that the regular fire fighters had on. The chaplain started by saying, "Dear Lord please bless these souls that have lost their lives tonight." He went on to say a few prayers and a short reading from the Bible, as a firemen held a flashlight above him. The chaplain finished and stood directly over the burned bodies and blessed them. He turned and asked us if we wanted his blessing and every man in that room stayed in the kneeling position and received the blessing.

I can tell you as I write this story many years later, I can still picture the scene in that room. I don't think any movie maker could ever reenact the absolute horror in that room that night. The smell of a burned body is something that cannot be described. As we prepared to continue the investigation, smoke was still coming off of what remained of the bodies. I do not want to get to graphic, more graphic then I already have, but when a body burns, the skin literally burns off the body. If the fire is intense, as it was in that fire, the bones actually start to burn. In most fire fatalities, we would normally move the bodies to take a closer look. We would do that to make sure there are no wounds on the body that were inflicted prior to the fire. In this case that would prove fruitless.

I can tell you that the breakdown of the nine bodies was determined later: there was a seventy-eight year old grandmother, a forty-six year old father, a forty-two year old mother, and six children ranging from eight months old, up to thirteen years old. The family had moved into the home about two months prior to the fire. From all accounts given by the neighbors, they were decent hardworking people. We later found out that the electricity to the home had been cut off two weeks prior to the fire.

We stayed on the fire scene until daylight and watched as what was left of the bodies was removed by the Medical Examiner's Office personnel. It was a job that the faint of heart could not have done. Even these trained men from the ME's office had a difficult time dealing with this scene. It took three trips to get all the bodies transported to the ME's office. They were wrapped in plastic body bags. It was one time that I would not have wanted that job for all the money in the world.

The fire had been so intense on the second floor that it made the investigation very difficult. The only determination that could be made by the fire investigators was that there was no electricity in that home. They most likely may have been using candles to illuminate the rooms.

Bill and I went to the office to finish our reports and on the way, we really didn't do much talking. It had been a heartbreaking and draining experience. All we wanted to do was to write the reports, go home, and appreciate life a little more than we probably did prior to that fire.

RETIREMENT – LEAVING WHAT I LOVED

As with any job, there comes a time to call it quits and that's what I did in March 1990. I had positioned myself in the police department to spend the last eight years in the Arson Unit. I had made several contacts with insurance company Special Investigation Units. I knew that working fire investigation would eventually lead me to a second career in the insurance industry. I also knew that at age forty-six it was time to make the move. I knew that waiting a few more years would put me near fifty years old and maybe I would not be as employable. I was fortunate to be retiring at age forty-six with twenty- five years with the department: thanks to the retirement rules being changed in 1990. I can remember that it was in early March that I made the decision. After roll call, I went up to city hall where the city retirement unit was located. My first intentions were to just check it out, but after talking to the retirement counselor, I made the decision to sign the retirement papers that day.

I decided that my retirement date would be March 28, 1990. This would give me a few weeks to make contact with a company that I knew was interviewing for an insurance investigator's position. When I got back to the arson office from city hall, I ran into my boss, Lieutenant Don Kent, who I had known for over twenty years. He said, "What's happening?" I said, "I'm out of here." He asked what I meant and I told him that I was retiring. He just laughed and said, "Quit kidding and let's get some lunch." I told him that I was serious. I had been to city hall and filled out my retirement papers.

As we were talking, my good friend and number one menace for years, Pete Bailey came by. Pete, who was at that time a lieutenant in the Burglary Unit, said "Come on man, quit bullshitting us, you can't retire. You're too young. What the hell would you do?" Well, they all laughed and had so many reasons why I should not retire. I listened, but none of them made any sense to me. Nothing they said would make me tear up the retirement papers. I knew that I had done the right thing. I immediately notified Nationwide Insurance that I would like to interview for the investigator position. They told me to submit a short resume and they would get back to me with the dates they were interviewing.

When I left the building that day, I drove around the city. I drove in no particular direction; I was just driving and thinking to myself, did I do the right thing. I was thinking, what were the good things about staying on the department, as opposed to retiring? What were the benefits of starting a new career with the insurance company? The more I thought about it, the more I knew that I was making the right decision.

About two weeks later, I interviewed with Nationwide Insurance. Prior to the interview, I discovered that a few of my friends were also going to be interviewed and the total number of people to be interviewed was about twenty. I was interviewed for the job on a Friday afternoon at the Nationwide Insurance Regional Office in Annapolis, Maryland. I was surprised that the only person interviewing me was the manager of the Special Investigation Unit. He seemed like a real nice guy. When we were talking, he told me that some other candidates that he had interviewed told him that they knew me. I was very relaxed at the interview and if I must say so, I had an excellent resume'. I knew that the experience that I had obtained from working in the Arson Unit in the police department would be a plus for me in the insurance industry. The interview went well and the Nationwide Insurance manager told me that he had completed all the interviews. He told me he would think about all the applicants over the weekend and make his decision by Monday.

Well, it was Friday and I left the interview feeling pretty good. I knew that a few of my buddies would be drinking at a happy hour downtown, so I went and met with them. I stayed with them until late that night: a little later than I wanted to. I was feeling pretty good, both from the drinks and the excitement I had about leaving the department. When I got home to my apartment, I checked my messages and one of the messages was from the Nationwide Insurance manager. The message on the machine was that he had thought about all the interviews and that I seemed more qualified for the job than the others. His message went on to say, although he originally said he would think about it over the weekend, he did not want me to wait that long. The job was mine!

I sat there in the apartment and was thinking how fortunate I was to be retiring after doing something that I loved for twenty-five years. I would now be embarking on a new career that sounded too good to be true. I was like a little kid with the excitement running through me. I sat there for awhile and the same thoughts came back that I had when I put in the retirement papers: am I doing the right thing, will the insurance job be satisfying, and will I miss my cop buddies? Most of all, I was thinking that I might be jumping the gun. I was actually taking advantage of the retirement age being lowered. Was this a knee jerk reaction or the right thing to do?

I pondered all these thoughts in my head and must have stayed up until the early hours of the next day. I actually got some paper and made a list of the good and bad. I know that I fell asleep from the exhaustion of running this back and forth in my head. The morning came quick and I was getting ready to meet my Saturday morning tennis group. I was about to leave the apartment and started to look at the list again. This time, the things listed on the good side of the paper, made a whole lot more sense than the side with the bad stuff. I was leaving the apartment and decided to add one more thing to the good side; I would be able to play more tennis.

THE RETIREMENT PARTY

The guys in the Arson Unit planned a retirement party for me. It was to be held on my official retirement date of March 28, 1990. The guys got the fire hall in southeast Baltimore where a lot of police and firefighter retirements were held. As the date approached, I was told that the ticket sales were really going good. Hell, I was so excited about retiring, that if the sales were not going good, I would have probably bought them up and passed them out on the street. I was told that they expected a crowd of over a hundred and fifty people and this included my family, which would be at least thirty relatives.

The party was on a Friday and had a start time of 7 PM. My start time was about 1 PM just after I got the official retirement papers from the police commissioner in his office. This was the formality for cops retiring from the job. The commissioner that gave me my retirement papers was Eddie Woods, who I had worked with earlier in my career. The ceremony in the police commissioner's office is usually attended by just a few of your cop friends and maybe your supervisors. They take photos, the commissioner says some nice things, and then you are out the door. They give you a retirement plaque and a badge that has your rank on it and the words, "Retired" at the bottom of the badge. It is a nice ceremony and then you usually go back down to your unit and say all your goodbyes and everyone wishes you well. I did all the goodbyes in the Homicide Unit and the Arson Unit; it was a strange feeling. I was shaking hands with some guys in the Homicide Unit as they were coming in the office, fresh from a homicide scene. As I was leaving the office,

I watched as they brought in witnesses and then a suspect was brought in and put in the interview room. I stood there for awhile; it was a sad moment. I knew this was the end of what I had loved for so many years. I felt like I wanted to just jump in one more time and play the bad guy. Maybe the guy I saw in handcuffs knew something about the Doctor Russo murder; maybe he knew who stabbed Doctor Thompson; maybe I was just delaying the process of getting my retired ass out of the building for the last time.

I was dressed up for the retirement ceremony, so I figure what the hell, I might as well go and have a few nerve settling drinks before the big party. I went to the bar with a few of my close friends. It was working hours for them, but what the hell; they can take some time for a former police officer. I wanted to have a couple of goodbye drinks with the guys that I had worked with for all those years. I also figured that a few drinks would settle my nerves. I knew that I would have to make a speech at my retirement party and I was nervous about that. I knew that the agenda for the party called for some high ranking police and fire officials to be there. It was the custom to present retirees with some plaques and certificates.

I left the bar at about 6 PM and I actually felt pretty good. I think I talked more than I drank at the bar, so I was fine. I was starting to realize that most of these guys I might never see again. As I approached the fire hall, I was starting to get a little nervous. I could not wait to get there and get my drink of choice, which was gin and tonic. I used to kid with the guys that I could drink gin and tonic all night and it did not affect me. That was not quite the truth; it actually felt like I was anesthetized after drinking gin and tonic for a period of time.

I got to the hall and the biggest surprise was at the front door. A friend of mine, who was also a Marine, had made arrangements for two Marines in full dress blue uniforms to be at the front door to greet people. As I walked through the door, the Marines snapped to attention and gave me a crisp salute that made me feel like a million dollars. I took time to talk to these two Marines, who looked like they were kids. I asked them to stay for the party, but one of them said, "Sir, we are Marines and we are not allowed to drink in uniform." I was impressed with their answer, but I responded kiddingly and said, "I didn't ask you to drink, I only asked you to stay for the party." I think they stayed for awhile, but they appeared to be nervous. I saw that they were getting ready to leave and I thanked them again. I was glad that my friend thought of the Marines; it was the topping for a very special night.

I did have time to grab one gin and tonic. Shortly after I got there, the crowd started to arrive. I positioned myself at the front door and greeted everyone who came in. That was draining. It was also remarkable, because some of the people that came I had not seen for years. It was a great feeling that they would share this night with me. The guys that put the party together did a great job of finding friends and police officers from the past and present. They made sure that my entire family was there and that is a job, as I have a large family.

After greeting people for about an hour, I decided it was time to start the celebration. I found my way to the bar. I didn't even have to order a drink, the bartender handed me a gin and tonic. I stayed at the bar for awhile, talking to some cops. We were telling stories. The stories never change, they are the same old stories that we hash around whenever we get together.

Later during the party, I did have to get up to the podium and stand there while the certificates were read off from the fire department, police department, the ATF, and a few other agencies. I received a proclamation from the mayor and the governor thanking me for my twenty-five years of service. I was getting overwhelmed when the inscriptions were read from the certificates and plaques. It was flattering. I just stood on the platform and would shake hands with whoever presented the plaques. I knew my time was approaching when I would have to take the microphone and thank everyone. I would try to talk about my twenty-five years in the police department and do it in the shortest amount of time. I had made some prepared notes, but in all the excitement, I did not use them. It turned out that I made it through without getting too emotional. It makes you nervous to be on the stage, as you look out and see all the faces. It is like a motion picture of your life being played and it is a private showing, only you can see the action. It is amazing how the brain reacts at moments like that. You are talking and remembering at the same time and hoping that all the right things come out of your mouth.

I didn't want to go on for a long time, because we were there to celebrate and not listen to me. I thanked everyone for coming. I thanked my family and especially my two children; it was great to share this night with them. I thanked all the police brass, fire officials, and politicians that attended. I especially thanked those that had presented me with plaques, certificates and gifts. I remember briefly talking about what it meant to be a part of a great police family and how I would really miss it. As I stood on that podium, I don't even know if at times I was talking. I talked about everything I did in those twenty-five years or it seemed like I did. I could tell it was starting to get to me and I was feeling a lot of emotion. I knew I had to end it real soon or I would break down in front of all these great people and Marines don't cry. I closed by saying that I would remember this day for the rest of my life. I told them that each and everyone in the room had touched me in some way, either in my personal life or on the department. I also told them that I hope that I could stay a part of the police family in the future. I actually felt like a politician or a sports figure, because when I ended my talk, the whole place stood up and gave me a standing ovation. At that point I lost it and I knew it was gin and tonic time again. I thanked everyone and made a quick exit off the stage. I made my way to the men's room and threw some water on my face. I stayed in the men's room long enough to make sure the tears were gone…Marines don't cry.

The party was supposed to end at 11 PM, but we were still there well after midnight. I was sitting there talking to some cops and my thoughts were that I hoped it would never end. I was thinking, maybe we could party for days, but reality set in when the bartender announced it was last call. I was feeling pretty good and I stood close to the door and I thanked every person as they left the hall. I was excited that as they left, everyone said that it was one of the best retirement parties that they had ever attended and that made me feel good.

ALL SHORT STORIES MUST END

I have taken about three years to write these stories and that's not bad for a guy that took seventeen years to get a two year degree from a community college. I really don't want to end it, because it has been a real experience for me to go back and put all these stories on paper. I did not pull any punches or hold anything back. I told you the truth. I would assume, that you do realize, I am not real proud of some of the stories, but I wanted to tell them nevertheless. The bottom line to all these stories is that I survived. I not only survived, but I am extremely proud of my career in the police department.

I have jotted down so many notes while I was writing this book. I would like to include more stories and there are more. I want to try and get this book out before they send me to the old age home. I don't want them to put me in a wheelchair up against the wall, with my hands tied to the sides, baby food dripping out the side of my mouth, my pants smelling like several dogs died in them, nobody visiting me, and nobody giving a fuck if I live or die. Wow, that was some serious shit and I got a little carried away. In reality, I hope that I never go to an old age home. If I do, I hope it's an old age home for retired cops, so we can sit around all day and tell cop stories. We won't allow all that bullshit I mentioned above to occur. We will kick some ass if necessary!

Before the old age home, I hope to continue to meet with my cop friends at breakfast, lunches, retirements, birthdays and yes, the now famous yearly homicide reunion. I meet with some guys now and it is inevitable that someone will start a story and they get to the middle of the story and all of sudden they can't remember the name of the person they are talking about. They stumble and say things like: you know who I mean, the big guy, the red headed guy, the fat guy, and we all try to help each other. Even if we don't know who is being talked about, we just say, oh yeah, I remember that guy. We just finish the story and about ten minutes later when someone else is telling another story, we just blurt out the name. At that point, everybody pauses and says, yeah that's the guy and then we go on with the new story and this goes on for the entire time we are together.

I enjoy every minute of the time spent with retired cops. We have something special in common. In a way, we have been through a hell of a lot and lived to talk about it. I think in the future when we meet and we are older and really can't even remember how we even got to the restaurant; I will carry some copies of my book and when we get stuck, I will just pass them around.

FINAL THOUGHTS

If I haven't said it several times in this book, which I know I have, I loved my time in the Baltimore Police Department. I can honestly say, even up to this day and having been retired for several years, I still have dreams of my days on the job. Most of the dreams are about homicides and I make sure I never wake up until they are solved. I have a better clearance rate now, than I did while on the job.

I have a lot of guys that I want to thank for all they did for me while on the police department. I don't want to wait and have to say it at a funeral or in the retired cops' nursing home. I always mark my calendar for police events, so I don't forget. I want to hear all the cop stories I can before I hit final roll call. When the day comes that I can't get myself there, I hope that some young cop will do something nice and take an old-timer to meet some old-timers. Maybe they will hang around and listen to some great stories.

I have never written a book before. I guess some of you are saying, that's real obvious, but I hope not. I did my best on these stories and that's all I wanted to do when I started this a long time ago. I don't want to just say... the end; that seems like if I did, I will regret it later when it gets published. I know that when it is published, I will think of all the things I left out. Not really knowing how to properly end a book, I am assuming this is the part where I say thanks to some people. These people have been a major part of my life; without them, I don't think I would have made it for twenty-five years on the police department, much less write a book.

The first person I want to thank is the most important person in my life.

Without my wife, Sharon, I would not have ever completed this book. She is my wife, my best friend, my adviser and my editorial review expert. I love her very much. Sharon is a retired school teacher. She has worked with me on the editorial review of this book. During the review, she has found out some things for the first time. Sharon and I were not married when I was on the police department and that my friends is a damn good thing.

I would like to mention just a few guys that have meant a lot to me throughout my career on the job. Frank Perkowski was my partner in the Homicide Unit and remains one of my closest friends today. Frank not only taught me a lot about patience when working on murders, he also taught me a lot about life. Many nights I sat in the bar with Frank while he listened to and advised me on issues going on in my life. Frank was a top notch homicide investigator, but most important, he was my friend. Another guy that is mentioned in my book, Pete Bailey is a guy that was always there for me when I needed someone to vent my frustrations. Pete and I are still very close friends today and yes, he still calls me "goof". When we are together for breakfast or lunch, you would not know we are close friends. We argue about everything, we disagree all the time, we get loud toward each other, we fight like brothers and guess what, I love the guy. Another guy, that although he is no longer with us, I think of him all the time. I have talked about him in the book and that is my former sergeant, Rod Brandner. What I learned from Rod over the years has helped me to be a better person. Rod was an extraordinary individual and I have mentioned in this book some of his "antics" that he pulled on us in the Homicide Unit.

I could go on with thanking numerous people for helping me along the way, but one that I need to mention, is my former captain in the Homicide Unit, Jim Cadden. I wrote a lot about him in the book. He had the most influence on me in the police department. We grew up in the same Irish neighborhood and although he is much older than me, I respected him on and off the job. He is a real American hero, having fought in World War II. I mentioned in the book that he was an absolute legend in the police department. He was my captain during some turbulent times in my life and for that, I will always be grateful to him. He is getting up in age now. When I see him, it appears that he probably doesn't remember me. It's okay that he doesn't remember me or what he did for me over the years. I remember all that he did and that's enough remembering for the both of us.

I know that thanking people can be an enduring process. I could name many others that meant a lot to me during my time on the police department. Over the span of twenty-five years, you meet some great people and I would not trade those years for anything.

Police work is a great career, but it is not for everyone. It does take a special person to want to dedicate your life to helping others. When you first come on the job, you have the mindset of wanting to solve the problems of the world. It does not take long to realize that there are people who don't want your help. I knew early on in my life that I wanted to be a cop. I was raised by a cop. In the neighborhood that I grew up in, it seemed like there was a cop family on every block. I feel that becoming a cop is in your blood; I know it is in my family. As you progress through the years in your career in law enforcement, you will know when and where you made a difference. Writing this book, took me back over my twenty-five years and I am more convinced than ever, that I definitely made a difference in Baltimore. Did I make a difference in the lives of those kids on the Kennedy Playground over forty years ago? I don't know the answer, but those kids are fathers and grandfathers today. Did they have more respect for cops after my small gesture of playing baseball with them?

It was amazing writing this book, because as I put each story into print, I had vivid memories of the time. The mere fact that I have written a book is amazing to me. It was a laborious task at first. I didn't know if I could finish it, but one story led to another and then I knew it was something that I had to finish. I hope I am around for a long time, but if I am not, my book will. I can walk down the street one day and someone will say, "Hey, that's Dick Ellwood, he was a cop." The other person will say, "Yeah, that's him all right and he wrote a book."

I never envisioned I would get to this point, but this is the end. I will leave you with one thought. I sincerely mean this for everyone, especially any young person who feels they have a calling to be a police officer.

I know that the will of God, will never take you where the grace of God will not protect you.

Semper Fi